Problems and Promises of Computer-Based Training

Edited by

Theodore M. Shlechter
U.S. Army Research Institute
for the Behavioral and Social Sciences

 ABLEX PUBLISHING CORPORATION
NORWOOD, NEW JERSEY

Printed in the United States of America

Library of Congress Cataloging-in-Publication Data

Problems and promises of computer-based training / edited by
    Theodore M. Shlechter.
        p.   cm.
    Includes bibliographical references and index.
    ISBN 0-89391-657-9 (cl). — ISBN 0-89391-658-7 (pp)
    1. Computer-assisted instruction.   I. Shlechter, Theodore M.
LB1028.5.P7197   1991
371.3'34—dc20
                                                                    90-26977
                                                                        CIP

Ablex Publishing Corporation
355 Chestnut Street
Norwood, New Jersey 07648

This book is dedicated to my late brother,
Laurence Jay Shlechter,
who taught me many things about life.

Contents

Preface

Even though computer-based training (CBT) holds tremendous promise for restructuring education, this medium has not been fully utilized by educators. This volume offers both pragmatic and theoretical solutions to obstacles associated with develping, implementing, and using this medium. These obstacles include problems with hardware and software, mismanagement of the CBT implementation, and inadequate training of teachers and other school personnel. The solutions to these problems are based upon the lessons learned from the development and implementation of previous CBT systems and the research literature. Also, some of these chapters provide a glimpse of future directions in CBT.

This book presents viewpoints on CBT development and implementation from the entire spectrum of professionals associated with this medium—developers, evaluators, instructional designers, school administrators, and schoolteachers. These professionals have been listed in alphabetical order, not in order of importance, as they are all equally important in the successful use of any instructional medium. This book is thus useful for all professionals and students interested in CBT.

This volume differs from previous volumes on CBT in several important ways. One, very few books have presented both the practical and theoretical issues associated with CBT. Most books tend to focus solely on either the practical or theoretical issues; this text covers both. Two, lessons learned from previous CBT implementations are rarely discussed in the literature. Hence, this volume includes a discussion of implementation issues and problems from the perspective of the users, for example, teachers and other practitioners, which is rarely found in other CBT books.

It is not the aim of this work to discuss all the possible issues and problems associated with CBT; such a task is impossible. Rather, this volume describes some of the more salient issues which may affect any CBT project. I hope that this volume succeeds in making the reader more aware of the potential problems and promises of CBT. It is a most exciting time for education with great promises for wide-sweeping and long-lasting changes. Certainly, CBT will be a part of this new frontier of education.

The chapters of this book are grouped into the following sections: (a) an overview of CBT development and application; (b) specific issues in CBT development and application; (c) lessons learned from the development and application of previous CBT systems; and (d) a summary chapter.

Chapter 1 (Theodore Shlechter) provides an overview of the history of CBT and some of the promises and problems associated with this medium, which are further discussed in this volume. Chapter 2 (Brenda Sugrue) provides an overview of several CBT projects which were implemented in Europe and the United States. This chapter describes the similarities and differences in policy implementation found in Europe and America. Chapter 3 (Steven Robinson) overviews the role of technology for educationally mildly handicapped populations in special and mainstream educational settings. This chapter also discusses technology-supported group instruction as a powerful new role for technology in special education. Chapter 4 (Thomas Reeves) delineates a dozen constraints on the application of CBT in higher education. The chapter concludes with a description of some optimistic developments with respect to CBT in universities and colleges.

The next section on specific issues in CBT development and application starts with chapter 5. This chapter (Carol Carrier and Allen Glenn) examines the current status of programs which train teachers to use computers effectively in the classroom and suggests the actions which these programs should initiate to meet the challenge of preparing tomorrow's teachers. Chapter 6 (Nira Hativa) discusses some of the most critical problems with several widely used CBT program which teach arithmetic skills. She also provides solutions to these problems. Chapter 7 (George Semb, John Ellis, William Montague, and Wallace Wulfeck) discusses the potential of self-paced instruction as part of an effective instructional delivery system, with particular emphasis on the concept of a system of instruction. Chapter 8 (Michael Pyryt) gives special attention to the need of integrating the characteristics of the gifted with software/hardware design considerations. Chapter 9 (Sharon Derry and Lois Hawkes) discusses the instructional design and computer system components necessary for a successful ICAI system.

The section on lessons learned starts with chapter 10 (Joel Colbert), which discusses the experiences of the Los Angeles Unified School District with its large-scale implementation of CBT. This author was an important player in this implementation program. Chapter 11 (William Schultz and Nancy Higginbotham-Wheat) explores the problems and frustrations that classroom teachers have experienced with using CBT. The two authors of this chapter have been classroom teachers with much CBT experience. Chapter 12 (William Deaton) describes the promises and problems of using computers in higher education as seen from the perspective of a dean in a college of education. Chapter 13 (Lois Wilson) provides a checklist of planning activities necessary to promote successful implementation of CBT in a community college. This chapter is based upon the author's experiences with implementing TICCIT in community colleges.

Chapter 14 (Robert Branson) discusses the major issues in designing and implementing a CBT program to teach basic skills to adults in both the private and public sector. The author's insights are founded upon his experiences with developing and implementing the Job Skills Education Program. Chapter 15 (Fred Romney) presents case studies from the Jefferson County (Louisville), KY School District of using computer technology to help severely disabled students to more effectively manage their daily lives and to reach their educational goals. This author has directed this program for a number of years.

This book's final section consists of a summary chapter (by Barbara McCombs) that reviews the current status of CBT as presented in this book and presents recommendations for future directions in CBT practice and research.

I would like to give a special thanks to four people who were instrumental in the successful completion of this book: Dr. Barbara McCombs, whose insightful comments were very helpful and much appreciated; Dr. Sandor Klein, a special friend, who was always there to give much needed support and encouragement; Mrs. Dorothy Gilbert of the Louisville Free Public Library, who was always able to provide me with key sources through inter-library loan, a feat that is quite remarkable as some of these articles and books were located in only one or two libraries in the United States. Most of all, I want to thank my wonderful wife, Rae Shepherd-Shlechter, who proofread each draft of every chapter, and whose marvelous patience and sense of humor rarely waned during the many long hours that I devoted to this project.

1
Promises, Promises, Promises: History and Foundations of Computer-Based Training

Theodore M. Shlechter
Army Research Institute

Computer-Based Instruction (CBI) has been hailed as a truly revolutionary instructional medium. As the Office of Technology Assessment (OTA) Report (1988) states:

> These innovations (e.g., computer technology) can radically change the performance and structure of the educational system. The new generation of technologies...is qualitatively different from the film strips, television shows, and other techniques that have been used to augment instruction in the past. They represent something fundamentally new...(pp. 242–243)

Computer-Assisted Instruction (CAI) and Computer-Managed Instruction (CMI) are the traditional methods of computer use in the classroom. In CAI, students receive instruction directly from the computer system. CMI involves using the computer for such instructional management issues as scoring, recording, and interpreting test results. Computers can also be used as instructional tools. Students, for example, are using computers as word processors to complete written assignments.

This book focuses on examining the promises and problems of using computers for a wide variety of educational settings and purposes from elementary schools to adult educational programs and from educating the gifted to educating the severely disabled. This book also examines the future directions of CBI.

This chapter provides an overview of the promises and problems with CBI. A brief history of this technology is also discussed.

A BRIEF HISTORY OF CBI

As is the case with most revolutions, the CBI revolution is the result of several evolutionary forces. One set of these forces concerns societal changes and pressures. Since similar societal pressures and changes have been found for most technological societies, the history of CBI in America can be seen as a microcosm of its development in other societies.

Computer Development and Society's Need for Protection

Ellul (1967) notes that a society's need for protection has been an important catalyst for technological change. This need has certainly been an important force for the technological changes that have occurred in American society during the last 50 years.

The demands of World War II helped accelerate the development of the computer. According to Goldstine (1972), who worked on the first-generation computer, a prime reason for the development of the computer was to help prepare the firing and bombing tables urgently needed by the U.S. Military for World War II. This computer, which was termed "ENIAC" (Electronic Numerical Integrator and Calculator), consisted of 18,500 vacuum tubes, 70,000 resistors, and 10,000 capacitors and was capable of 5,000 computations per second (Kinzer, Sherwood, & Bransford, 1986).

During the Cold War period from 1946 to 1966, the Pentagon was the primary source of funds for the research and development of the second and third computer generations (Goldstine, 1972). These two generations of computers were distinguished by several important hardware breakthroughs which led to faster, smaller, and more efficient computers. The hardware breakthroughs for the second-generation computers included the use of transistors and the reproducing electronic punch system as the input-output medium. The third-generation computers were marked by the development of integrated circuitry, which made it possible for hundreds of transistorlike elements to be placed into a small computer chip. This generation of computers was also marked by the development of "time sharing" which allowed users at different (military) installations to have access to the same computer.

The need for economic protection has also been a major impetus for the development of computers in America. For example, the Japanese threat to the economic security of America has led to a national effort by the U.S. to develop the fifth generation of computers. These computers are characterized by their ability to (a) use natural language; (b) make inferences; and (c) make intelligent decisions. The Japanese are already using such computers to help operate their superspeed train system.

Educational Technology and Society's Need for Protection

The U.S. went to war three times during the last 50 years. Each war involved the use of a new training medium to meet the challenges inherent in providing standardized training for countless thousands of enlisted personnel. Training films were developed during World War II on such topics as personal hygiene, recognition of the enemy, and basic military equipment. These films involved the efforts of many of Hollywood's leading film makers and personalities, for example, Frank Capra and Ronald Reagan. Televised instruction came into use by the armed services during the Korean conflict. Fritz, Humphrey, Greenlee, and Madison (1952) concluded that this medium allowed the Army to have its best instructors available for universal training.

With the Vietnam War came the first widespread usage of CBI. This training medium was initially developed by IBM for corporate training purposes and had limited experimental use in the civilian educational sector. The impetus for using computers in military training came from a 1965 memorandum released by Secretary of Defense Robert McNamara for the secretaries of the Army, Navy, and Air Force (Fletcher & Rockaway, 1985). This memorandum directed the different services to examine new innovations for military training (Fletcher & Rockaway, 1985). McNamara's goal was to provide standardized and cost-efficient training for the war effort.

Each of the different services then invested a great deal of effort and funds into developing and implementing CBI. One such project was the development of a 102-hour CAI course in basic electronics for enlisted Army personnel (Long, 1972). The computer system for this course was an IBM 1500 instructional series, which consisted of a mainframe time-sharing computer system with 32K memory and 20 student terminals linked to a control unit. The courseware was a basic programmed learning package for procedural training. Longo found that CAI was a viable instructional system within an operational Army training program.

These early military CBI projects led to marked improvements in CBI courseware. Ford, Slough, and Hurlock (1972), for example, discussed several ways in which the Navy's CBI system for electricity/electronics training represented an instructional improvement over previous CBI ventures. The designers of this system made a number of advances in branching technology, which made the courseware more adaptive to individual needs. This CBI system was also one of the first to use a combination of program and student control over the instructional sequences.

The military has continually supported the research and development of CBI throughout the 1970s and 1980s. One major focus of the military's recent CBI efforts is the development of remedial training programs. Branson

(Chapter 14) discusses the research and development of the Army's Job Skills Education Program (JSEP). This program provides remedial training for soldiers with deficiencies in the basic skills needed for their jobs. JSEP is probably the largest, special purpose, CBI curriculum yet developed (see Chapter 14).

Another major focus has been the research and development of intelligent computer-assisted instruction (ICAI). ICAI is a product of the movement toward the fifth-generation computer system of artificial intelligence as "smart technology" has been used to help train students (Gray, Pliske, & Psotka, 1985). Such "smart technology" can serve as both a functional simulator and mechanism for causal explanation in which learners can develop their own problem-solving strategies (Nawrocki, 1985).

Another catalyst for CBI development was the Russian launching of Sputnik. In order to protect the national interest, President Eisenhower pledged a national commitment to the teaching of science and mathematics. CBI prototypes were then developed to answer this call. Vinsonhaler and Bass (1972) noted that the vast majority of the major CBI projects in the 1960s dealt with teaching mathematical skills. One such project was Suppes' (1966) CBI program for teaching elementary arithmetic skills. This project was important because its adaptive drill-and-practice and branching schemes have been incorporated into many other CBI programs.

PLATO (Programmed Logic for Teaching Automated Operations) was also rooted in the response to Sputnik. The concept of PLATO was devised by Dr. Donald Bitzer of the University of Illinois in 1959 and was initially used to assist science teachers (Meyers, 1984; Smith & Sherwood, 1976). The PLATO project was also instrumental in the development of CBI as many of the initial ideas and concepts behind this medium came from the work done by Bitzer and his colleagues. Plato II was designed, for example, with the "teaching logic" (courseware) determined by programs within the central computer, and changes were made in the "teaching logic" by rewriting the computer programs (Bitzer, Braunfeld, & Lichtenberg, 1962). The PLATO project thus demonstrated the feasibility and flexibility of using computers to assist in the teaching process (Bitzer et al., 1962; Meyers, 1984).

CBI and Adaptation

To cite the need for protection as the sole driving force behind the development of computers and CBI is a great oversimplification. Another element in this developmental process has been the need to adapt to new societal demands.

Radical changes in the U.S. student population have played an important role in the development of CBI. This population nearly doubled in the

25 years between 1950 and 1975—from 31,151,000 in 1950 to 60,496,000 in 1975 (Snyder, 1987). Correspondingly, educational expenditures dramatically increased during that 25-year period from nine million dollars spent for education in 1950 to over 100 million dollars in 1975 (Snyder, 1987). Computers were thus expected to help the educational system handle these reported increases in enrollment and expenditures by allowing the horde of new students to receive a quality education without the need to hire a proportionate number of new staff.

Political pressures to deal with new societal demands have also played an important role in the development of CBI. President Johnson's attempt to form a "Great Society" in which all citizens could receive a quality education was a great spur to the CBI movement. The passage of the *Elementary and Secondary Education Act of 1965* led the Federal Government to double the proportion of money spent on education (Oetinger & Marks, 1967). Some of these additional federal revenues were certainly spent by local schools to develop CBI.

President Johnson also directed the National Science Foundation (NSF) to take the lead in supporting computer use in the schools (OTA, 1988). NSF funds, for example, were now provided to the University of Illinois to further develop the PLATO system into a large-scale CBI system. Through the use of time-sharing, the same PLATO courseware was used by students at many different remote locations. Previous funding for this system had come from corporate and military sources.

NSF funds were also provided for the development and implementation of several new large-scale CBI systems. NSF awarded the MITRE Corporation a multimillion dollar grant to develop and implement the TICCIT (Time-Shared Computer-Controlled Information Television) system (see Chapter 13). NSF also stipulated that the first application of TICCIT was to be at the community college level (see Chapter 13). This stipulation was seemingly made to meet the needs of a rapidly increasing student population and the desires of the "Great Society" for a quality education for all its citizens.

Politicians and educators have recently been arguing for CBI as a means of helping Americans to develop the job skills necessary for this technological world (Bok, 1986; Bonner, 1984). Two recent congressional reports have stressed the need for using computers in the classroom to meet future economic needs (OTA, 1986, 1988). Also, Congressmen, for example, Albert Gore of Tennessee, have emphasized the enormous importance and potential of CBI to meet the educational challenges of preparing people to live in this society which is dominated by the computer (Bonner, 1984).

Educational adaptation to the demands of a computer-oriented society has also been instrumental in the aquisition of computers for classroom use. As indicated by Deaton (see Chapter 12), the task for educators became one of getting computers involved in the educatonal situation. The number of computers in the school systems has thus dramatically increased during the 1980s (see Chapter 2).

The development and implementation of CBI has also been structured by other forces within this computer society. Hardware and software manufacturers, for example, have been a strong mediating force in the use of computers by American schools (Chapter 2). These commercial interests have vigorously encouraged school systems to use computers because they needed a huge market for their products. This encouragement has often taken the form of donating computer hardware to the schools without proper planning for using the equipment (Chapter 4).

Commercial interests have also been instrumental in determining changes with CBI. Manufacturers have always claimed that the new generation of their product represents a significant leap forward. Manufacturers of CBI products have not been any different. CBI based upon the use of time-sharing has for the most part been replaced by the use of microcomputers which in turn will shortly be replaced by the use of ICAI. Such changes in CBI hardware have occurred despite the lack of evidence for the educational superiority of one system over another.

CBI DEVELOPMENT AND INSTRUCTIONAL THEORIES

CBI development and implementation have seemingly been determined by societal pressures rather than by educational theories. Again, this is an oversimplification of the history of CBI as educational theories have had an important role in its development. This section briefly discusses a few of the important educational theories associated with the development of CBI.

CBI Development and Behavioral Theories of Learning

The behavioral theories of learning, especially B.F. Skinner's theory (1954, 1961) of operant conditioning, have had a tremendous influence on the development of the early CBI systems. Among the basic learning principles of Skinner's theory are the following: (a) personalized instruction, (b) "controlled operant," (c) immediate feedback, (d) linear sequence of learning, and (e) instructional prompts. Controlled operant involves the presentation of a stimulus situation which lasts until the student makes the one and only correct response to that situation (Zeman, 1959). The student must then immediately receive a reinforcing stimulus for that response (Zeman, 1959). Skinner (1954) has also argued that the instructor must control the learning situation.

The designers (Bitzer et al., 1962) of the PLATO II Computer System embraced Skinner's learning principles. Students were required to individually proceed through a fixed "main" sequence of instruction controlled by the computer and to answer correctly each question posed in this sequence. Feedback to each response was immediate. The students, however, could avail themselves of a supplementary help sequence (prompts) to answer a particularly troublesome question.

Other early CBI programs used instructional designs which were less similar to Skinner's approach to instruction. One major change from Skinner's theory involved the use of a branching sequence. The branching sequence, which was devised by Crowder (1962), involved the use of remedial subsequences. Students who experienced problems mastering a particular set of materials would then be branched to a remedial set of instructions. This instructional approach was found in the CBI program described by Ford et al. (1972) for training Navy personnel and was the basis for an adaptive sequencing found in the updated PLATO systems (e.g., Avner, Moore, & Smith, 1980).

CBI and Cognitive Theories

As CBI progressed, many CBI programs changed from a behaviorist instructional orientation to a more cognitive orientation. The cognitive orientation comes from a belief that students need to develop an understanding of the underlying concepts associated with any task, and that this understanding is developed by allowing the students to interact actively with the environment.

The TICCIT's instructional design, for example, contains elements of the cognitive orientation (Merrill, Schneider, & Fletcher, 1980). Under this instructional design, students are usually presented with an initial series of RULE frames, which have been designed to present the (a) definition of the concept, (b) the list of steps in the procedure, and (c) the statement of relationship between concepts. After these RULE frames, the student may either want to view the EXAMPLE frames or the PRACTICE frames. The EXAMPLE frames demonstrate the procedure or show an application of the principle while the PRACTICE frames allow the students to apply the rule to a specific object or event (Merrill et al., 1980). As demonstrated, the designers of TICCIT's instructional design were interested in developing the students' understanding of the underlying concepts. They also believed that learner control of the instructional sequence was necessary for such understanding to occur (Merrill et al., 1980).

Piaget's theory of cognitive development has also influenced many CBI designers. Papert (1980), who helped design the LOGO system, was greatly influenced by Piaget's theory. A basic assumption of Piaget's theory is that a different type of assimilation and accommodation occurs at each stage of development (Flavell, 1963). A person, for example, must wait until the final stage of development—the formal operational stage—to develop the cognitive structures necessary for dealing with abstract environmental relationships.

While basically agreeing with Piaget about the assimilation and accommodation process, Papert (1980) argues that cognitive development can be expedited by providing the child with more formal operational experiences. A child can acquire these needed experiences by programming a computer with the LOGO authoring language (Papert, 1980). A young child can develop computer graphics of different geometric forms by using and combining different LOGO commands. If the child has provided the system with a wrong set of messages then he or she must systematically debug the program. Using and combining different commands to form a coherent computer graphic and debugging a program are examples of formal operational experiences.

Cognitive theories and issues, such as metacognition, mental algorithms, and mental models have also been important in the development of ICAI (Chapter 9, Solomon, 1988). Development of this educational medium has been shaped vis-à-vis insights into such cognitive issues as metacognition, mental models, mental algorithms, and expert knowledge bases. Lantz, Bregar, and Farley (1983) have devised, for example, a prototype ICAI system to teach problem solving for high school algebra word problems, which includes a model of an expert's algorithms to these problems. See Chapter 9 for a more detailed account of the theoretical underpinnings of ICAI.

Instructional Theories and Hardware Development

It is interesting to note that the cognitive influence became more prevalent as computer technology became more sophisticated. The PLATO II computer system, for example, had a high-speed electrostatic memory of 1024 40-bit words and an average multiplication time of 700 microseconds (Bitzer et al., 1962). Of course, the capacities of the computers associated with ICAI programs have been infinitely greater. The LISP Machines used for ICAI programming have the storage and memory capacity of 2000 microcomputers (Pliske & Psotka, 1986).

Two basic questions arise from this relationship between hardware development and instructional theories. One, does this relationship provide further support for the notion of Ellul (1967) that technical advancement is needed for scientific (and educational) changes to occur? Bitzer et al. (1962) noted that the memory limitations with their computer system did limit their educational program. Or is the relationship between computer development and instructional theories purely coincidental? Skinner's theory was popular with American psychologists and educators during the 1950s and 1960s while Piaget's theory became popular in the early 1970s.

THE PROMISES OF CBI

As previously indicated, CBI was expected to help improve the American educational system by helping educators to accomplish the following goals: (a) stabilization of educational costs, (b) increase in student achievement, (c) handling of individual differences and needs, and (d) increase in student motivation. This section presents some of the arguments and evidence for these expectations.

A caveat must be made for this discussion of the promises of CBI. As discussed by Clark (1983) and Shlechter (1988), some of the evidence supporting instructional advantages of CBI may be problematic. The reader is thus referred to these works for a more conservative view of the promises of CBI.

Stabilizing Educational Costs

Many CBI reports (e.g., Chapter 14; Hofstetter, 1983; Seidel, 1980; Chapter 13) have suggested that such systems are cost effective and would eventually lead to some savings in educational expenditures. Branson (Chapter 14) has noted, for example, that a MicroTICCIT system could save an educational institution nearly $1,130,000 during its life cycle. His argument was partially based on data which showed that CBI drastically reduced training time. Training time savings would reduce military and civilian adult educational expenditures because less money would be spent on students. Also, more students would be able to complete a course without the hiring of additional instructors.

It has also been an expectation that CBI could allow educational systems to solve continuing financial problems by reducing the need to expand their instructional and support staffs. Wilson (Chapter 13) suggests that CBI can provide students with additional courses of instruction without greatly increasing the number of teachers. Computers, as indicated by Deaton (Chapter 12), can help the clerical staff deal with the exponential increases in paperwork without the need to hire a proportional amount of new staff.

Levin (1988) finds limited empirical evidence for the cost-effectiveness of CBI. By combining the effects per student and the costs per student for an educational intervention, he finds at one educational site that CBI is a more cost-effective educational intervention than are adult tutoring, longer school days, and smaller class sizes. This finding, however, has not been replicated at another educational site because that system has not been fully utilized.

Increasing Student Achievement

A major assumption behind implementing CBI is the medium's positive impact upon students' learning processes. As previously discussed, using computers in the classroom was expected to facilitate students' cognitive development. And many CBI professionals and educators (e.g., Bok, 1986; Kearsley et al., 1983) have indicated that CBI has led or will lead to the development of superior instructional materials.

Empirical evidence does exist which supports the claims about CBI's positive impact upon students' learning processes. Several reviews of the CBI research have shown that CBI does moderately raise students' levels of achievement (Hasselberg, 1984; Bangert-Drowns, Kulik, & Kulik, 1985; Neimic & Walberg, 1985). Neimic and Walberg, who examined the effects of CBI for all educational levels, have found an average increase of .42 standard deviations in students' achievement levels as a function of CBI.

Several chapters in this volume also present evidence of CBI's effectiveness (e.g., Chapter 14, Chapter 5, Chapter 13). Wilson (Chapter 13) notes that CBI is more effective than conventional instruction for teaching certain areas of mathematics to community college students. Carrier and Glenn claim that using word processsing systems helps students to produce more and higher quality work.

Handling Individual Differences and Needs

Handling individual learning differences has long been a difficult problem for educators. As indicated throughout this chapter, many educators and researchers (e.g., Avner et al., 1980; Bok, 1986; Carrier, 1979) believe that computers are ideally suited to handle individual learning differences. "To many educators, the computer represents the ultimate individual difference machine" (Carrier, 1979, p. 25).

Evidence shows that a CBI system can help educators to deal with differences in cognitive abilities (Bangert-Drowns et al., 1985; Neimic & Walberg, 1985; Zemke, 1984). Bangert-Drowns et al., and Neimic and Walberg have both found that CBI has the most pronounced effect for increasing the test scores of low-ability students. It must be noted that drill-and-practice programs are still primarily used to instruct low-ability students. These types of programs thus appear to provide low-ability students with needed additional structure of and practice with the instructional materials (Becker & Sterling, 1987).

Several chapters in this volume demonstrate the usefulness of CBI for handling individual needs (Chapter 8, Chapter 3, Chapter 15). Pyryt provides an account of using computers in the classroom to help challenge gifted students. On the other extreme, Romney described several computer programs that have been implemented by the Jefferson County, Kentucky school system, which are designed for dealing with severely handicapped students. He quite vividly demonstrates how computers can ease the hardships faced by such students. Finally, Robinson has described a group CBI training program for dealing with mildly handicapped students. Group CBI presentation has allowed mildly handicapped students to interact with and learn from nonhandicapped students.

Increasing Student Motivation

Another pervasive contention of CBI advocates has been that this medium increases students' motivation to learn the instructional materials (Lepper & Gurtner, 1989). As advertisements of CBI products have claimed, learner motivation is high for a particular CBI program because the system is easy and fun to use.

Avner and associates (Avner, 1981; Jones, Kane, Sherwood, & Avner, 1983) in a series of evaluations found that University of Illinois' students favored PLATO over other instructional media. For two semesters, Chemistry 100 students were asked to rate several different media with regard to helpfulness in learning the class materials. These media were PLATO, the textbook, lecture, labs, and quiz sections. For both semesters, the system received the highest ratings of 4.5 on a 5-point scale.

It has been an assumption that using computers in the classroom might also help motivate students to be more creative. Some students, such as this author, hate to write and do art work because of problems with producing a "perfect" final product. Word processors and computer graphics, by eliminating such drudgery, can help motivate students to write more and do more art work. Evidence does exist for this argument (Chapter 5; Jefferson County Public Schools, 1988). As reported by a teacher in the Jefferson County, Kentucky school district, "With the computer there is more motivation and constant writing; whereas in the classroom there was a need for more encouragement" (p. 4).

Final Thoughts about the Promises of CBI

Computer technology can also help the educational process in a number of other ways. For one thing, the motivational aspects of CBI may help "at-risk" students to complete the educational program. Wilson (Chapter 13) notes that the completion rates for CBI community college classes have met or exceeded those of conventional classes. This effect for CBI, however, occurred only after more rigorous instructional management strategies were put in place (Chapter 13). As noted in nearly every chapter in this volume, computers can also help with the administrative aspects of teaching. CMI programs, for example, have been shown to relieve instructors of tedious grading and management chores (Chapter 13). Consequently, freed from these chores, teachers have more time to devote to their students. Computer technology can also help educators to maintain quality instructors in remote areas (OTA, 1988). Specialized classes in the sciences and mathematics, for example, can be brought to schools that have neither the number of students nor the appropriate complement of specialized teachers to offer such courses (OTA, 1968). Finally, computers —by simulating complex equipment and hazardous situations—can provide science and vocational training which cannot easily be provided by other means (Chapter 5; Department of Defense Memorandum from the Assistant Secretary of Defense, September 9, 1985).

PROBLEMS WITH CBI USE

With all the cited advantages of using computers in the classroom, it is hard to believe that computers are still not being fully utilized by educators. Fisher (1987) notes that only half of the kids in American elementary schools will actually use computers in any year. Also, Becker (1985) has found that the median number of computers at an American high school is 20; at a middle school/junior high it is 13; and at an elementary school the number is 9.

Among the many barriers to full CBI implementation are the following: (a) inadequate funding, (b) inadequate software, (c) inadequate planning and preparation, and (d) unrealistic expectations. These barriers are briefly discussed in the next few pages.

Inadequate Funding

Even though the costs for computers have dramatically decreased in the last few years, an extensive capital investment is still required for implementing and using CBI. School systems should expect to spend $1,000 per computer; $400 per printer; and $200 per software package (OTA, 1988; Becker, 1985). There are also hefty expenditures associated with the following: (a) maintenance and upgrading of the system, (b) teacher training, (c) power for terminals, (d) peripheral equipment, (e) support personnel,

(f) disk storage space, and (g) lifetime authoring privileges for some systems (OTA, 1988; Shlechter, 1988). For example, the American school system annually spends nearly $700 million for maintaining and upgrading its computer systems (OTA, 1988).

Insufficient funds for these expenditures are noted by state agencies, school systems, and educators (see OTA, 1988; Gleason & Read, 1985; Strudler & Gall, 1988; Chapter 2). Gleason and Read have found that 80 percent of their sample of representative Wisconsin educators cited insufficient funding as the most serious constraint to CBI implementation. And Wisconsin is a relatively progressive state with regards to funding education and CBI.

This lack of funds for CBI is associated with an absence of financial commitment from the federal government to education and educational technology. For fiscal year 1987, the federal government provided only 15 percent of the funds spent for computer-based technology in the classroom —$29 million out of $200 million. Sugrue (Chapter 2) indicates furthermore that the order of magnitude for CBI funding is local sources (e.g., parent–teacher associations, school districts, and businesses) followed by state and federal agencies.

Sugure (Chapter 2) concludes that wealthier school districts have more resources for hardware, software, and teacher training, a conclusion that unfortunately has been substantiated by the research literature (Becker & Sterling, 1987; National Task Force on Educational Technology, 1986). Black students have been much less likely to attend schools with computers and with computer-using teachers than has been the case for white students (Becker & Sterling, 1987). The National Task Force on Educational Technology has emphatically recommended that the federal government take steps to end this inequitable distribution of educational technology. (See Chapter 11 for a further discussion of problems with using CBI in an inner-city school.)

Indequate Software

Another traditional complaint by educators of CBI is the lack of adequate software (e.g., see Chapter 6; Linn & Fisher, 1984; National Task Force on Educational Technology, 1986; Walker, 1984). After 30 years of CBI, the curricula for this medium are still in their infancy (Strudler & Gall, 1988). Hativa (Chapter 6) describes some of the problems with current drill-and-practice programs for teaching mathematics. She also offers some remedies for these problems.

There are several factors that have led to the development of inadequate software. For one thing, CBI developers have concentrated on the hardware rather than on the courseware aspects of this medium. This situation is unfortunate because the heart of any CBI system is the courseware, not the hardware (Holmes, 1982). Secondly, teachers have rarely been involved in developing commercially published software (Shlechter, 1988; Walker, 1984). Most schools do not have the technological capabilities to run some of the more sophisticated software applications associated with artificial intelligence (OTA, 1988). Finally, educators may have perpetuated the marketing of problematic courseware because of problems with selecting courseware (Linn & Fisher, 1984).

Several chapters in this volume discuss methods of improving CBI courseware (e.g., Chapters 4, 6, 8, and 10, respectively). Reeves discusses the importance of providing faculty support for the development of CBI courseware. As he has noted, "Parallel incentive and support structures (as found for research) must be found for CBI if a sufficient quantity of quality courseware is to be provided for Higher Education" (p. 5). And Colbert (Chapter 10) details the procedures needed for a large urban school system (e.g., the Los Angeles Unified School District) to select quality courseware.

Inadequate Planning and Preparation

As emphasized throughout this volume, a successful implementation of this instructional medium requires careful planning and preparation. The National Task Force on Educational Technology (1986) reports, however, that adequate planning and preparation are frequently not carried out for integrating the technology into the educational system. Hence, as previously reported, available computers are not being fully utilized by teachers and students.

Conscientious planning is needed, first of all, to determine the feasibility of using CBI for a particular course. Not all courses are suited for CBI. Wilson (Chapter 13) notes that CBI can teach grammar rules but cannot teach creative writing. Wilson then provides some basic guidelines for making a decision about using CBI. There are also some more elaborate media selection models (e.g., Reisser & Gagne, 1983) available to help determine the feasibility of using CBI; however, these models only provide a very general framework.

Planning for CBI involves determining the CBI program most appropriate for the particular course. Some courseware may be more appropriate for certain educational situations. Computer simulations, for example, seem to be most suitable for supplementing astronomy, ecology, and meteorology courses (Chapter 8); however, drill-and-practice courseware seems to be best for teaching basic mathematics (Chapter 13). Pyryt also suggests that some types of courseware may not be appropriate for certain

types of students. Drill-and-practice courseware, for example, may alien-
ate gifted students (Solomon, 1986). As previously argued, however, such
courseware may be best for teaching "at-risk" students. Educators must
then be aware of possible aptitude-treatment-interactions (Cronbach &
Snow, 1977) when choosing a CBI program.

Careful planning is also needed to coordinate the resources and efforts
of the many different professionals involved in a CBI implementation.
Several reports have shown that a successful CBI implementation requires
the long-term commitment and participation from school superintendents
to school administrators to teachers (e.g., Chapters 10 and 14, respectively;
Shlechter, 1988). Personnel from the school superintendent's office must
help to coordinate and lead the implementation process (Chapters 10 and
14, respectively). Furthermore, a system is rarely successfully implemented
without the participation and full support of the school's administration
and is rarely used without the participation and support of teachers. As
noted by Strudler and Gall (1988):

> [T]eachers expressed being less resistant to change when they can influence
> the "fit" between their curricular responsibilities and the computer program.
> (p. 7)

A simultaneous top-down and bottom-up approach is thus needed for successfully implementing this medium (Chapter 14).

Educators must also be prepared to make changes associated with using
CBI. School administrators must be able to deal with the organizational
changes which occur vis-à-vis CBI implementation (Suppes & Fortune,
1985). A school district needs, for example, a computer coordinator in
order to help integrate the CBI curricula into the district's curriculum. As
discussed throughout this volume, teachers will also have to be trained to
use and integrate the CBI materials into their program (Chapter 5; Wiske
& Zodhiates, 1988). Wiske and Zodhiates have found that using computers, initially, makes teaching more difficult. They have also noted that
planning is needed, for example, to sort out the logistics of the who,
when, and where of using the equipment.

Planning for successfully implementing CBI into the educational system
must also involve the coordinated efforts of federal agencies. Educational
innovations have only flourished with a financial and philosophical commitment from the federal government. Also, the federal government can
best provide the coordination needed for a united effort in the development
and implementation of CBI for all students. Washington's role in the implementation of CBI is further elaborated upon by Branson (Chapter 14)
and Sugrue (Chapter 2).

Unrealistic Expectations

Another major problem facing long-term CBI implementation is teachers' unrealistic expectations of this system (Shlechter, 1988; Green, 1984). Since the phonograph, each new educational innovation has promised to be an educational panacea and each new technology floundered when it failed to deliver educators to the promised land (Bok, 1986; Shlechter, 1988). Skinner (Green, 1984), for example, claims that programmed instruction faltered because the people selling the programs made all kinds of outlandish claims for the materials. Educators then became discouraged with using programming learning packages when these promises were not met. Skinner warns us that CBI may be facing a similar problem.

SOME FINAL WORDS

Several points have been underscored throughout this chapter. CBI does have a tremendous potential to help the world meet future educational challenges. This potential will only be realized through a national and international commitment to this medium. Educators, educational researchers, CBI professionals, politicians, and concerned citizens must work closely together to understand and overcome the barriers to successful CBI implementation. They must also realize that computers are not an educational panacea, but rather another instructional program and tool which must be carefully integrated into established instructional programs. The remaining chapters in this volume will provide further insights into CBI's potential and will discuss procedures for successfully integrating computers into the classrooms of the 21st century.

REFERENCES

Avner, R.A. (1981, February). *Update of PLATO-Based physics teaching.* (Unpublished data). Urbana: University of Illinois.

Avner, R.A., Moore, C., & Smith, S. (1980). Active external control: A basis for the superiority of CBI. *Journal of Computer-Based Instruction, 11*(3), 85–89.

Bangert-Drowns, R.C., Kulik, J.A., & Kulik, C-L., C. (1985). Effectiveness of computer-based education in secondary schools. *Journal of Computer-Based Instruction, 12*(3), 59–68.

Becker, H.J. (1985). *The second national survey of instructional uses of school computers: A preliminary report.* Paper presented at the World Conference on Computers in Education, Norfolk, VA.

Becker, H.J., & Sterling, C.W. (1987). Equity in school computer use: National data and neglected considerations. *Journal of Educational Computing Research, 3,* 289–311.

Bitzer, D.L., Braunfield, P.G., & Lictenberger, W.W. (1962). PLATO II: A multiple-student, computer-controlled, automatic teaching device. In J.E. Coulson (Ed.), *Programmed learning and computer-based instruction* (pp. 205–216). New York: John Wiley & Sons.

Bok, D. (1986). *Higher education.* Cambridge, MA: Harvard University Press.

Bonner, P. (1984). Computers in education: Promise and Reality. *Personal Computing, 8*(9), 64–77.

Carrier, C.A. (1979). The role of learning characteristics in computer-based instruction. *National Society for Programmed Instruction Journal, 18*(5), 22–25.

Clark, R.E. (1983). Reconsidering research on learning from media. *Review of Educational Research, 53*(4), 445–459.

Cronbach, L.J., & Snow, R.E. (1977). *Aptitudes and Instructional Methods.* New York: Irvington Publishers, Inc.

Crowder, N.A. (1962). Intrinsic and extrinsic programming. In J.E. Coulson (Ed.), *Programmed learning and computer-based instruction* (pp. 58–66). New York: John Wiley & Sons.

Cuban, L. (1986). *Teachers and machines: The classroom of technology since 1920.* New York: Teachers College Press.

Ellul, J. (1967). *The technological society.* New York: Vantage Books.

Fletcher, J.D. & Rockaway, M.R. (1985). Computer-based training in the military. In J.A. Ellis (Ed.), *Military contributions to instructional technology* (pp. 171–213). New York: Praeger.

Fisher, G. (1987). Is the computer movement dead? *Instructor, 95*(9), 27.

Flavell, J.H. (1963). *The development psychology of Jean Piaget.* Princeton, NJ: D. Von Nostrand.

Ford, J.D., Jr., Slough, D.A., & Hurlock, R.E. (1972). *Computer assisted instruction in Navy technical training using a small dedicated computer system: Final report* (Research Rep. No. SRR 72-13). San Diego: Naval Personnel and Training Research Laboratory.

Fritz, M.F., Humphrey, J.E., Greenlee, J.A., & Madison, R.L. (1952). *Survey of television utilization in Army Training* (Human Engineering Report SpecDeveCen 530-01-1). Ames, IA: Iowa State University.

Gleason, G.T., & Reed, T. (1985, April). *Computers in the Schools: How will educators cope with the revolution?* Paper presented at the Annual Meeting of the American Education Research Association, Chicago, IL.

Goldstine, H.H. (1972). *The computer from PASCAL to Von Neumann.* Princeton, NJ: Princeton University Press.

Gray, W.D., Pliske, D.J., & Psotka, J. (1985). *Smart technology for training: Promise and current status* (ARI Research Rep. No. 1412). Alexandria, VA: U.S. Army Research for the Behavioral and Social Sciences.

Green, J.O. (1984, February). B.F. Skinner's technology of teaching. *Classroom Computer Learning,* pp. 23–29.

Hasselberg, T.S. (1984, July). *Research on the effectiveness of computer-based instruction* (Tech. Rep. No. 84.1.3). Nashville, TN: The Learning Technology Center of George Peabody College of Vanderbilt University.

Hofstetter, F.T. (1983). The cost of PLATO in a university environment. *Journal of Computer-Based Instruction, 9,* 148–155.

Holmes, G. (1982, September). Computer-assisted instruction: A discussion of some of the issues for would-be implementors. *Educational Technology, 22,* 7 – 1 2 .

Jefferson County Public Schools. (1988, March). *The new kid graduates.* Unpublished report. Louisville, KY: Jefferson County Public Schools.

Jones, L.M., Kane, D., Sherwood, B.A., & Avner, R.A. (1983, June). A final-exam comparison involving computer-based instruction. *American Journal of Physics, 51*(6), 533–538.

Kearsley, G., Hunter, B., & Seidel, R.J. (1983). *Two decades of CBI research: What have we learned* (HUMRRO Professional Paper 3-83). Alexandria, VA: Human Resources Research Organization.

Kinzer, C.K., Sherwood, R.D., & Bransford, J.D. (1986). *Computer strategies for education. Foundations and content-area applications.* Columbus, OH: Merrill Publishing Company.

Lantz, B.S., Bregar, W.S., & Farley, A.M. (1983). An intelligent CAI system for teaching equation solving. *Journal of Computer-Based Instruction, 10*(1,2), 35–42.

Lepper, M.R., & Gurtner, J-L. (1989). Children and computers: Approaching the twenty-first century. *American Psychologist, 44*(2), 170–178.

Levin, H.M. (1988). Cost-effectiveness and educational policy. *Educational Evaluations and Policy, 10*(1), 51–69.

Lin, M.C., & Fisher, C.W. (1984, June). *The gap between promise and reality in computer education: Planning a response* (Eric Document ED 249 598).

Longo, A.A. (1972). *A summative evaluation of computer assisted instruction in the U.S. Army Basic Electronics Training* (Tech. Rep. No. 72-1). Fort Monmouth, NJ: U.S. Army Signal Center & School, Computer Assisted Instruction Division.

Merrill, M.D., Schneider, E.W., & Fletcher, K.A. (1980). *The instructional design library (Vol. 40): TICCIT.* Englewood Cliffs, NJ: Educational Technology Publications.

Meyers, R. (1984). PLATO: Historical roots, current applications and future prospects. *Training Technology Journal, 1*(2), 33–37.

National Task Force on Educational Technology. (1986). Transforming American Education: Reducing the risk to the Nation. *Technological Horizons, 14*(1), 58–67.

Nawrocki, L.H. (1985). An intelligent computer assisted instruction system for maintenance training. *Proceedings of the NATO symposium on computer-based instruction in military environments.* Brussels: Belgium: Belgium Defense Staff Headquarters.

Neimic, R.P., & Walberg, H.J. (1985). Computers and achievement in the elementary schools. *Journal of Educational Computing Research, 1,* 435–550.

Oetinger, A.G., & Marks, S. (1967). *Run computer, run: The mythology of educational innovation.* New York: Collier Books.

Office of Technology Assessment (OTA). (1988). *Power on! New tools for teaching and learning* (OTA-SET-379). Washington, DC: U.S. Government Printing Office.

Office of Technology Assessment. (1986). *Assessment, technology, and the American economic transition: Choices for the future* (OTA-TET-283). Washington, DC: U.S. Government Printing Office.

Papert, S. (1980). *Mindstorms: Children, computers and powerful ideas.* New York: Basic Books.

Pliske, D.B., & Psotka, J. (1986). Exploratory programming environments for designing ICAI. *Journal of Computer-Based Instruction, 13*(2), 52–57.

Reisser, R.A., & Gagne, R.M. (1983). *Selecting media for instruction.* Englewood Cliffs, NJ: Educational Technology Publications.

Salomon, G. (1988, April). *Artificial intelligence and natural wisdom: How cultural artifacts can cultivate the mind.* Paper presented at the Annual Meeting of the Dutch Education Research Association, Leuven, Netherlands.

Seidel, R.J. (1980). *It's 1980: Do you know where your computer is?* (HUMMRO Doc. No. IR-008-536). Alexandria, VA: Human Resources Research Organization.

Shlechter, T.M. (1988). An examination of the research evidence for computer-based instruction. In R.T. Hartson & D. Hix (Eds.), *Advances in human-computer interactions* (Vol. 2, pp. 316–367). Norwood, NJ: Ablex.

Skinner, B.F. (1954). The science of learning and the art of teaching. *Harvard Educational Review, 24,* 86–97.

Skinner, B.F. (1961). Learning theory and future research. In J.P. Lysaught (Ed.), *Programmed learning: Evolving principles and industrial applications.* Ann Arbor, MI: Foundations for Research on Human Behavior.

Smith, S.G., & Sherwood, B.A. (1976). Educational uses of the PLATO computer system. *Science, 192,* 344–352.

Snyder, T.D. (1987, May). *Digest of education statistics 1987.* Washingaton DC: Office of Educational Research and Improvement, U.S. Department of Education.

Solomon, C. (1986). *Computer environments for children.* Cambridge, MA: The MIT Press.

Strudler, N.B., & Gall, M.D. (1988, April). *Successful change agent strategies for overcoming impediments to microcomputer implementation in the classroom.* Paper presented at the Annual Meeting of the American Educational Research Association, New Orleans, LA.

Suppes, P. (1966). The uses of computers in education. *Scientific American, 215,* 206–211.

Suppes, P., & Fortune, R.E. (1985). Computer-assisted instruction: Possibilities and problems. *NASSP Bulletin, 69*(480), 30–34.

Vinsonhaler, J.F., & Bass, R.K. (1972). A summary of ten major studies on CAI drill and practice. *Educational Technology, 12,* 29–32.

Walker, D.F. (1984, February). *Computers in schools: Potential & limitations. II: The software problem.* Educational Brief. San Francisco: Far West Laboratory for Educational Research and Development.

Wiske, M.S., & Zodhiates, P. (1988, March). *How technology affects teaching.* Prepared for the Office of Technology Assessment. Springfield, VA: National Technical Information Service.

Zeman, D. (1959). Skinner's theory of teaching machines. In E.H. Galanter (Ed.), *Automatic teaching: The state of the art* (pp. 167–176). New York: John Wiley & Sons.

Zemke, R. (1984, May). Evaluating computer-assisted instruction: The good, the bad and the why. *Training, 21*(5), 22–47.

2

A Comparative Review of European and American Approaches to Computer-Based Instruction in Schools*

Brenda M. Sugrue
Sugrue & Associates Training, Dublin, Ireland

INTRODUCTION

As the title suggests, this chapter attempts to compare the predominant approaches to the implementation of computer-based instruction (CBI) in schools in Europe and in the United States. Since Europe is made up of more than 20 independent countries, each with its own political, social and cultural identity, and educational system, it might seem misleading to identify a general "European" approach. It would be equally inappropriate to refer to a general "American" approach, given the lack of centralization of educational policy and the absence of a national agency with responsibility for computers in schools in the U.S. However, there are indeed some trends which appear to be distinctly American and distinctly European. There are also many similarities in the uses of computers in schools on both sides of the Atlantic. The main similarities between the European and American approaches to CBI in schools are as follows:

1. Local funding and initiatives in the acquisition and use of computers in schools are at least as important as state or national efforts.

---

* The author wishes to acknowledge Elizabeth E. Oldham, Trinity College Dublin, for her help in locating sources and clarifying ideas discussed in this chapter.

2. In both the U.S. and Europe, teacher training for the use of computers across the school curriculum is minimal, with a few notable exceptions.
3. CBI in elementary schools lags behind CBI in secondary schools, although the difference between the two is greater in Europe than in the U.S.
4. Secondary schools in the U.S. and Europe have concentrated on teaching about the computer rather than on using it as an instructional device.

The main differences between the European and U.S. developments are as follows:

1. U.S. schools appear to have about twice as many computers per student as their largest European counterparts.
2. European software tends to be developed and evaluated within the education sector, often supported by grants from central government bodies. U.S. educational software tends to be developed more by private and business initiatives, and evaluation is conducted by schools and universities (if at all).
3. There is greater diversity of hardware and software for CBI in European schools than in schools in the U.S.

Since the use of computers in schools was not widespread, even in the U.S., until the 1980s, when microcomputers brought the cost of the technology within reach of school budgets, this chapter focuses on activities in the past decade. Firstly, developments in the U.S. and Europe are described separately under the headings influences and goals, funding, hardware, software, types of instructional use, teacher training, and evaluation. Secondly, similarities and differences between approaches are discussed. Thirdly, changing trends and promises for the future of CBI in schools in the U.S. and Europe are discussed. Finally, critical factors, necessary for realization of those promises regardless of country or culture, are isolated.

DEVELOPMENTS OF THE PAST DECADE

United States

Influence and goals. Pressure for the widespread adoption of the computer as an instructional technology with the potential of "revolutionizing" American schools came from a variety of sources. Most pressure stemmed from the prevailing cultural, corporate, and political desire to improve the achievement levels of students in U.S. schools, with the ultimate goal of producing more engineers, mathematicians, scientists, and technicians, and reducing the levels of illiteracy among U.S. high school graduates (Cuban, 1986). Pressure manifested itself simultaneously from the top down (i.e., from federal government to state to local school districts to school) and from the bottom up (i.e., from parents to teachers to school principals). A mediating force was that of commercial interests, namely hardware and software manufacturers who saw schools as a potentially huge market for their products.

Although policy on CBI in schools differs from state to state, activities have been concerned with four areas: (a) hardware acquisition, (b) software acquisition, evaluation, and distribution, (c) staff training and development, and (d) integrating the technology with ongoing instruction. Some state policies suggest "curriculum approaches while others outline detailed strategies for implementation, or establish graduation and teacher certification requirements" (U.S. Congress, Office of Technology Assessment, 1988, p. 205).

Funding. It is estimated that $2 billion was spent on hardware for instructional computing in schools in the U.S. in the last decade (U.S. Congress, Office of Technology Assessment, 1988). That represents a cost of about $5 per student per year, an insignificant fraction of total annual educational expenditures. Costs and funding mechanisms vary from state to state. The order of magnitude of funding from greatest to least is local (parent–teacher associations, school districts, business contributions), followed by state, followed by federal funding. Therefore, wealthier school districts have more resources for hardware, software, and teacher training.

State funding for educational technology (including CBI) often comes from federal grants and is usually mixed with funding from business and industry, software publishers, hardware vendors, and private foundations. Information obtained from an Office of Technology Assessment survey in 1987 indicates that specific allocations for 1987 ranged from less than $200,000 (Oregon) to $41 million (New York). Two-thirds of the states reported that insufficient funding hampered the implementation of technology in schools (U.S. Congress, Office of Technology Assessment, 1988).

Hardware. Between 1981 and 1987, the percentage of American schools with one or more computers intended for instruction grew from 18 percent to 95 percent. There are now between 1.2 and 1.7 million computers in the 81,000 public schools alone (servicing 40 million students); this number translates to approximately one computer for every 30 students. In practice there is a wide disparity between schools, some having one computer in every classroom, others having clusters of computers in a library or in classrooms, others having designated computer laboratories. Great latitude is afforded local school districts in the choice of hardware. However, the Apple computer has been the most frequent choice for educational uses. Although computers are widely distributed and access to them by students has increased significantly during the past decade, "the vast majority of schools still do not have enough of them to make the computer a central element of instruction" (U.S. Congress, Office of Technology Assessment, 1988, p. 6).

Smaller schools have proportionally more computers than large schools, giving students in smaller schools greater access to computers. Wealthier schools have acquired computers more rapidly than schools with students of predominantly low socioeconomic status (U.S. Congress, Office of Technology Assessment, 1988). Elementary schools are approximately two years behind secondary schools in terms of hardware acquisition (Becker, 1986).

Software. More than 10,000 software products intended for instructional use with stand-alone computers in schools are now on the market in the U.S. While in the 1970s practically all programs on the market were in the drill and practice or tutorial mode, the 1980s have seen a diversification into more experiential or simulation-type programs which might promote "higher order thinking" in students. There are about 900 suppliers (all private and commercial), most of them small companies. Tool programs (e.g., generic programs for word processing and data management) have become the best sellers in the late 1980s, reflecting the recent shift toward using the computer as a tool rather than as a stand-alone tutor.

The extent of state involvement in software development is limited to small-scale projects. Most software in use in schools is developed and sold by commercial software publishers. One state which has particularly supported software development is Minnesota. The Minnesota Educational Computing Corporation (MECC) was established in the 1970s and now sells its software to schools all over the U.S. There are some multistate collaborative projects, such as the Software Evaluation Exchange Dissemination Project (SEED) involving Alabama, Florida, Georgia, Mississippi, North Carolina, and South Carolina. The main aim of such collaborations is to avoid duplication of effort and to exchange information such as software evaluations and practical classroom applications.

Types of instructional use. Actual student utilization of computers depends on more than just the availability of hardware and software. There is substantial variance in the use of computers across schools of different size, demographic composition, and location. Not all students use computers and it is estimated that those who do spend on average a little more than one hour per week on the computer, 4 percent of their instructional time. The National Assessment of Educational Performance (NAEP) report on computer competence found in its 1985–86 survey of third-, fifth-, and eleventh-grade students that computers were seldom used in subject areas, but were used almost exclusively to teach about computers, that is, computer literacy or computer science programs (Martinez & Mead, 1988). Some schools set up computer laboratories that all students use for a certain amount of time each day, month, or year. Other schools target CBI at selected groups, for example, to teach low-achieving students basic skills or to provide integrated learning systems for certain grade levels.

At Johns Hopkins University, Henry Becker has conducted two national surveys of school uses of microcomputers in 1983 and 1985 (Becker, 1984, 1986). In 1983, he found that the teaching of programming (98 percent in BASIC) was the main use, followed by the use of packaged programs for either mathematics or language drills. At that time, tool software, such as word processing programs, was beginning to be used in secondary schools but was not yet visible in elementary schools. In general, the focus was on computer literacy or learning about computers as opposed to learning with the computer. At elementary school, Becker estimated that, in 1983, 16 percent of students used the computer for 20 minutes per week, with usage increasing with grade level; in secondary schools, students in the upper grades used the computer for an average of 45 minutes per week.

In 1985, Becker found that a typical student computer user was getting about twice as much computer time than in 1983, and that the number of students actually using computers in both elementary and secondary schools had also doubled. These increases reflected the quadrupling of the number of computers in schools during that two-year period (Becker, 1986). As for the main types of uses of computers in schools in 1985, Becker found that, on the average, across all school levels, student time divided more or less evenly among computer-assisted instruction (CAI), that is, prepackaged tutorial and drill programs, programming, and other academic work including discovery-based programs and content-free tool software. However, a much higher proportion of time in secondary schools than in elementary schools was spent on programming and on the use of applications software. In elementary schools, the computer was mostly used as a medium for delivering mathematics drill and practice or tutorial programs.

There is very little statistical information about current trends in classroom computer uses. While the trend in the late 1980s appears to be towards more integration of the computer as a tool in all subject areas, through the use of content-free applications software similar to that used in society at large for information management, the picture is by no means clear. As Cuban wrote in 1986: "Determining what levels of teacher use now exist is like trying to snap a photograph of a speeding bicyclist" (p. 78). According to Cuban (1986), many of the classroom uses that get a lot of publicity (for example, Papert's work with children using Logo or Dwyer's work with discovery-oriented mathematics programs) remain far outside the mainstream of public schooling.

Teacher training. Undoubtedly, the most critical factor in CBI is the knowledge and skill of the classroom teacher, or what Thompson (1988) calls the "liveware." However, "the vast majority of teachers in the U.S. have had little or no training on how to apply computers in teaching" (U.S. Congress, Office of Technology Assessment, 1988, p. 98). It seems that as teachers become competent in using computers, they leave the classroom to become computer curriculum coordinators or to take jobs in industry.

In the U.S., 18 states require and 8 recommend that teachers seeking certification take computer-related courses or become familiar with using technology in instruction. However, preservice training is hampered by lack of federal funding, state restrictions on teacher education curriculum, and a lack of adequate equipment and faculty with the expertise to teach beyond basic introductory computer courses. Almost every state provides or supports in-service technology activities through a combination of ongoing activities at technology centers. Of the 20 states that allocate funds specifically for technology training, annual funding ranges from $15 million to less than $20,000. Most teachers receive CBI training through their local school district but the state is an important source of training programs and assistance.

According to the Office of Technology assessment, the most recent data available indicate that only one-third of all K–12 teachers have had as much as 10 hours of computer training and much of this training focuses on learning about computers, not learning how to teach with computers (U.S. Congress, Office of Technology Assessment, 1988, p. 18).

Evaluation. One can evaluate the impact of computers on schools along two dimensions: effectiveness and efficiency. Most evaluation research in the U.S. during the past 30 years was concerned with the effectiveness of drill and practice and tutorial programs in basic mathematics and computation skills. This research was conducted primarily by academic researchers, sometimes funded by federal grants. The results of many of these studies, which focused on the outcomes of instruction as opposed to the learning processes induced (Shlechter, 1988), appeared to indicate that CBI improved performance levels on standardized achievement tests by .5 standard deviation (Kulik, Bangert-Downs, & Williams, 1983). However, many of the studies had severe methodological flaws; the observed achievement gains could be accounted for by novelty and instructional design variables which were independent of the computer (Clark & Sugrue, 1988). More recent research on other types of CBI, such as the effects of LOGO on higher order thinking skills, are equally disappointing (Pea,

Kurland, & Hawkins, 1985). Becker suggests that most of the CBI evaluation literature is obsolete and does not generalize beyond the particular school or schools in which it was conducted (Becker, 1987).

Evaluation of the efficiency or cost-effectiveness of CBI in schools has been minimal. The Office of Technology Assessment (1988) has reviewed a number of cost-effectiveness studies and concludes that (a) CBI can be more cost-effective than other nontechnological methods of achieving similar goals among particular groups of students; (b) some forms of CBI are more cost-effective than others; and (c) the cost-effectiveness of learning technologies is very sensitive to particular characteristics of schools and classrooms where they are implemented.

Europe

Influences and goals. In the 1980s, the typical European response to the potential of microcomputer technology for schooling has been the establishment of coordinated nationwide development programs under the responsibility of public authorities. These national programs have been generally preceded and accompanied by more "spontaneous" activity at a local or "grass roots" level. The forces underlying the "official" response have been predominantly economic, social, and political, for example, the demand in the labor market for specialized manpower, or the changes in society as new technologies are adopted. The relative importance of these economic, social, and political pressures varies from country to country, as does the form of new initiatives in relation to CBI in schools in terms of curriculum and equipment policies, target populations, scale of investment, and demands on teachers. In general, policies have responded instrumentally and pragmatically to a "web of influences" (OECD, 1986, p. 26). Most policies have been short term, with a maximum time perspective of five years. No policy has aimed at altering the existing structure of the educational system. The organization of European initiatives reflects the organization of the educational systems. France has a highly centralized program, whereas the UK, West Germany, and the Netherlands give much more autonomy to regional authorities. The scale of programs reflects the size and wealth of nations, the UK and France, and more recently the Netherlands, having the most extensive programs.

It was concern about the economic position of the Netherlands among the great industrial powers which pushed the Netherlands to develop a five-year national plan in 1984, the National Information Stimulation Plan (NISP). The goals of the program were the improvement of the quality of the "human capital," that is, high school graduates, and the preparation of ordinary citizens for information technology as a social phenomenon. The goals were to be realized along three channels: distribution of hardware; production and distribution of software; provision of in-service training for teachers (Van Deursen, 1988).

One of the main differences in policy between countries has been the segment of the school population at which initial CBI initiatives have been targeted. The Netherlands gave top priority to the vocational education sector. France and the UK adopted a more "comprehensive" approach with investment at all levels of the school system, and the goal of computer literacy for all. However, all countries, with the exception of the UK, have tended to neglect the elementary school sector. Every other country in Europe is noted as making a conscious decision to introduce computing into the secondary school curriculum first (Aston & Templeton, 1988). The 1981–1986 UK national program, the Microelectronics Education Programme (MEP), was based on the perceived need to prepare children for life in a society in which systems based on microelectronics would be commonplace. The MEP had three main goals: the establishment of information services, the in-service training of teachers, and the publication and distribution of materials (Fothergill & Anderson, 1981). The program was replaced in 1986 under the direction of the Microelectronics Education Support Unit (MESU). The overall policy was one of encouraging the use of the computer as a tool for teaching and learning across the curriculum. A separate subject, computer studies, had been on the curriculum of UK secondary schools since 1975. This situation reflects a general pattern in European countries, with the notable exception of France, whereby the computer is first introduced into the secondary school curriculum as an object of study in its own right and is followed some time later by an attempt to integrate the computer into all subjects on the curriculum.

The French government-sponsored "informatique pour tous" (computer literacy for all) plan came into effect early in 1985. The objective to be attained by the end of the year was to train 100,000 teachers in computer science, and to install 120,000 micros in schools throughout the country. The French approach differs from that of the Netherlands, the UK, West Germany, or Ireland in that the French had a sizeable national program as early 1973 and had started by attempting to integrate the computer into the curriculum without creating a separate discipline of computer studies. The more recent programs in France have introduced "informatics" (i.e., information technology) as an optional separate subject on the curriculum.

Funding. Regardless of the extent of centralization of the educational system, in Europe national programs are funded by the national government, usually through joint investment by the Department of Education and the Department of Trade and Industry, reflecting the influence of economic pressures on the drive for CBI in schools. The largest investment has been made by the French government with the equivalent of approximately U.S. $300 million allocated in 1985 alone (OECD, 1986). Funding for the Dutch NISP started with about $140 million in 1984, almost one-third of that coming from the Ministry of Economic Affairs (Van Deursen, 1988). From 1989, a continued budget of approximately $25 million per year has been allocated for hardware replacement and software acquisition. In the UK, funding has also come from both the Department of Education and Science (DES) and the Department of Trade and Industry (DTI); the DES provided the equivalent of over U.S. $40 million with the DTI providing a similar amount in hardware subsidies to schools. The UK government has provided almost U.S. $20 million in Educational Support Grants for CBI in the 1988–1989 financial year for England and Wales (Gardner, Fulton, & Megarity, 1988). The Spanish and Portuguese governments have, since 1985, made substantial investments in computer equipment for schools (OECD, 1986). The Irish government has provided more than $2 million for the supply of computers to Irish secondary schools since 1981.

In all countries, national programs have been paralleled by nongovernment-sponsored local-level initiatives in the field of education and beyond; parents and school boards bought computers out of their own funds and sent their teachers on training courses; parents started fund-raising activities; businesses gave donations of hardware; industry trained unemployed graduates to become microcomputer operators and programmers. It was mainly such "grass roots" activity that funded CBI in Europe, particularly CBI in elementary schools. Generally, in most countries, more money for CBI has come out of the normal equipment budgets of schools and local educational bodies than from special central funds supporting official policy (OECD, 1986).

Hardware. Many countries limit equipment to that manufactured within the country. For example, the UK is committed to the BBC microcomputer, the French to Thomson, and the Irish to Apple computers. Often computer manufacturers have made offers of subsidized hardware that governments and schools could not refuse. However, some countries place no restrictions on the type of hardware that schools can purchase. Due to the freedom of learning materials policy in the Netherlands, the government was unable to prescribe guidelines for the choice and purchase of computers; any prescription would have violated the schools' freedom to arrange their own educational system. However, the Dutch government did encourage standardization on MS-DOS microcomputers (Plomp, Steerneman, & Pelgrum, 1988). In all countries, the independent activities of schools, school boards, and parents have led to a maximum amount of variation in hardware in schools. The result is a lack of standardization of equipment between countries and, in some cases, within countries.

It is difficult to obtain accurate figures for the numbers of computers in schools in the various countries. The OECD in 1986 estimated that computers were present in up to 80 percent of secondary schools, but in less than 5 percent of elementary schools in Europe (OECD, 1986). In the UK there was an average of one computer per 95 secondary school students, and an average of one per 150 elementary school students. In France the ratio at the end of 1985 was one computer per 70 students. The common situation in most other countries is a very uneven distribution of hardware, schools in better socioeconomic locations being better equipped. Countries with specialized educational sectors such as technical, commercial, and professional sectors at the secondary level have concentrated hardware in particular sectors. For example, in 1985, Austria had a ratio of one work-station to every two students in commercial schools (OECD, 1986).

Software. Government investment in software development has been minimal in comparison with investment in hardware for CBI in schools in Europe. However, most European software is produced within the educational system and not by commercial companies. There is much government-sponsored software development. In the Netherlands attempts were made to create the conditions for software development through the design of a standard methodology for courseware development; funding for courseware development; software coupons for all secondary schools to buy commercial programs; and training of 90 teachers to be courseware writers. In 1987, the Netherlands began a four-year project, called POCO, to produce courseware for both the separate subject of informatics and also for other subject areas, including writing and science simulations (Van Weering, 1988). The goal is to produce 1,000 hours of courseware by 1990 and to turn the project into a fully commercial company. In the UK, the MEP funded regional software development projects which would meet known national needs and have high transferability (McMahon & Anderson, 1980). In the UK, teachers have developed 25 percent of the software they use (OECD, 1986). The software programs developed in the UK were mainly simulation and problem-solving programs rather than drill and practice or tutorials (Kelly, 1987), for example, the program "L," a "mathemagical" adventure game, written by a group of enthusiasts from the Association of Teachers of Mathematics, or the program "Bank," which allows students to set up and carry out life-like bank transactions and accounting procedures; "Bank" was developed by the Scottish Microelectronic Development Project.

There is some production of software by commercial companies in Europe and also importing of software from other countries. To monitor the quality of software being produced by commercial companies, the Dutch government instigated a software evaluation project—Software and Courseware Evaluation Netherland (SCEN). Programs are evaluated for their user friendliness and suitability for application in educational programs. The reports are published every two months. The Dutch government tried to influence the software policy in schools by setting up projects which showed "exemplary" software plus indications of how they could be used (Van Deursen, 1988). The MEP in the UK issued guidelines for teachers writing software, and also issued lists of approved software. Local publications of computer user groups in many countries publish reviews of software. Teacher centers and regional information centers also play a role in the evaluation and distribution of software (OECD, 1986).

Types of instructional use. Most countries in Europe have a new subject, called either informatics, computer science, or computer studies on the secondary school curriculum, usually in the senior years. This subject is more technical than "computer literacy" which is concerned with the use of computer applications rather than with studying computer architecture and programming. In many computer studies programs, students learn more than one programming language and the emphasis has been on learning structured languages rather than on BASIC. In 1985, the number of entries for Computer Studies in the O-level examination in England ranked seventh in the list of subjects, just below the number of entries for Physics and above the number for French (Gardner et al., 1988). In the junior curriculum of European secondary schools, the focus is on computer literacy. In elementary schools in Europe the computer is mostly used as a medium for a variety of types of programs, generally with more of a focus on problem solving than on tutorial or drill programs.

While the primary focus in European schools has been on computer studies and computer literacy programs, the most recent trend is towards integrating the computer across the curriculum at both elementary and secondary school levels. The UK is often cited as being most successful in integrating the computer into a variety of subject areas. Each conventional subject area incorporates appropriate packages and subject-specific applications, for example, data logging in science experiments, composition in music class, graphics in art and design classes, desktop publishing in English class, databases in history class.

Teacher training. While most European countries specifically list teacher training as one of the main aims of their programs for implementing CBI in schools, the level of training received has been generally minimal or nonexistent (OECD, 1986). Most of the training is in-service rather than preservice. Elementary teachers tend to receive more training than do secondary teachers. France has made the greatest investment in teacher training; by mid-1985, 2,500 teachers had received extensive training and 45,000 had undergone more introductory programs, with another 110,000 being initiated by the end of 1985 (OECD, 1986). In the UK more than 80,000 teachers have received training in CBI. Although the initial dominant use of computers in UK schools was for computer studies, the MEP took action to foster more cross-curricular use of the resources by deliberately targeting in-service courses at teachers in the humanities and arts subjects (Gardner et al., 1988). However, the average length of time spent by each teacher was only 1.7 days. More recently, the UK policy on teacher training has shifted from trying to train all teachers to training a smaller group of information technology specialists (Malletratt, 1988). In many countries—for example, Ireland—there has been development in preservice training and also the introduction of one year postgraduate diplomas, but these are generally geared towards teachers of Computer Studies rather than to teachers interested in using the computer across the curriculum (Oldham, 1986).

Evaluation. There has been little formal evaluation of CBI in schools in Europe. One of the last actions of the MEP in the UK was to commission reports from the various subject associations on the penetration of the technology into their teaching/learning domains. Many of those reports highlight three main constraints in the progress of integrating CBI into their subjects: low hardware resource levels, poor software quality, and insufficient in-service training (Gardner et al., 1988). These three problems are evident in all countries. The results of a study in the Netherlands indicate that computers are not yet integrated into the secondary school curriculum at either school or subject level (Plomp et al., 1988). Even schools regarded as forerunners had hardly passed the stage of grass-roots developments. However, most countries appear to have succeeded in having the computer accepted as a regular feature of schooling. Most government and school board budgets now show continued reservation of funds for continuation of the activities begun by initial national programs.

The International Association for the Evaluation of Educational Achievement (IEA) has started an international study in which data will be collected regarding the content and outcomes of the introduction of computers in education in more than 20 different educational systems. The study focuses on national and school policies and practices, the type of use of the computers by teachers and students, and the consequences of computer use on achievement and attitudes of students with respect to computers themselves as well as to the traditional subjects. The design of the study provides opportunities to investigate the change in these aspects over time. The data collection for the first stage of the study is planned for the end of 1988 and the beginning of 1989. Thirteen European countries, Canada, the U.S., and some Asian and East European countries will participate. Reports of the study should be available in 1994 (Pelgrum & Plomp, 1988).

SIMILARITIES AND DIFFERENCES

The growing demand for computer-related skills in the labor force has contributed to the promotion and growth of CBI in schools in both the U.S. and Europe during the past decade. This increasing demand has led to the introduction of some form of computer studies and computer literacy as part of the secondary school curriculum in all countries. CBI in schools has manifested itself most consistently in the teaching of computer programming and the use of data processing software for its own sake or for the purpose of preparing students for life in the "information age." The more purely educational goal of revolutionizing the process of instruction itself remains less tangible and less easily operationalized. More lip service seems to have been paid to this goal in the U.S. than in Europe, perhaps indicating that either the European approach to education is more utilitarian or that European educators are more satisfied than their American counterparts with the instructional methods and media that already exist in their schools.

The initial form taken by CAI programs in the U.S. was far from revolutionary, focusing as it did on using the computer for drill and practice and linear tutorial programs. While these uses of the computer for instruction have been imitated in European schools, there has been a greater emphasis in Europe than in the U.S. on the use of the computer as a problem-solving environment and as a tool for simulating, modeling, and controlling processes that previously could not be done very easily in the classroom, for example, using the computer to control scientific experiments and to analyze data. CBI in schools in the U.S. is currently moving away from using the computer as a tutor to using the computer as a tool in a variety of subject areas. The difference between the existing tool-oriented European approach and the recent tool-oriented approach in the U.S. is that the more recent trend involves using subject-independent software such as word processing, database, and data analysis software, whereas the earlier European approach utilized subject-specific software. It appears that developments in CBI in schools are becoming more and more similar between nations, with both economic and educational goals being pursued in tandem.

In Europe, there have been more national government initiatives and support for CBI in schools than in the U.S. However, grass-roots activity has been more important than state-sponsored initiatives in most nations. Both in Europe and in the U.S., it is the dedication and enthusiasm of particular teachers, schools, and teacher educators that have raised the awareness of parents, school boards, and government departments to the point where they are now committed to CBI. In the U.S. and in Europe, similar problems have hampered the widespread and consistent integration of the computer in the instructional activities of schools. The inadequate pre- and in-service training of teachers and the scarcity of hardware in the schools continue to be the main obstacles to realization of the promises of CBI in schools everywhere. Continued investment in hardware and the prioritization of the preparation of teachers for their new role indicate that the main obstacles to CBI may eventually be eliminated.

FUTURE TRENDS

While the history of CBI in schools in the U.S. is older than in Europe, the problems encountered and the goals envisioned by all countries have become increasingly similar. There is now similarity of hardware and software, recognition of two parallel goals for CBI (the promotion of computer literacy and the improvement of the instructional process itself), and a growing focus on teacher training in both the U.S. and Europe. It is difficult to predict where the most extensive and innovative activity will be in the next decade. Europe has perhaps two advantages: Firstly, the fact that CBI is a newer phenomenon there may lead to more energy and enthusiasm on the part of teachers, teacher educators, and curriculum designers; secondly, the advent of a more unified European Community in 1992, with a pooling and standardization of resources, may result in a more coordinated and concerted effort to modify school practices to accommodate the capabilities of the computer. There are no similar reasons that might lead to equal standardization or rejuvenation of effort in the U.S. Equally, there is no reason to expect that the U.S. will not retain its lead in the area of research on the effects of CBI on learning and instruction.

In schools themselves, it appears that the emphasis will be on the cross-curricular use of applications software, in effect merging the development of computer literacy and the use of the computer as a tool for problem solving and extending the nature and range of activities possible within each subject area. It is not clear what direction teacher training will take. The targeting of a small number of teachers to act as specialists in their schools has led to many of those teachers leaving the teaching profession or to the separation fo CBI from the normal activities of each teacher. On the other hand, where attempts have been made to provide some training for all teachers, the amount of training has been too little to give teachers either the confidence or the skills to integrate the computer into the curriculum. While in-service training is important, perhaps the most it can hope to achieve, given the scarcity of resources, is the creation of favorable attitudes towards CBI among existing teachers. It would be more profitable to focus resources on preservice training, particularly on those teacher educators who integrate the computer into their own programs and who train student teachers to develop creative applications of existing software in particular subject areas.

CRITICAL FACTORS

Most successful implementations of CBI may be attributed to local variables, such as the management/organization of resources or the attitudes and skills of teachers within particular schools or school districts. The identity of the critical factors for the successful implementation of CBI are not yet clear, mainly because there are no standard criteria for evaluating the success of CBI. Achievement outcomes as measured by traditional tests of basic skills may not be appropriate; tests of improvement of the learning process or of students' thinking skills are not yet sufficiently reliable and valid; examination of the cost-effectiveness of CBI is just beginning. In the case where the computer is used as a stand-alone tutor, it is the design of the tutorial programs which is the critical factor related to student achievement. Just as in the case of traditional instruction, the teacher variable appears to be most critical to the success of CBI, particularly CBI in which the computer is not used as a stand-alone tutor. Since the trend in CBI in schools is toward more teacher-dependent applications, then the instructional design and management skill of the teacher, as well as his/her ease and skill in the software being used, will become increasingly important.

CONCLUSION

There is a tendency in education to view each new technology as the one which will revolutionize education. It seems that existing educational practices are very difficult to modify and therefore each new technology is seen as the vehicle for change. No new instructional technology, since the printed book, has caused a significant change in instruction in schools. More global changes in the goals and orientation of the curriculum itself and in the training of teachers are needed to bring about school reform. After 25 years of experience with CBI, educators are still looking for the magical innovation that will "dramatically change what we teach and how we teach it" (Charp, 1988/89). In comparing activities in the U.S. and Europe, it is evident that while an addition has been made to what we teach, by introducing new subject matter (computer studies) into the curriculum of secondary schools, little or no widespread change has occurred in how teachers teach.

American educators have perhaps been more optimistic than European educators regading the promises of the computer for education. The U.S. began by seeking purely instructional uses for the computer, whereas most European countries have begun by teaching about computers. At this point there has been movement in all countries to move beyond teaching about computers to innovatively teaching with the computer. At least the promises are becoming more realistic and the caveats accompanying them more specific. However, until there are more computers in schools and more teachers can perform the function of instructional designer of computer-related activities, then neither the goals of Western schools nor the knowledge acquired by students will change dramatically. This may seem like a pessimistic conclusion for what started out as a comparative review of approaches to CBI in schools. Some more positive and immediate conclusions are that (a) CBI is now viewed as a permanent feature of schools in both Europe and the U.S., (b) there is much exchange of ideas and practices between countries, (c) countries that have adopted CBI more recently seem to be avoiding some of the mistakes made by countries that adopted it earlier, and (d) there has been a definite learning curve in terms of identification and utilization of the most instructionally beneficial types of CBI and it appears that schools and teachers (at least the more innovative ones) are gradually moving to uses that do not isolate the computer from the mainstream of classroom instruction.

REFERENCES

Aston, M.H., & Templeton, R. (1988). Prospects and Problems: A pan-European perspective on technological innovation and educational practice. In F. Lovis & E.D. Tagg (Eds.), *Computers in education: Proceedings of the International Federation for Information Processing Technical Committee 3 1st European conference on Computers in Education* (pp. 443–447). Amsterdam: North-Holland.

Becker, H.J. (1984). *School uses of microcomputers: Reports from a national survey* (Issues 1–6). Baltimore, MD: The Johns Hopkins University, Center for Social Organization of Schools.

Becker, H.J. (1986). *Instructional uses of school computers: Reports from the 1985 national survey* (Issues 1–6). Baltimore, MD: The Johns Hopkins University, Center for Social Organization of Schools.

Becker, H.J. (1987). *The impact of computer use on children's learning: What research has shown and what it has not.* Paper presented at the annual meeting of the American Educational Research Association, Washington, DC.

Charp, S. (1988/89). Editorial. *Technological Horizons in Education, 16*(5), 8.

Clark, R.E., & Sugrue, B.M. (1988). Research on instructional media, 1978–1988. In D. Ely (Ed.), *Educational media and technology yearbook* (pp. 19–36). Denver, CO: Libraries Unlimited.

Cuban, L. (1986). *Teachers and machines: The classroom use of technology since 1920.* New York: Teachers College Press.

Fothergill, R., & Anderson, J.S. (1981). Strategy for the Microelectronics Education Programme (MEP). *Programmed Learning and Educational Technology, 18*(3), 121–129.

Gardner, J., Fulton, J., & Megarity, M. (1988). The in-service education of teachers (INSET) in information technology (IT): A UK perspective. In F. Lovis & E.D. Tagg (Eds.), *Computers in education: Proceedings of the International Federation for Information Processing Technical Committee 3 1st European conference on Computers in Education* (pp. 131–138). Amsterdam: North-Holland.

Kelly, H.B. (1987). The British are coming! The British are coming! *Incider, 5*(5), 65–68.

Kulik, J.A., Bangert-Downs, R.L., & Williams, G.W. (1983). Effects of computer-based teaching on secondary school secondary school students. *Journal of Educational Psychology, 75,* 19–26.

Mallatratt, J. (1988). Teacher education and teacher training: The identification of in-service requirements to support computer usage across the curriculum. In F. Lovis & E.D. Tagg (Eds.), *Computers in education: Proceedings of the International Federation for Information Processing Technical Committee 3 1st European conference on Computers in Education* (pp. 157–162). Amsterdam: North-Holland.

Martinez, M.E., & Mead, N.A. (1988). *Computer competence: The first national assessment* (Report No. 17-CC-01). Princeton, NJ: Educational Testing Service.

McMahon, H.F., & Anderson, J.S. (1980). Building a springboard: Regionalization within the Microelectronics in Schools and Colleges Development Programme. *British Journal of Educational Technology, 11*(3), 201–220.

Oldham, E.E. (1986). Computers in teacher training: Initial and inservice. *Report on Computers in Primary Education Conference.* Dublin, Ireland: Irish National Teacher's Organisation.

Organization for Economic Co-operation and Development (OECD). (1986). *New information technologies: A challenge for education.* Paris, France: OECD, Centre for Educational Research and Innovation.

Pea, R.D., Kurland, D.M., & Hawkins, J. (1985). LOGO and the development of thinking skills. In M. Chen & W. Paisley (Eds.), *Children and microcomputers: Research on the newest medium.* Beverly Hills, CA: Sage.

Pelgrum, W.J., & Plomp, T. (1988). The IEA study "Computers in Education": A multinational longitudinal assessment. In F. Lovis & E.D. Tagg (Eds.), *Computers in education: Proceedings of the International Federation for Information Processing Technical Committee 3 1st European conference on Computers in Education* (pp. 433–437). Amsterdam: North-Holland.

Plomp, T., Steerneman, A.H., & Pelgrum, W.J. (1988). Curricular changes as a consequence of computer use. In F. Lovis & E.D. Tagg (Eds.), *Computers in education: Proceedings of the International Federation for Information Processing Technical Committee 3 1st European conference on Computers in Education* (pp. 503–508). Amsterdam: North-Holland.

Shlechter, T.M. (1988). An examination of research evidence for computer-based instruction. In R.T. Hartson & D. Hix (Eds.), *Advances in human–computer interaction* (Vol. 2, pp. 316–367). Norwood, NJ: Ablex.

Thompson, A. (1988). *Liveware: The next challenge in computer education.* Paper presented at the annual meeting of the International Association for Computers in Education, New Orleans, LA.

U.S. Congress, Office of Technology Assessment. (1988). *Power on! New tools for teaching and learning* (OTA-SET-379). Washington, DC: U.S. Government Printing Office.

Van Deursen, J.I. (1988). Computers in Dutch education: Results and analysis of a stimulation plan. In F. Lovis & E.D. Tagg (Eds.), *Computers in education: Proceedings of the International Federation for Information Processing Technical Committee 3 1st European conference on Computers in Education* (pp. 23–31). Amsterdam: North-Holland.

Van Weering, I.H. (1988). A national curriculum informatics for lower secondary education. In F. Lovis & E.D. Tagg (Eds.), *Computers in education: Proceedings of the International Federation for Information Processing Technical Committee 3 1st European conference on Computers in Education* (pp. 421–425). Amsterdam: North-Holland.

3
Computer-Based Instruction in Special Education

Steven L. Robinson
Amherst H. Wilder Foundation

In 1978 when Public Law 98-142 (The Education of All Handicapped Children Act) took effect, the United States became legally as well as philosophically committed to providing "equal" individualized educational opportunities for handicapped and nonhandicapped children. Furthermore, the law mandated that the regular school environments should be architecturally and instructionally modified to accommodate handicapped children to the greatest extent possible.

Unfortunately, the commitment to such instruction for handicapped children has not automatically translated to the achievement of the goal. Teachers already faced with the task of managing 25 and more "normal" students are justifiably concerned about providing quality instruction to additional exceptional students. Also, responsibilities for the education of these exceptional children extend beyond instruction. Careful attention must be given to the diagnostic and classification decisions that result in prescriptions for instruction. Additionally, Public Law 94-142 requires a written individualized educational plan (IEP) for each exceptional child which must be approved and closely monitored by a team of professional educators.

Despite the difficulties inherent in serving the handicapped, the obligations remain. Consequently, educators must consider any instructional alternatives which help the classroom teacher to better meet the needs of these students. This chapter will explore the use of computer-based training (CBT) to help the school staff in the task of providing more effective instruction for mildly handicapped students. The term "mildly handicapped" refers to learning disabled, educable mentally retarded, and emotionally disturbed students who are served in the "regular" classroom.

This chapter discusses the following issues in teaching these students: (a) basic principles of effective instruction, (b) current applications of CBT for such students, and (c) group applications of CBT. Using computer-controlled prosthetic devices designed to increase mobility or enable the handicapped to more easily utilize computers will not be discussed in this chapter (see Chapter 15 for a discussion of such devices).

EFFECTIVE INSTRUCTION
FOR MILDLY HANDICAPPED STUDENTS

Surprisingly, very little is known about specific effective instructional interventions for the mildly handicapped. After reviewing special education research, MacMillan, Keogh, and Jones (1986) concluded:

> We (educators) have not been successful in teaching mildly handicapped learners, regardless of where we place them (special or regular classes) or what we call them (EMR, LD, or "normal"). (p. 711)

This statement does not mean that the mildly handicapped do not learn or that their learning is not influenced by instruction. Rather it means that specific variations in instruction have not produced demonstrable variations in the achievement of such students.

Despite the lack of a validated effective instructional program for the mildly handicapped, there is a body of knowledge regarding basic principles of effective instruction. Fisher et al. (1980) have noted that effective teachers were able to do the following : (a) diagnose the students' skill levels, (b) prescribe appropriate tasks, (c) interact with students frequently, (d) monitor the students' performance, and (e) provide feedback to their students. Effective instruction for mildly handicapped students should also include the above-mentioned instructional components of effective teaching (e.g., Bickel & Bickel, 1986; Brophy & Good, 1986; Gersten, Carnine, & Woodward, 1987; Rosenshine & Stevens, 1986).

Other instructional techniques for effectively teaching mildly handicapped students can be found in the following instructional models: (a) Gersten et al.'s (1987) Direct Instruction approach, (b) Bloom's (1985) Mastery Learning approach, and (c) Hunter's (1976) Instructional Theory into Practice (ITIP) approach. A primary tenet of these models is that instruction must be explicitly stated in small sequential steps with error-free performance being the intended instructional outcome. These models also demand high levels of active learner involvement. Stallings and Krasavage (1986), for example, summarize the five elements of ITIP as:

1. Lessons start with a whole class activity in which the objectives are clearly stated.
2. Instruction is in small segments using demonstration and modeling with frequent checks for student understanding.
3. Guided practice and feedback are used.
4. A closure activity is employed to make sure that students can perform with few errors.
5. Independent practice gives students a chance to overlearn the skill.

Conducting formative evaluations must also be done when teaching the mildly handicapped child. Formative evaluation is basically a methodology for monitoring student progress (Fuchs, 1986). Such monitoring of the mildly handicapped child is important for two reasons. One, P.L. 94-142 mandates that each IEP include evaluations of the student's progress toward the academic goals. Second, performance monitoring is the law because educators recognize the uncertain effects of instruction for the mildly handicapped. The success of any instructional intervention program for the mildly handicapped can only be determined by individual assessments. The readers are referred to Fuchs (1986) and Deno (1985) for a more detailed discussion of formative evaluation procedures.

As previously indicated, these cited techniques for effectively teaching the mildly handicapped are usually not implemented. Delaquadri, Greenwood, Whorton, Carta, and Hall (1986) found that mildly handicapped children were not actively engaged in work. Reid (1986) also found that mildly handicapped students rarely responded in the regular classroom setting. Zigmond, Kerr, and Schaeffer (1986) found that regular high school classroom teachers asked approximately two questions per period to their mildly handicapped students. Furthermore, these teachers rarely answered the mildly handicapped students' requests for academic help.

Thus, the American public has cause for concern. The educational system is not accomplishing the goal, mandated by public concern, to educate exceptional students. While it may be tempting to criticize teachers for "not doing their jobs" such criticism oversimplifies the issue. Certainly to some extent improved preservice and inservice training is required. Even with well-trained and supportive teachers, the job of providing individually appropriate instruction for the mildly handicapped is a difficult and sometimes overwhelming task. Teachers must balance their teaching time with such management chores as writing reports, preparing and organizing instruction, and conducting formative evaluation for each student. These management chores compete with the exceptional students' need for attention. The fundamental complexities inherent in providing effective instruction to the mildly handicapped are a primary reason behind the interest of educators in CBT for such students.

COMPUTERS IN SPECIAL EDUCATION

Computers would seem to be an excellent instructional medium for teaching mildly handicapped students. Computers enable highly interactive instruction that caters to the characteristics of the individual learners. Computers can also support carefully sequenced instruction which requires frequent responding and provides instantaneous feedback to the learner about their performance. Teachers can also use computers to help with formative evaluation and other chores, for example, preparing reports. Computers would thus seemingly help teachers to put into practice the cited techniques for effectively teaching mildly handicapped students.

As indicated, there are many potential applications of computers to the task of implementing more effective instruction for the mildly handicapped. These applications can be classified into four basic areas: (a) computer-assisted instruction (CAI), (b) interactive media, (c) computer-managed instruction (CMI) and administrative tools, and (d) instructional tools. These applications will be discussed in the next few sections.

CAI and Special Education

As discussed by Shlechter (Chapter 1) and by the U.S. Congress, Office Technology Assessment (1988), there are two fundamental principles behind CAI. One, students progress through the instructional sequence, in small steps, without the need for a teacher. Second, basic instructional decisions are transferred from the teacher to the curriculum developer (U.S. Congress, Office of Technology Assessment, 1988). The curriculum developer designs the nature and sequence of instructional events, the responses required from the students, and the extent and timing of feedback. Even though the research evidence on CAI is contaminated with methodological flaws (see Clark, 1985; Shlechter, 1988), using CAI to teach children with learning problems is supported by the research literature (Torgesen, 1984).

An important variable in the success of any CAI program is the courseware. Gerber (1988) suggested that teachers should carefully consider characteristics of software packages before using them with the mildly handicapped. He found that a basic "drill-and-practice" courseware for teaching spelling to mildly handicapped students led to higher levels of achievement than did an arcade-style courseware. The arcade course did, however, lead to higher levels of motivation. Gerber suggested that the arcade courseware was appealing to these students but was distracting and interfered with their ability to pay attention. It must be noted that the "drill-and-practice" format accounts for nearly 80 percent of the CAI courseware for special education (Male, 1988).

Another example of an effective drill-and-practice CAI courseware for mildly handicapped students is discussed by Trifiletti, Frith, and Armstrong (1984). This courseware involved a mastery learning approach to teach mathematical skills to learning disabled students between the ages of nine and fifteen. Instruction was carefully sequenced in a hierarchy of small steps. That is, a student proceeded to the more advanced instructional step after completing all the requested math problems for the previous level. Daily feedback about a student's performance was also provided to the teacher and to the student. The students were presented this courseware for an entire school year in daily 40-minute sessions. Trifiletti et al. compared these students' learning to that of a parallel group of learning disabled students who received comparable mathematical training in their resource room. The CAI students learned twice as much as the other group.

Another promising area for CAI with the mildly handicapped is the instruction of problem solving, reasoning, and basic skills which have been difficult to teach by traditional means. The HOTS program (Higher Order Thinking Skills) (Pogrow, 1987) is a widely known and effective CAI program for teaching such skills to low-achieving students. With HOTS, the computer is viewed as a tool to provide students with a private but active learning environment. Students are provided on a computer with problems in mathematics or reading which focus on the development of metacognitive strategies, inference skills, and generalization. It must be noted that the teacher, not the computer, is the key in the HOTS program. Learning in HOTS comes from the dialogue between the teacher and students around ideas presented by the software. The computer is thus used by teachers as a tool to highlight important elements of the instructional materials.

Other researchers (e.g., Collins, Carnine, & Gersten, 1987) have also shown that CAI can be used as a valuable supplement in the training of problem-solving and basic reasoning skills. Stand-alone applications of CAI have not been supported by the research. Even in cases where the software is designed to be self-contained, teachers must understand how to (a) operate the software, (b) modify the software for use with mildly handicapped students, and (c) integrate it into the content of all instruction. The teacher's ability to be an interface between the mildly handicapped student and the computer thus seems to be the most critical element of successful CAI use.

Interactive Video and Mildly Handicapped Students

The use of visual and auditory media for teaching the mildly handicapped has strong appeal. Media-based applications provide different avenues to important competencies for these children (Bransford, Sherwood, & Hasselbring, 1988). Carnine (1989), for example, claimed that the average high school science textbook required students to master 3,000 terms and symbols which might be quite a difficult task for the mildly handicapped students.

Visual and auditory media offer many advantages that may help attenuate the problems associated with language-based instruction. One of these advantages is variety. As the willingness of children to engage in lengthy periods of television viewing attests, images and sound attract and maintain attention. A television presentation should help augment the attention span of the mildly handicapped student. Multimedia presentations may also augment the mildly handicapped students' ability to organize the instructional materials. The relationship between apparently unrelated facts or events may be more understandable when graphically depicted.

Also, multimedia presentations can help create a more enjoyable and meaningful learning situation for the mildly handicapped students. Many critical life skills (e.g., arithmetic and reading) may be more easily grasped when related to interesting nonclassroom events. These events may help the mildly handicapped child to make sense of the seemingly senseless. Bransford et al. (in press) used segments of the *Raiders of the Lost Ark* to demonstrate the contextually rich aspects of using film as a teaching medium. One segment showed Indiana Jones jumping across a pit. Students were then asked to use cues from the segment to estimate the length of the pit. Discussion consequently involved such issues as examining the realistic possibility of such a jump. As previously indicated, putting instructional materials into the context of an Indiana Jones film could be most helpful to the mildly handicapped student.

Interactive video can help increase the instructional options associated with the use of visual and auditory media. Interactive video consists of the computer acting as a media control device for group or individual applications. A branching routine can then be programmed into the video presentation. This routine allows the instructional program to depart from the traditional "straight-line" use of media in which an "instructional film" (e.g., the Indiana Jones film) is presented from start to finish and then is discussed by the class. A branching "instructional film" can be programmed to show a segment, stop, request input from the learner, and then show a different segment vis-à-vis the learner's needs.

A good example of an interactive video for the mildly handicapped students was discussed by Friedman and Hofmeister (1984). An interactive video system was utilized to deliver instruction in telling time to elementary level, mildly handicapped students. The instruction was adapted from a paper-and-pencil package and was recorded on a videodisc which looks like a 12″ phonographic record. The disc can store 54,000 still-frame images and about 30 minutes of audio and full-motion video. Also, these images are read by a laser beam which makes the disc very resistant to wearing out. Friedman and Hofmeister programmed the computer to play an instructional segment on the television screen. The segment ended with questions that the student answered by touching the screen. If the answer was correct, the student was advanced to the next segment. If incorrect, the student would be branched to a remedial segment. Students consistently mastered the objectives at or above the criterion of 80 percent without any teacher intervention (Friedman & Hofmeister, 1984).

Interactive video has been used to teach thinking, reading, and writing skills to hearing-impaired students as well as basic and social skills to the mentally handicapped and behaviorally disordered students (Elting & Eisenbarth, 1986). Applications of interactive video to teacher training programs have also benefited the handicapped. This medium has been used to demonstrate teaching concepts and to create simulations of teaching the mildly handicapped (Salzberg et al., 1987).

Computer-Managed Instruction (CMI)

CMI employs the power of computers to help the teacher with administrative chores. Computers are, for example, a natural application to the tasks of monitoring and grading the student's progress.

There are two types of CMI systems. One type of CMI system (CAI-CMI) integrates the instructional aspects of CAI with the administrative aspects of CMI. These systems provide carefully sequenced instuction across a range of grade levels. Detailed printouts and reports are provided describing individual and group progress toward mastery. Some of these CAI-CMI systems will make suggestions for remediation while others will create and administer Individual Education Plans (IEPs) for special education students. CAI-CMI systems have been found to be particularly effective for teaching low-achieving children (Jamison, Suppes, & Wells, 1974). See Tyre (1988) for a listing and description of the major CAI-CMI systems.

The other type of CMI systems are solely for assessment functions. These systems are especially useful for assessment of students' progress by molar school district level units. Stevenson, Edwards, and Bianchi (1978), for example, reported on a goal-based educational management system (GEMS) to be used by several schools. Gems was designed to support diagnostic-prescriptive teaching for mastery learning in reading, mathematics, and English. Reading results from 32 schools showed that students made educationally significant gains with the GEMS model. This type of CMI tends to benefit mildly handicapped and other lower-achieving children because their academic difficulties are quickly identified and communicated to the teacher.

Curriculum-based measurement (CBM) (Deno, 1985) is a paper-and-pencil assessment system designed for special education. Teachers collect weekly performance samples drawn from the students' curriculum materials. Performance is then charted over time. Fuchs, Fuchs, Hamlett, and Hasselbring (1987) developed and tested procedures to implement CBM with computers. They found that the CBM program offered no advantage over paper-and-pencil methods in terms of implementation efficiency. Teachers however, felt that the CBM was easier to use with a computer. If computers appear to make CBM manageable, perhaps they will then be more willing to use this program for their monitoring.

Computers are also useful in special education for the purpose of test administration and scoring—two extremely important activities since student scores on standardized tests are a required component in almost all classification decisions. The validity of these scores is influenced by the manner in which the test has been administered and scored. Computers can help eliminate the following problems in testing: (a) negative reactions by students to the tester, (b) mistakes in scoring the test, and (c) mistakes in interpreting the test data. Correspondingly, computer programs have been written to emulate an expert's scoring and interpretation of the results. These programs consider and weigh the multiple variables important in referral and/or placement decisions (Haynes, 1988).

Finally, a powerful application of computers to special education is administrative management. Special education students demand much attention and monitoring throughout their education. Computers have been invaluable aids to help administrators keep track of student numbers, services, staff allocations and program effectiveness.

Computers as Instructional Tools

"Tool" programs in the areas of writing, drawing, and computation represent other applications of computers for the mildly handicapped. Just as prosthetic devices facilitate movement and communication for the physically handicapped, so may word processors, graphics software, and calculators make academic work more manageable for mildly handicapped students.

Word processing programs have been touted as a panacea for students who have difficulty writing, a problem stereotypic of almost all classifications of mildly handicapped students but particularly synonymous with learning disability. LD students' writing is typically described as being garbled, containing letter reversals, indiscriminate punctuation, omitted words, broken sequences, incomplete words and thoughts, and illegibility. The editing and revision capabilities of word processors can simplify writing production to a point which will allow the mildly handicapped student to produce an improved written paper.

Research and narrative reports have supported the benefits of word processing programs for the mildly handicapped. Teachers have reported that word processing programs allow them to spend less time teaching writing mechanics (Morocco & Neuman, 1986). Students have reported that word processors make them feel more in control and better able to produce a quality document (Morocco & Neuman, 1986). Also, reports from writing projects for LD college students have claimed that word processors improve students' writing quality and reduce their spelling errors and writing apprehension (UPDATE, 1988).

Using a word processor has also been shown to have a positive effect upon the likelihood that a essay would be revised; however, using a word processor did not have any impact upon the essay's quality, length, and structure (Graham & MacArthur, 1988). Also, Vacc (1987) did not find any differences in the quality of letters produced by mildly handicapped students as a function of writing these letters by computer or by hand. Other potentially useful computer tools for the mildly handicapped are graphics and music composition programs. Graphic programs allow the mildly handicapped students to draw and print by moving a pointer on a screen and selecting drawing options. The computer then produces the design. An added benefit of graphics for instruction is their visual nature. As previously discussed, visually presented information may be more meaningful to the mildly handicapped students than is information presented in text. Music programs enable students to create and experiment with sound patterns, lyrics, and other musical operations without requiring mastery of a musical instrument. Again, the multisensory characteristics of these programs are particularly advantageous.

LOGO is another highly publicized computer tool. As discussed by Papert (1980) and Shlechter (chapter 1), LOGO is a programming language which permits children to engage in exploration and problem-solving behaviors. This multisensory learning environment may be helpful for mildly handicapped students in the areas of thinking, problem solving, communicating, and organizing the learning situation (Male, 1988). The major focus in special education by the LOGO developers at MIT, however, has been with children having physical and communicative disabilities. Direct evidence of the benefits of LOGO for enhancing the academic or cognitive skills of the mildly handicapped is lacking.

PROBLEMS WITH USING COMPUTERS FOR TEACHING THE MILDLY HANDICAPPED

As previously stated, computers seem to be ideally suited for helping educators to meet the educational needs of the mildly handicapped. Unfortunately, this promise of computers for teaching the mildly handicapped has not been actualized (U.S. Congress, Office of Technology Assessment, 1988; Russell, 1987).

Problems with fitting computers into classroom instruction is one obstacle to successful use of computers. In the rush to obtain computers, school districts have not spent enough time with the important issues associated with technology integration. Lacking are administrative systems which coordinate and plan purchasing of equipment and software, provide information and support to schools and teachers, train teachers, and maintain the equipment. Teachers have thus been given computer materials which do not meet their needs, and they have been charged to use these materials without the necessary training and information with regards to integrating them into current operations. Successful CBT implementation thus requires the school system to develop a systematic planning scheme which is coordinated with school administrators and classroom teachers.

Correspondingly, teachers' unpreparedness for their role vis-à-vis instructional technology is another obstacle to effective use of computers for educating the mildly handicapped. Teachers were led to believe and apparently view computer use as an auto-instructional, teacher-free activity which would reduce their instructional burdens (Rieth, Bahr, Polsgrove, Okolo, & Eckert, 1987). Nothing can be further from the truth. Even with the best software, teachers are required to engage in explaining, discussing, and managing the computer-based instructional materials. In fact, CAI may have increased some instructional burdens. Hansen, Miller, Roth, Miller, and Jones (1988) have estimated that teachers must make between 60 and 90 "non-trivial" instructional decisions per hour when students are engaged in CBT as compared to 10–30 decisions per hour when engaged in a highly interactive, lecture-discussion format. More typical lecture/discussion periods result in 1–3 decisions per hour. It is no wonder that teachers, who are not prepared for these new demands, are unwilling to utilize computers in their classroom (Morocco & Zorfass, 1988).

Another obstacle to successful CBT use is a lack of viable courseware. Problems with courseware were frequently cited in a national survey of teachers and administrators as another major problem with using technology effectively (Russell, 1987). Courseware problems are especially prevalent for teaching the mildly handicapped students. For one thing, there is a limited amount of courseware being developed for teaching the mildly handicapped. As Sandals and Hughes (1988) have pointed out, commercial companies are unlikely to devote resources to develop such courseware given the limited market and high developmental costs. A second problem is that the developed courseware has not been validated with a sample of mildly handicapped students. Hence, the quality of the available courseware is questionable.

There is also a lack of available computers. Even though 95 percent of American schools have computers, the ratio of computers to students is still only one computer to 30 students (U.S. Congress, Office of Technology Assessment, 1988). It has been estimated that a ratio of one computer to ten students is needed for this medium to have any effect on academic performance (Torgesen, 1984). Furthermore, the available computers are almost exclusively used for teaching programming to the most advanced students (U.S. Congress, Office of Technology Assessment, 1988).

Again, software and hardware problems can only be properly resolved when school districts have detailed the procedures for using computers to help educate mildly handicapped students. Schools must define the software needed and the hardware required to teach these students. This planning will drive the development of quality CBT courseware and the availability of needed hardware. Commercial developers, for example, will be more than willing to invest in such software if they know that a market does indeed exist.

This section has shown that the exciting uses of computers for teaching the mildly handicapped are isolated examples in the overall educational context. A primary reason for the underutilization of computers is that the planning for this medium has been minimal. Another reason is that educators have focused too narrowly on the individualized paradigm of computer applications and have consequently underestimated the difficulty of integrating such a model for training mildly handicapped students with current educational practices. The next section will focus on using computer technology for group teaching.

GROUP CBT: THE NEGLECTED ALTERNATIVE

A central fact of academic work in regular and special education classrooms is that such work occurs in groups and groups create problems for effective instruction. Why? In groups, as the number of students per teacher increases, accommodation to individual learners in terms of critical instructional events decreases. The teacher cannot elicit and monitor the performance of individuals as well in groups, cannot provide adequate individual feedback, cannot engage in high levels of teacher/student interaction. Consequently, as Gagne, Briggs, and Wager (1988) said, "The influence of instructional events in the large group is only probable. The teacher's communications...and their effects on individual students cannot be monitored with certainty" (p. 280). The result is that capable students tend to manage their own learning while less capable students fall behind.

Despite the fact that group instruction is difficult to manage, and presents problems in terms of critical learning events, it is not the case that children should exclusively learn alone, even if that goal could be achieved. Group environments are important for socialization, attitude formation, problem solving, and other learning where exposure to alternative perspectives is important. Such learning is socially mediated and is learned via dynamic communication, social interaction, and the building of shared meanings (Stone, 1989). For the mildly handicapped, group contexts are particularly problematic. Studies of participation structures (Doyle, 1983) indicate that low-ability students do not have these and other important group skills (such as the ability to interpret the flow of events in a discussion).

Unfortunately, a focus on the capabilities of computers to provide individualized instruction and the rush to provide students with computer access resulted in a failure to consider ways in which computers could be used to help teachers more effectively deal with the problems of everyday instruction. The move to make computers "stand-alone teachers" and to design curricula that was "teacher-proof" (Calfee, 1983) diverted attention from exploring alternatives for technology to enhance and not impede social interaction in classrooms. Methods were also not explored for using computer technology to assist teachers in interpreting and elaborating upon students' responses to the instructional materials.

Several CBT systems have thus been recently devised for group instruction. Carnine (1989), for example, has reported on a group-based videodisc instructional program. One videodisc player was used to present daily 40-minute chemistry lessons to an entire class of at-risk students. The students responded chorally to questions posed by a narrator. They also, individually, wrote answers to a series of problems. If more than 20 percent of the students missed key items, the explanations from the videodisc were then presented to the class. Homework was included in the instructional program and subsequent lessons began with a short quiz on previously covered concepts. The videodisc program also included remediation and extra review segments. This instructional program lasted for four weeks. Carnine found that the posttest scores of these at-risk students did not differ from those of "normal" students in an advanced placement chemistry class.

Group response systems are another type of technology for classroom instruction. A good example of a simple group response system is Teacher Net (Woodward, Carnine, Moore, Noell, & Hayden, 1986). Teacher Net provides up to 16 students in a classroom with numerical keypads connected to one computer. Students enter multiple choice or numeric answers on their keypads. The computer screen is divided into separate squares for each student. Students view the entry displayed in their square. Computer software signals students if their answers are correct and provides progress reports. Teacher Net has been found to be a useful classroom tool for the management of classroom instruction and for student learning.

The Discourse® R&D Project

A description of the Discourse® system. The Discourse® Educational Communication System (Discourse®) is another recently developed CBT system for group instruction. The Amherst H. Foundation in St. Paul, Minnesota has spent five years investigating this system with the collaboration of the 3M Foundation, the University of Minnesota, and the St. Paul Public School District. Over 200 teachers and 4,000 students in three elementary and two high schools participated in this project to investigate applications of the technology with at-risk and mildly handicapped students.

The Discourse® system was designed to be a classroom management device to enable increased teacher control over (a) communication between the teacher and students, (b) presentation of subject content, and (c) record keeping. Each student (up to 32) is provided with a response device. Each device has a "QWERTY" keyboard with a 32-character display line. Students use the devices to respond to the instructional materials. Meaningful sentences of 20–25 words can be entered into a device. These responses are then instantly organized and displayed on the teacher's monitor. A computer and a printer are also located at the teacher's workstation (see Figure 3.1).

The Discourse® system thus allows the teacher to significantly increase students' active learning and to closely monitor students' responses. Remediation efforts can then be quickly directed to students who need the most help. Monitoring students responses can also help stimulate classroom discussion as the teacher can ask students to elaborate upon their answers.

The Discourse® system has several other important instructional features. The teacher can use an on-line authoring system to prepare and organize instruction. The system also scores and stores student answers to multiple-choice or whole-word test items, provides instant feedback to the students, and delivers information about an individual's and/or group's performance on the test. Instant visual and printed reports are also available to the teacher.

This system can also facilitate the use and control of media for presentation purposes. Teachers may manually control a slide projector, videodisc player, and videocassette recorder from the computer keyboard. Or the teacher can use the authoring system to program the media control system. Options for producing graphic and text displays on a large monitor for classroom viewing are also available.

Research results regarding Discourse®. Initially, the R&D team led by Robinson examined the impact of this system upon the time required for correcting papers (Robinson, 1985). They found that the Discourse® system instantaneously scored the spelling tests of fourth graders (It did take 5 minutes to "program" the system to score the tests.) while teachers needed

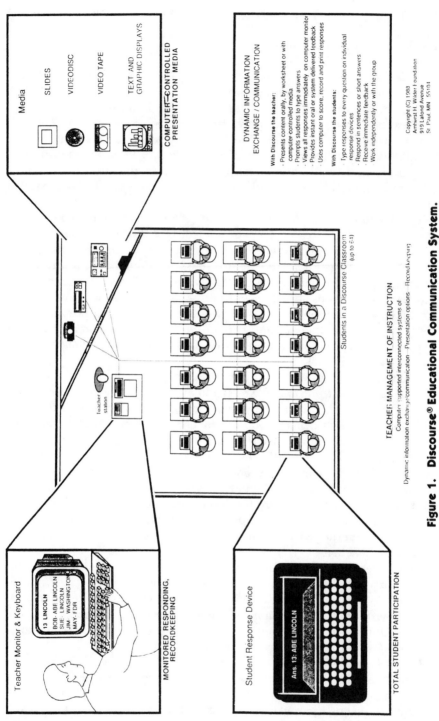

Figure 1. Discourse® Educational Communication System.

52

12 minutes to hand-score tests for a class. The Discourse® teachers were able to provide immediate feedback and did not have to grade these tests after school. The other group of teachers was forced to provide delayed feedback because tests were graded after school. This study's findings were replicated in another study (Robinson, Roberts, & Nakra, 1988) with third- and fourth-grade students completing mathematics worksheets. With the technology, students received immediate item-by-item feedback. Without the technology, the teacher had to tell the few students who were not finished to complete the worksheets as homework. The worksheets for the entire class were then collected the next day. The teacher scored the whole set of worksheets that night and returned them to the students the following day, two days after most of the students had completed the assignment. The Discourse® system had a dramatic effect on the time the teachers spent on grading tests and the duration between the students' taking a test and receiving feedback.

Robinson and his colleagues (Robinson & DePascale, 1985; Robinson, DePascale, & Deno, 1988; Robinson, DePascale, & Roberts, 1989) have also shown that the Discourse® system had a dramatic effect upon active student engagement and participation during instruction and effective monitoring of students by teachers. Robinson and DePascale (1985) found that low-achieving reading students were more actively involved (e.g., answering questions and student/teacher discussion) in the instructional program when using the Discourse® system than when participating in a traditional question-answer session with the teacher. In a second study, Robinson, DePascale and Deno (1988) found that teachers who used the Discourse® system were better able to monitor and give corrective feedback regarding students' spelling performance than those teachers who used more traditional teaching methods (e.g., tutoring the students). More importantly, the mastery of words for the LD students in the Discourse® condition far exceeded those of the LD students in the more traditional teaching conditions and the increments were maintained two weeks later.

Other studies also showed positive results for achievement. Robinson and Brown (1989) found that in the context of regular classroom instruction and in comparison to control groups, low achievers who used the system had significantly higher scores in math and reading on standardized tests. Robinson, DePascale, Espin, and Deno (1987), Robinson, Wilson, and York (1989), and Brown, Robinson, and Dellenbach (1989) found that instruction developed and delivered around the components of effective teaching models was effective in producing significant achievement gains with handicapped children in the areas of spelling, basic math, reading, and math estimation skills.

Putting Discourse® into practice. As previously mentioned, a major focus of the Wilder Discourse® R&D program was to bridge the gap between research and practice. Most research conducted in schools ends when the investigation ends. Integration of the developed instructional program or technology has been infrequently done by R&D teams. The task of translating research into practice has been therefore left to the schools who may not have the resources or expertise to do the job. Compounding the problem of integrating research into practice has been the reality that school environments are not controlled research environments. What worked well in the research situation may not work in practice.

In recognition of the problems with putting research into practice, the Wilder R&D team secured a long-term agreement with the St. Paul School District. The agreement stated that the schools would participate in the R&D program if Wilder would assist the teachers who used the system for everyday instruction. This agreement was primarily designed to build a level of on-site staff expertise so that the technology would continue to be used productively after the research program ended. A corresponding goal was to create a situation where researchers and practitioners could learn from each other.

Several important lessons were learned from this experience. One prominent lesson was that CBT advocates and developers have greatly underestimated the complexity of issues related to changes in the instructional environments for both "normal" and mildly handicapped students. That is, many CBT advocates and developers do not fully understand the complex nature of the classroom environment. The R&D team found the classroom environment to be an imposing and demanding setting, even for the most highly skilled teachers. Teachers have been required to provide constant, long-term, quality instruction in 5–7 content areas for 25 or more students from multiple language groups, multiple cultural groups, and widely divergent skills levels. In addition, the class day was seldom consistent. Over the term of this R&D project, interruptions to classroom routines by other teachers, parents, principals, special events, and students were the rule rather than the exception. The R&D team was amazed that any quality instruction could occur in such a chaotic environment, yet for the most part it did. However, it was easy to understand why mildly handicapped students do not generally fare well academically in mainstream classrooms.

Correspondingly, another impotant lesson learned was that teachers are primarily concerned with utility. New methods and procedures will always be developed; they will attract support and a few disciples will carry them forward. However, if innovations do not make classroom environments more manageable for teachers, they will not be widely used. The reason for this statement is a simple but overlooked truth. As discussed above, teachers must operate in very complex environments. Innovations must fit the way these environments operate. Teachers need innovations which make their lives easier not harder. Any new innovation will not receive the necessary commitment of teachers and will not survive unless this condition is met.

The teacher's skill level was also a critical variable in the success of the implementation process. Teachers with limited management/organizational skills and with limited knowledge of instructional principles presented problems to the R&D team. Most of the teachers were highly competent professionals; however, a sizeable number were not. The R&D staff realized that training to use the technology would not be successful for these latter group of teachers without instruction in basic teaching and management skills.

A final lesson learned was the need for the appropriate level of support from administrators at the school and district levels. Of course, the technology could not have been placed at school sites without the support of the school principal. Surprisingly, "successful" schools were characterized by principals who were only moderately supportive of the technology. High levels of support produced a perception by teachers of "principal's project" which in turn diminished their commitment to the project. On the other hand, moderately supportive principals introduced the technology to potentially interested teachers, and then let these teachers explore the technology and report back to them.

The Wilder Discourse® project went well in part because it had the strong backing of the school superintendent. However, the most important role of the district came into play at the project's end. The extended utilization of Discourse® by the St. Paul School District, of course, depended on the district's willingness to produce sufficient plans and resources for continually using the system. Producing these plans and resources was a lengthy but successful process.

THE FUTURE OF CBT IN SPECIAL EDUCATION

In the future, computers will be faster, less expensive, and hold more information; software will be more comprehensive and sophisticated. As technology develops, alternatives for teaching mildly handicapped children will develop as well. Expert systems will serve as advisors and consultants in areas of administration, diagnosis, prescription, and ongoing instruction. Hypermedia software (Rogers, 1988) will allow visual, textual, and auditory exploration of subject matter at levels appropriate to individual users. In classrooms, group response systems will be combined with CAI systems; management software will help the teacher more efficiently track and orchestrate instruction that is appropriate and powerful for all children.

Although the future almost certainly holds many exciting advanced in CBT for the mildly handicapped, it is uncertain whether, as is currently the case, CBT applications will remain interesting but, in large part impractical. Ultimately, the success of any computer application is dependent on teachers. With luck, future educators will abandon the pursuit of "teacher-proof" technology and, in recognition of the realities of instruction, will produce innovations that can be easily implemented, integrated, and managed on a broad scale.

SUMMARY

This chapter has documented the thesis that a variety of computer applications have excellent potential as resources for providing mildly handicapped students more effective instruction. CAI, interactive video, CMI, and tool applications such as word processing and graphics programs all offer important options for implementing critical components of instruction such as diagnosis, prescription, active involvement, continuous monitoring, feedback, frequent evaluation, and so on.

Another recent and valuable application of computers to instruction is technology-based instruction in groups. Group technology systems focus on supporting the teacher as a manager in the typical, one-teacher-to-many-students classroom. Research was reviewed which showed that this alternative to the CAI model of computer use is an effective tool for mildly handicapped and nonhandicapped students alike.

Unfortunately, while computer applications show much promise, many factors such as limited resources, poor planning, lack of training, and a general ignorance of the needs and conditions of teaching in classrooms have limited their impact. Hopefully, the future of CBT in special education will see these problems resolved. What is needed is less an interest in computers themselves as interesting devices than an increased understanding of the processes of change, integration, and utilization. Advances should be based on the realities of teaching and the needs of the students. Until this happens, computers will be interesting but will always remain a promise unfulfilled.

REFERENCES

Bickel, W.E., & Bickel, D.P. (1986). Effective schools, classrooms, and instruction: Implications for special education. *Exceptional Children, 52*(6), 489–500.

Bloom, B.S. (1985). Learning for mastery. In C.W. Fisher & D.C. Berliner (Eds.), *Perspectives on instructional time* (pp. 73–96). White Plains, NY: Longman.

Bransford, J., Sherwood, R., & Hasselbring, T. (1988). Effects of the video revolution on development: Some initial thoughts. In G. Foreman & P. Pufall (Eds.), *Constructivism in the computer age* (pp. 173–201). Hillsdale, NJ: Lawrence Erlbaum Associates.

Brophy, J., & Good, T. (1986). Teacher behavior and student achievement. In M. Wittrock (Ed.), *Handbook of research on teaching* (3rd ed.). New York: Macmillan.

Brown, S.L., Robinson, S.L., & Dellenbach, K. (1989). *Preparing students for the St. Paul School District reading competency examination: An evaluation of materials and procedures designed for delivery with the Discourse® Educational Communication System* (Tech. Rep.). St. Paul, MN: Wilder Research Center, Amherst H. Wilder Foundation.

Calfee, R. (1983). Computer literacy and book literacy: Parallels and contrasts. *Educational Researcher, 14*(5), 8–13.

Carnine, D. (1989). Teaching complex content to learning disabled students: The role of technology. *Exceptional Children, 55*(6), 524–533.

Clark, R.E. (1985). Confounding in educational computing research. *Journal of Educational Computing Research, 1*, 137–148.

Collins, M., Carnine, D., & Gersten, R. (1987). Elaborated corrective feedback and the acquisition of reasoning skills: A study of computer-assisted instruction. *Exceptional Children, 51*(3), 254–262.

Delaquadri, J., Greenwood, C., Whorton, D., Carta, J., & Hall, R. (1986). Classwide peer tutoring. *Exceptional Children, 52*(6), 535–542.

Deno, S.L. (1985). Curriculum-Based Measurement: The emerging alternative. *Exceptional Children, 52*(3), 219–232.

Doyle, W. (1983). Academic work. *Review of Educational Research, 53*(2), 159–199.

Elting, S., & Eisenbarth, J. (1986). *Interactive video for special education*. ERIC clearinghouse on handicapped children 1986 digest. Reston, VA: The Center for Special Education Technology at The Council for Exceptional Children.

Fisher, C., Berliner, D., Filby, N., Marliave, R., Cahen, L., & Dishaw, M. (1980). Teaching behaviors, academic learning time, and student achievement: An overview. In C. Denham & A Leiberman (Eds.), *Time to learn* (pp. 7–32). Washington, DC: National Institute of Education.

Friedman, S., & Hofmeister, A. (1984). Matching technology to content and learners: A case study. *Exceptional Children, 51*(2), 130–134.

Fuchs, L.S. (1986). Monitoring progress among mildly handicapped pupils: Review of current practice and research. *Remedial and Special Education, 7*(5), 5–12.

Fuchs, L.S., Fuchs, D., Hamlett, C.L., & Hasselbring, T.S. (1987). Using computers with curriculum-based monitoring: Effects on teacher efficiency and satisfaction. *Journal of Special Education Technology, 8*(4), 14–27.

Gagne, R.M., Briggs, L.J., & Wager, W.W. (1988). *Principles of instructional design*. New York: Holt, Rinehart & Winston, Inc.

Gerberg, M.M. (1988). *Effects of microcomputer game environment on spelling drill and practice for learning handicapped students*. Paper presented at the American Educational Research Association annual meeting, New Orleans, LA.

Gersten, R., Carnine, D., & Woodward, J. (1987). Direct instruction research: The third decade. *Remedial and Special Education (RASE)*, 8(6), 48–56.

Graham, S., & MacArthur, C. (1988). Improving learning disabled students' skills at revising essays produced on a word processor: self-instructional strategy training. *The Journal of Special Education*, 22, 133–152.

Hansen, E.G., Miller, R.L., Roth, S.F., Miller, H.L., & Jones, P.E. (1988). *The potential of intelligent instructional support tools for high technology class-rooms and schools*. Paper presented at the Association for the Development of Computer-based Instruction Systems (ADCIS) annual meeting, Philadelphia, PA.

Haynes, J. (1988). *CAPER: An expert system to support referral, diagnosis and instructional planning in culturally diverse elementary schools*. Invitational Research Symposium on Special Education Technology. Reston, VA: The Center for Special Education Technology, Council for Exceptional Children.

Hunter, M. (1976). *Prescription for improved instruction*. El Segundo, CA: TIP.

Jamison, D., Suppes, P., & Wells, S. (1974). The effectiveness of alternative instructional media: A survey. *Review of Educational Research*, 44, 1–61.

MacMillan, D.L., Keogh, B.K., & Jones, R.L. (1986). Special educational research on mildly handicapped learners. In M.C. Wittrock (Ed.), *Handbook of research on teaching* (3rd ed., pp. 686–726). New York: Macmillan.

Male, M. (1988). *Special magic: Computers, classroom strategies, and exceptional students*. Mountain View, CA: Mayfield Publishing Company.

Morocco, C.C., & Neuman, S.C. (1986). Word processors and the acquisition of writing strategies. *Journal of Learning Disabilities*, 19(4), 243–247.

Morocco, C.C., & Zorfass, J. (1988). Technology and transformation: A naturalistic study of special students and computers in the middle school. *Journal of Special education Technology*, 9(2), 88–97.

Papert, S. (1980). *Mindstorms: Children, computers and powerful ideas*. New York: Basic Books.

Pogrow, S. (1987). *A thinking skill approach to using computers to improve the basic skills of at-risk students: Experience with the HOTS program*. Tucson, AZ: University of Arizona.

Reid, E. (1986). Practicing effective instruction: The exemplary center for reading instruction approach. *Exceptional Children*, 52(6), 510–519.

Rieth, H., Bahr, C., Polsgrove, L., Okolo, C., & Eckert, R. (1987). The effects of microcomputers on the secondary special education classroom ecology. *Journal of Special Education Technology*, 8(4), 36–45.

Robinson, S.L. (1985). *A summary of finding from the first year of research with the Discourse Educational Communication System*. St. Paul, MN: Educational Technology Research Program, Amherst H. Wilder Foundation.

Robinson, S.L., & Brown, S. (1989). *Computer-supported, group-based instruction in elementary school reading and mathematics*. Paper presented at the American Educational Research Association annual meeting, San Francisco, CA.

Robinson, S.L., & DePascale, C. (1985). *Effects of a technology-based communication system on student responding and teacher questioning*. Unpublished Research Report. St. Paul, MN: Educational Technology Research Program, Amherst H. Wilder Foundation.

Robinson, S.L, DePascale, C., & Deno, S.L. (1988). *Technology and group in-*

struction: An investigation of enhanced teacher monitoring, correction and student feedback. Paper presented at the American Educational Research Association annual meeting, New Orleans, LA.

Robinson, S.L., DePascale, C., Espin, C., & Deno, S.L. (1987). *The effects of technology-aided direct instruction in large groups.* Paper presented at the American Educational Research Association annual meeting, Washington, DC.

Robinson, S.L., DePascale, C., & Roberts, F. (1989). Computer-delivered feedback in groupbased instruction: Effects for learning disabled students in mathematics. *Learning Disabilities Focus, 5*(1), 28–35.

Robinson, S.L., Roberts, F., & Nakra, O. (1988). *A comparative study of discourse, teacher and peer worksheet grading processes.* St. Paul, MN: Educational Technology Research Program, Amherst H. Wilder Foundation.

Robinson, S.L., Wilson, L., & York, C. (1989). *Technology-supported classroom instruction: Facilitating effective teaching practices with hearing impaired and learning disabled children* (Tech. Rep.). St. Paul, MN: Wilder Research Center, Amherst H. Wilder Foundation.

Rogers, M. (1988). Here comes Hypermedia. *Newsweek, 112*(14), 44–45.

Rosenshine, B., & Stevens, R. (1986). Teacher behavior and student achievement. In M. Wittrock (Ed.), *Handbook of research on teaching* (3rd ed.). New York: Macmillan.

Russell, S.J. (1987). *Microcomputers in special education: Beyond drill and practice* (Final report, Grant No. G008430071). Washington, DC: U.S. Department of Education.

Salzberg, C.L., Rule, S., Chen, J., Fodor-Davis, J., Morgan, R., & Schulze, K. (1987). *Videodisc technology in teacher training: Advantages and limitations.* Logan, UT: Logan State University, Department of Special Education.

Sandals, L.H., & Hughes, J. (1988). Computer software for those with special needs: What is really needed? *Canadian Journal of Special Education, 4*(1), 23–41.

Shlechter, T.M. (1988). An examination of the research evidence for computer-based instruction. In R.T. Hartson & D. Hix (Eds.), *Advances in human-computer interactions* (Vol. 2, pp. 316–367). Norwood, NJ: Ablex.

Stallings, J., & Krasavage, E.M. (1986). Program implementation and student achievement in a four-year Madeline Hunter follow-through project. *The Elementary School Journal, 87*(2), 117–129.

Stevenson, G., Edwards, P., & Bianchi, E. (1978). *GEMS Goal-based educational management system. A computer supported management system developed to support diagnostic prescriptive teaching for mastery learning.* Program report. Jordan School District, Sandy, UT.

Stone, C.A. (1989). Improving the effectiveness of strategy training for learning disabled students: The role of communicational dynamics. *Remedial and Special Education, 10*(1), 35–42.

Torgesen, J.K. (1984). Instructional uses of microcomputers with elementary aged mildly handicapped children. In R.E. Bennett & C.A. Maher (Eds.), *Microcomputers and exceptional children.* New York: NY: The Haworth Press.

Trifiletti, J.J., Frith, G.H., & Armstrong, S. (1984, Winter). Microcomputers versus resource rooms for LD students: A preliminary investigation of the effects on math skills. *Learning Disability Quarterly, 7*, pp. 69–76.

Tyre, T. (1988, December/January). CMI seen as possible solution to quality of education issue. *T.H.E. Journal*, pp. 17–25.

UPDATE. (1988). *The newsletter of the LD college writers project V3.1.* Minneapolis, MN: University of Minnesota-General College.

U.S. Congress, Office of Technology Assessment. (1988). *Power on! New tools for teaching and learning* (OTA-SET-379). Washington, DC: U.S. Government Printing Office.

Vacc, N.N. (1987). Word processor versus handwriting: A comparative study of writing samples produced by mildly mentally handicapped students. *Exceptional Children, 54*(2), 156–165.

Wodward, J., Carnine, D., Moore, L., Noell, J., & Hayden, M. (1986). Teacher Net: A multipurpose computer networking system for the classroom. *Journal of Learning Disabilities, 19*(9), 558–561.

Zigmond, N., Kerr, M., & Shaeffer, A. (1986). *Behavioral patterns of LD, ED, and nonhandicapped adolescents in high school academic classes.* Unpublished manuscript, Program in Special Education, University of Pittsburgh, PA.

4
Implementing CBT in Higher Education: Unfulfilled Promises and New Directions

Thomas C. Reeves
Department of Instructional Technology,
College of Education, The University of Georgia

Just as the computer has become an integral part of many spheres of human activity including business, industry, transportation, medicine, and the military, the computer has become an essential component of the modern university. Registration, accounting, grade reporting, and research are just a few areas in which applications of computing abound in higher education. Roecks (1981) identified 13 uses of computers in higher education, including:

- administrative (accounting, attendance, and scheduling)
- curriculum planning
- professional development
- library applications
- research tool
- guidance, counseling, and special services
- test construction, administration, and scoring
- instructional aid
- instructional management
- computer awareness and literacy
- computer science and programming
- instructional coordination and networking
- computer-assisted instruction.

However, while the computer has been a widely used and effective tool for administration and communication in higher education, the computer's utilization in an instructional role has been severely limited (Heermann, 1988). Perhaps this should not be surprising or disappointing, given the general lack of success of computer-based training (CBT) in other fields of human endeavor (cf., Colbert, 1988; Ellis & Wulfeck, 1988; Shlechter & Kristiansen, 1988). McClintock (1988) argued that the computer is a relatively immature technology, and thus, like previous innovations such as the telephone, the automobile, and the television, the computer must evolve through many generations before its real potential is reached. And yet, despite the computer's apparent immaturity, its powers in activities such as financial accounting, data storage and retrieval, and electronic maintenance and control have been nothing less than astounding. Why has the computer not enjoyed similar success in education and training?

Promises regarding the instructional powers of computers in higher education have been made frequently in the past, and they continue to be made today. At EDUCOM '88, held in Washington, DC, Dr. Edward F. Redish, professor of physics and astronomy at the University of Maryland and creator of MUPPET (Maryland University Project Physics and Educational Technology), claimed that the computer can restore "flexibility and creativity. . . to subjects stifled by decades of repetitive and rigid presentations" (Redish, 1988). Two years earlier, at EDUCOM '86, Steve Jobs, founder of Apple Computer, Inc. and Next, Inc., proclaimed that "the real breakthrough. . . is going to come in the form of a few 100K byte programs that will forever change the way we teach and learn, forever change the way we conceive of higher education." Similar promises can be found in virtually every publication related to academic computing, and they are standard fare for keynote presentations at conferences such as EDUCOM. It seems appropriate to ask why these promises have not been fulfilled.

CONSTRAINTS ON APPLICATIONS
OF CBT IN HIGHER EDUCATION

Some of the earliest experiments and applications of computer-based training (CBT) have taken place on our college campuses (cf. Alderman, 1978; Levien, 1972; Suppes & Macken, 1978), and yet widespread use of instructional computing in academe is virtually nonexistent. There are many barriers to the effective use of CBT in higher education, including:

1. *There still exists a dominant view of teaching in academe as the flow of information from the teacher to the students instead of the development of generalizable problem-solving abilities and lifelong learning skills.* This traditional academic view supports the overwhelming usage of

the lecture as the primary instructional delivery mode in higher education. Even when CBT is used in higher education, its primary focus is in drill and practice and tutorial formats as opposed to potentially more powerful instructional applications such as simulations (Taylor, 1987; Turner, 1989).

Computer-based simulations, especially those incorporating interactive video capabilities, have been demonstrated as effective instructional methods in medical, industrial, military, and business contexts (Reeves, 1988). Interactive simulations are also being used for testing purposes, for example, the Internal Medicine portion of the Medical Board Examinations is being converted to interactive video. The high experiential value of interactive video simulations combined with sophisticated answer-judging routines and realistic feedback have potentially effective applications in a wide range of academic settings.

For example, several colleges of education are developing simulations for teaching classroom management methods and questioning skills to preservice teachers. "Project Athena" at the Massachusetts Institute of Technology and The "Intermedia" project at Brown University have both included the development of sophisticated instructional simulations in a wide variety of disciplines (Turner, 1989). Professional schools such as law (cf. Hoelscher, 1988) and medicine (cf. Abdulla, 1987) are developing interactive instructional simulations. Even history professors (cf. Semonche, 1989) have developed instructional simulations that enable students to be "responsible for making significant historical choices" regarding questions such as "Should the Southern States be Readmitted to the Union in 1865?" Despite these advances, the great bulk of academic departments have not begun to investigate, much less develop, these types of instructional simulations. At least part of this lack of enterprise must be traced to an unwillingness on the part of faculty to abandon the direct control of the instructional process which they maintain in traditional teacher-centered methods.

2. *Many developers of CBT attempt to make the computer replicate traditional teaching methods, and the result is a phenomenon called "the electronic page turner."* This often occurs because the developers base their instructional designs from the perspective of "what a teacher does to teach a subject" as opposed to "what a student does to learn it." Just as effective, efficient business software must be developed from the user's point of view (Shneiderman, 1986), instructional software must be developed from the learner's perspective.

The learner's viewpoint has been greatly enriched by recent advances in cognitive psychology. Gagné, Wager, and Rojas (1984) describe an instructional model for CBT which includes nine external instructional events designed to engage nine corresponding internal learning processes. The latter are based upon the cognitive research of Estes (1978), Klatzky (1980), and others. Johnson-Laird (1988), Levine and Rheingold (1987), and Winograd and Flores (1987) provide additional insights into the learner's perceptual states which should drive the design of CBT. For example, the first three steps of Gagné's model—(a) grabbing the learner's attention, (b) informing the learner of the lesson objectives, and (c) stimulating recall of prior learning—are believed to elicit corresponding cognitive states such as (a) alertness, (b) expectancy, and (c) retrieval to working memory. Unfortunately, the so-called "cognitive revolution" in education has not overthrown the didactic orientation of most CBT programs.

3. *There is a lack of support for faculty development of CBT.* A plethora of academic textbooks continue to be written, widely distributed, and adopted, primarily because there is a mature incentive structure that reinforces their production and because there is a sophisticated support and assistance structure provided by publishers' editors. The "publish or perish" atmosphere of many academic settings plus the potential financial rewards derived from popular textbooks stimulates the authoring of textbooks. Parallel incentive and support structures must be found for CBT if a sufficient quantity of quality courseware is to be provided for higher education.

However, support structures for CBT cannot be directly analogous to those provided for textbook publishing. Authoring complex interactive programs usually requires a close-knit team approach made up of people with diverse backgrounds and expertise (e.g., subject matter experts, instructional designers, programmers, graphic artists, etc.) whereas authoring a textbook usually involves one or more people with similar backgrounds and expertise (e.g., physicists) assisted indirectly by assorted professionals (e.g., editors, artists, typesetters, etc.). The authorship of CBT is often difficult to attribute to one or a few individuals whereas the authorship of a book is much more clearly established. Incentive and support structures for CBT must take these and other differences into account.

4. *The existing reward structure in higher education does not generally support quality instruction of any type, much less the development and implementation of effective CBT.* "Publish or perish" still predominates in most universities, and as a result, valuable intellectual work in digital form may go unrecognized and unrewarded. Ironically, the university often demands a share of profits derived from courseware, but rarely demands any part of publication profits!

In other instances, faculty have been forced to develop software to guarantee their access to "cutting edge" hardware without any hope of sharing in the profits or even recognition which may accrue to a program. When Carnegie-Mellon University began its ambitious "Andrew" project in 1982, the primary sponsor, IBM, which donated $35 million in development funds, expected to own all ensuing technology. Although IBM and other vendors seem to be accepting the position of many higher educators that software should be shared, the issue is still far from settled.

It is especially ironic that tenure and promotion committees rarely give electronic works which may receive widespread utilization and acclaim the equivalent weight of a paper published in the most obscure academic journal. Some of this inequity can be traced to ignorance of the creativity and effort involved in the development of CBT; more can probably be linked to the tendency of review panels to concern themselves with the form and quantity of academic "achievements" rather than their substance and quality. In any case, faculty seeking success within the traditional academic reward structure remain at risk if they devote themselves to the development of electronic as opposed to print works. In a recent report of *The Chronicle of Higher Education* (Turner, 1989), the need for increased recognition for the value of software development was cited as one of the three primary problems yet to be resolved before computing can be comfortably integrated into higher education.

5. *CBT development projects are rarely provided with systematic instructional design support and/or programming expertise.* Computer companies such as the International Business Machines Corporation, Apple Computer, Inc., and the Digital Equipment Corporation often donate computer hardware to institutions of higher education, and in return the universities agree to provide faculty with release time to develop courseware for the donated systems. However, few faculty members possess the instructional design and programming skills to develop effective CBT on their own. Further, it seems ludicrous to expect them to develop substantial expertise in areas far removed from their subject matter. Instead, colleges and universities should have a resource center of instructional designers, evaluators, media producers, and programmers to collaborate with faculty in a team-based approach to developing CBT. The comprehensive development and evaluation services available at Syracuse University's Center for Instructional Development (CID) (Diamond et al., 1975) provide good models for such a support unit.

As noted by Danielson (1985), the motto on university and college campuses seems to be "millions for equipment, but not one cent for staff." Johnson (1987) maintains that the typical split for campus-wide distribution of computing resources should be one-third for hardware, one-third for software, maintenance, and operation, and one-third for training and assistance. Usually, the last two thirds are ignored. Jacobson and Weller (1987) surveyed 144 faculty members at a large state university and found that lack of training and technical support were two of the four most critical issues identified as barriers to instructional computing. The belief that faculty members can be given 25 percent release time and subsequently develop effective, efficient courseware is simply fallacious (Bork, 1984).

6. *Highly touted "authoring systems" have not yielded effective CBT.*
The basic idea behind an authoring system as opposed to a programming or
authoring language is that it enables the subject matter expert to produce
effective interactive instruction without the aid of experienced programmers (Reeves, 1986a). The advertisements for these computerized lesson
generation programs often approach levels of incredulity. (For example,
one recent authoring system advertisement in an education journal pic-
tured a chimpanzee and suggested that the authoring system is so powerful and easy to use that even a monkey can program "your" instructional
lessons.)

Although authoring systems are constantly being improved, some with
the addition of "artificial intelligence" (AI) support (Begg & Hogg, 1987),
it seems reasonable to expect that the creativity of content experts and instructional designers will continue to outstrip the power of these systems
to automatically generate instructional code (Merrill, 1985). This should
be especially evident as more developers move away from a frame-oriented
question-and-answer format to the construction of elaborate instructional
simulations. The addition of AI capabilities to CBT as in the development
of expert systems also suggests that most authoring sytems will not provide
sufficient interactive options for sophisticated instructional applications.

7. *There has been a general failure to manage expectations with respect
to CBT on college and university campuses.* CBT has been represented as
a panacea to many of the instructional ills faced by higher education, and
it is threatened with suffering the same fate as many earlier instructional
innovations (e.g., radio, film, television, and programmed instruction)
(McClintock, 1988). If CBT is to be successful, it must be introduced
gradually by employing the procedures and tools of systematic instructional design and evaluation. Evaluation is key to the management of
realistic expectations.

The lack of sound evaluation may be the most damaging factor in efforts to develop and implement CBT in higher education. Reeves (1989)
has described a six-level model for the evaluation of interactive instruction. Level 1, *project documentation,* involves keeping records of when
and where various development and implementation activities occur,
what the activities cost, and who participates in them. Level 2, *assessment of the worth of project objectives,* is defined as a separate activity
because of the tendency of CBT designers and users to become so fixated
on specifying objectives and then accomplishing them that they fail to adequately examine the worth of their objectives, especially with respect to
the ultimate aims of higher education. Level 3, *formative evaluation,* involves collecting the opinions, suggestions, and criticisms of faculty, students, and other interested parties for purposes of revising and improving
aspects of CBT. Level 4, *immediate effectiveness evaluation,* is carried
out to assess the instructional effectiveness and efficiency of CBT within

the immediate temporal and spatial context of its implementation. Level 5, *impact evaluation*, looks at the effects of CBT on the long term goals of higher education, for example, teaching students how to learn once they leave the campus. Level 6, *cost effectiveness analysis*, involves the appraisal of CBT to determine the costs of specific effects, both immediate and long term.

Unfortunately, few evaluations of CBT in higher education can be found that utilize more than one of the levels described above. Nonexistent or inadequate evaluation insures that future CBT development projects will be uninformed by the successes and failures of past efforts. In addition, the conceptualization and conduct of evaluation must go beyond the predominant comparative model in which instructional innovations are pitted against other instructional technologies or the mythical "traditional instruction." A host of conceptual, methodological, and statistical problems plague these comparative studies which often leads to findings of "no significant differences" between instructional methods (Reeves, 1986b).

8. *Rampant misunderstandings of the benefits and findings of instructional technology and educational research exist, especially ignorance of the relationship between CBT and instructional design.* Ely (1987) lists some of the common misconceptions held by academics with respect to instructional technology, including:

1.   media equals instructional technology
2.   the use of media will automatically bring about learning
3.   one medium is superior to another.

Reviews of decades of media comparison studies (Clark, 1983) support the following conclusions which conflict with the perceptions commonly held by university faculty:

1.   How a medium is used (i.e., the quality of its implementation) is often more important than the choice of a medium.
2.   Because most of the variance in the differential performance of alternative instructional programs can be explained by aptitude differences among students, it is very difficult to directly attribute learning to any specific medium.
3.   Basic psychological principles such as requiring active, overt responses, giving immediate feedback, and providing cognitive scaffolding are the key features that can account for the effectiveness of media, not such technical elements as color, motion, and speed.

Clearly, the perception of CBT as a "magic bullet" for the solution of instructional problems must be balanced with a more informed view of the medium as a "vehicle" for well-designed instruction.

9. *Most univerisities and colleges lack a campus-wide direction or commitment to a "computer intensive environment" (Johnson, 1987).* The lack of commitment is evidenced by the inadequate or inappropriate physical plant for CBT on most campuses. Buerger (1987) interviewed 274 faculty members at a large liberal arts institution and found that lack of facilities for classroom use was perceived as the number of one impediment to CBT. While there is a proliferation of computing resources on many campuses to support word processing and data analysis, the establishment of instructional computing environments lags far behind. If CBT is to become a mainstay of the instructional repertoire of higher education, universities must establish a sense of purpose, policies, and standards with respect to instructional computing. Ideally, all the various computing resources should be integrated and networked.

In his keynote address at EDUCOM '87, John Sculley, chief executive officer of Apple Computer, Inc., painted an optimistic vision of the powerful academic communication and instructional capacities of computers in the next century. The video used to illustrate this vision featured a professor of the future preparing for an afternoon class by interacting with a computer-based instructional mentor. The mentor aided the professor as he analyzed data trends from multiple databases, collaborated via face-to-face telecommunications with a colleague on the other side of the continent, and prepared interactive instructional simulations. Sculley concluded this seemingly fantastic prediction with the statement that virtually all the tools and techniques required for such a seamless academic support system already exist (Sculley, 1987).

Ironically, the reality of today is that most academic departments are struggling with incompatibilities among the various computing resources used for such mundane tasks as word processing and data analysis. These types of incompatibility problems are increased geometrically when instructional applications are considered. While Sculley's claim that most of the tools and techniques for the "knowledge navigator" are incubating in the academic and industrial laboratories of today may be warranted, a corresponding "technological readiness" must be nurtured among the faculty of the future. Some estimates indicate that as many as one-third of all faculty in higher education will be replaced by the year 2000. There is little evidence that these new faculty members will be much better prepared to integrate computing into their instructional activities than the present faculty.

10. *There is a lack of quality commercial software for instruction (Lukesh, 1987).* Therefore, academics desiring to use CBT must attempt to develop the programs themselves. Unfortunately, many universities and colleges labor to develop CBT in isolation, wastefully duplicating efforts. Ironically, this can occur even on the same campus when various departments fail to collaborate and share expertise and experience.

Attempts to develop instructional software by consortia of universities and colleges are sometimes frustrated by the "not invented here" syndrome. Academics have a penchant for rejecting instructional media of any sort which do not completely reflect local theories and practices. As a result, some textbooks include only "safe" topics and theories, neglecting speculative or controversial ones for fear of decreased adoption. When this syndrome is added to the problems of hardware incompatibility, it is a small wonder that few, if any, instructional software programs enjoy widespread utilization in academic settings.

11. *There is insufficient evidence supporting effectiveness of CBT (Kulik, Kulik, & Cohen, 1980).* In fact, there is little strong research supporting the use of any instructional technologies. Some theorists attribute this lack of support to the inadequacy of research methodologies adopted from the "hard" sciences to account for and control the variables involved in human learning (Pagels, 1988). Others attribute the weaknesses of existing research to the paucity of instructional theory to drive educational research (Farley, 1982). Regardless of the origin, it is clear that instructional research has provided little concrete direction for the design and use of any type of instructional innovations (Phillips, 1980; Sanders, 1981). Until such support is forthcoming, many academics will continue to reject the adoption of CBT. There is a glaring need for alternative approaches to the conduct of research in instructional technology (Clark, 1989; Reigeluth, 1989; Reeves, 1986b).

12. *The costs of using CBT are kept artificially high because there is little understanding of how to buy software for campus use.* Site licensing agreements are complicated and volume discounts are not established clearly. The seemingly constant struggle for declining resources for higher education makes it extremely unlikely that major investments in CBT will be made unless economies of scale can be realized.

Many colleges and universities are establishing computer labs on their campuses, but these resources are often swamped by students using them for word processing, data analysis, and graphics production. The establishment of labs for strictly instructional purposes is rare. It is a classic "chicken and egg" problem, that is, the labs are not constructed because there is not enough CBT available and the CBT is not developed because there are not enough labs.

EDUCOM, a consortium of more than 500 colleges and universities involved in academic computing, commissioned a survey of the status of academic computing (Lukesh, 1987). Among the major findings of this study were:

1. 13% of the students in 211 respondent institutions own microcomputers.

2.   There are an average of 17 students and faculty per computer on the respondent campuses.
3.   Average 3 hours of access to computers is available per student each week.

The surveyors indicated that because of the nature of the responding institutions, these figures are high in comparison to those representing the entire populations of U.S. colleges and universities. Clearly, a major constraint to adequate integration of CBT into the academic program continues to be the sheer lack of an adequate base of computing availability.

NEW DIRECTIONS

Despite the "bad news" about CBT in higher education described above, there are some signs that the status of academic computing may be improving. Instances of "good news" include:

1. There are some notable success stories on some campuses. For example, Danielson (1985) described the development of an advanced state of computing integration at the University of Texas at Austin. The Air Force Academy, Clarkson College, and Drexel University are other examples of campuses with innovative and pervasive integration of instructional computing. The Air Force Academy has established a goal of providing each student with an interactive learning station in his or her room, and students take exams distributed over the local area network. In addition, the Academy leads the country in the implementation of interactive videodisc instruction, especially in the teaching of second languages. Carnegie-Mellon University, MIT, and Stanford have mounted notable instructional computing efforts, primarily through the provision of advanced workstations throughout their campuses.

2. There is continued and perhaps increased support for high level research and development for academic computing. For example, in the fall of 1988, Next, Inc. introduced a relatively low-priced powerful workstation for academic computing. A major purpose of this hardware is to implement what founder Steve Jobs calls "simulated learning environments" which are basically sophisticated simulations of labs and modeling (Jobs, 1986). Interestingly, when asked how the Next workstations might be purchased by those outside academe, Job advised would be buyers to "enroll." Not too surprisingly, however, Next recently announced the availability of its new computer to business and industry through a marketing arrangement with the Computerland chain. Apple Computer, Inc. responded to the Next challenge in September 1989 by releasing the Macintosh IIci, reportedly developed with academic users in mind. Meanwhile, IBM, in addi-

tion to its significant support of cutting-edge projects at Carnegie-Mellon, MIT, and Brown has funded "Advanced Education Projects" at 16 other institutions. Over 3,000 projects have been undertaken at the participating institutions, and over 300 software products have been made available to other colleges and universities (Turner, 1989).

3. EDUCOM, CONDUIT, and other recognized groups are establishing peer review evaluation processes for instructional software aimed at higher education (DeLoughry, 1988b). These services will enable purchasers of commercial courseware to make more informed decisions. The EPIE Institute and the MicroSIFT project at the Northwest Regional Educational Laboratory also provide important review services for instructional software. In addition, the establishment of prestigious recognition structures such as the EDUCOM/NCRIPTAL higher education software awards enhances the incentives for developing CBT for academic use.

4. There is increased interest in instructional software by textbook publishers (DeLoughry, 1988a). At the same time, innovative schemes for bypassing the slow-moving traditional publication process are being explored. (Regrettably, Kinko's Courseware Exchange, a novel approach to the dissemination of instructional programs for the Macintosh may be going the way of the albatross according to recent press releases.) Of course, it must be noted that the availability of large quantities of CBT will not automatically insure the availability of high quality CBT. The author's own view is that CBT for higher education has not bypassed the highly generalizable assertion that "90% of everything is crap."

5. Lukes (1987) reported that there is a general growth in the number of "computer intensive environments" at the nation's universities and colleges. These campuses generally take one of three directions:

1. Policies are established which require the purchase of a specific microcomputer.
2. Policies are established which recommend the purchase of a specific microcomputer.
3. Policies are established which provide pervasive access to and use of institutionally owned computers.

6. There is continued growth of inter- and intrainstitutional computer networks, such as BITNET, CSNET, NSFNET, and PROFS. These services provide academics with greatly enhanced methods for sharing information about instructional computing.

7. Newer technologies such as interactive videodiscs (IVD) are gaining important roles in classrooms as simulators of real life situations (DeLoughry, 1987). The "First National Conference on Postsecondary Utilization of Videodisc" at the University of Nebraska in Lincoln in early 1988, sponsored in part by the Annenberg-CPB project, brought together

many of the most important developers of IVD for higher education in the country, and several collaborative ventures have been derived from it. University students can anticipate the availability of powerful IVD simulations in diverse fields including physics, chemistry, ethics, music, nursing, and teacher education. Even newer technologies such as Compact Disc-Interactive (CD-I), Compact Disc-Read Only Memory (CD-ROM), Digital Video Interactive (DVI), and Laser Digital Video (LDV) will begin to be applied in academic settings in the coming months and years. In February 1989, a special conference called "Use and Development of Interactive Multi-Media in Higher Education" was held in Orlando, Florida to explore the potential of these newer optical technologies.

8. Membership and participation in professional associations such as EDUCOM, CAUSE, and the Association for the Development of Computer-Based Instructional Systems (ADCIS) enhance the general environment for the development and implementation of CBT in higher education. For example, ADCIS has established an active Special Interest Group dedicated to Academic Computing. Furthermore, attendance at EDUCOM's annual conference over the past few years has increased from several hundred to several thousand participants. In addition, these professional organizations are enjoying the increased support of commercial companies such as IBM, Apple, DEC, Aston-Tate, AT&T, MicroSoft, Zenith, and Next, Inc. The growing collaboration of higher education and business agencies, a hallmark of the defense industry for decades, holds enormous potential for the future of academic CBT.

A POSSIBLE FUTURE

In many academic departments, the computer has become an almost transparent medium for the creation and processing of printed materials. Given microcomputers and laser printers, faculty would no more think of writing a paper by hand and giving it to a secretary to type than they would think of riding a horse to work. And yet, most continue to utilize lecture (perhaps supported by overhead transparencies and spiced up with an occasional videotape) as the primary instructional delivery approach. When will the computer become a primary vehicle for instruction in higher education?

Predictions have a nasty habit of coming back to haunt one, but some portrayal of a short-term (five- to ten-year) future for instructional computing seems worth the risk. First, classrooms will become equipped with microcomputers linked to video projection systems so that faculty can make classroom presentations with interactive audiovisual support. (HyperCard stacks are already being used to support lectures in subjects as diverse as art history, microbiology, astronomy and research design.)

Second, computer laboratories devoted to instructional delivery will become prominent on campuses at every level of higher education. Third, syllabi and lecture notes will be provided to students in electronic form on a regular basis. Fourth, faculty and students will make increasingly more effective and efficient use of electronic communications such as bulletin boards and electronic mail. Fifth, CBT programs in the form of high fidelity simulations will enjoy increasing popularity, especially in technical subjects such as science and engineering.

SUMMARY

A number of significant constraints on the integration of CBT into postsecondary education have been identified. While some of these can only be remedied by the infusion of greater resources into the academic environment, others simply require modifications of the knowledge and attitudes of administrators, faculty, and students with respect to instructional computing. Successful CBT implementations in higher education must be exposed through meetings such as EDUCOM and ADCIS, teleconferences, site visits, and publications (e.g., Apple Computer's *Wheels for the Mind* journal). In the relatively short period of time that academic computing has existed, many hard lessons have been learned and it is up to each and every "learner" to share those lessons (FIPSE Technology Study Group, 1989).

Two major first steps toward the successful implementation of CBT in academe will be adjustment of the reward structure in higher education to recognize the value of electronic publications and the provision of instructional design and evaluation resources to support the development and implementation of CBT. Faculty are only human, and they require the same recognition and resources that are required by professionals in other fields.

At the same time that serious limitations exist, there is some room for optimism concerning the future of academic computing, especially with respect to the development of powerful workstations specifically designed for higher education. Furthermore, there is cause for enthusiasm regarding the enhanced application of computer integrated technologies such as interactive videodisc for the implementation of challenging and realistic simulations.

The college freshmen of the year 2000 were already in the first grade in the year 1988! Cetron (1988) predicts that the body of knowledge will have doubled four times between 1988 and 2000, and college freshmen in 2000 will be exposed to more information in one year of study than their grandparents were in a lifetime. How can the existing instructional infrastructure in higher education handle this sheer volume of information without widespread utilization of CBT? More importantly, how can higher education provide students with the experiential basis for lifelong independent learning without the adoption of sophisticated intelligent simulations? In the final analysis, it is not a question of whether higher education will adopt CBT, but how effectively and efficiently it will do so.

REFERENCES

Abdulla, A.M. (1987, February). *Use of interactive laser video, natural language and high fidelity simulation in medical education.* Paper presented at the Second Annual Conference on Learning Technology in the Health Care Sciences, Society for Applied Learning Technology, Washington, DC.

Alderman, D.L. (1978). *Evaluation of the TICCIT computer assisted instructional system in the community college.* Princeton, NJ: Educational Testing Service.

Begg, I.M., & Hogg, I. (1987). Authoring sytems for ICAI. In G. Kearsley (Ed.), *Artificial intelligence and instruction: Applications and methods* (pp. 323–346). Reading, MA: Addison-Wesley.

Bork, A. (1984). Production systems for computer-based learning. In D.F. Walker & R.D. Hess (Eds.), *Instructional software: Principles and perspectives for design and use* (pp. 96–115). Belmont, CA: Wadsworth.

Buerger, D.J. (1987, Summer). Computer usage in a liberal arts university. *EDUCOM Bulletin*, pp. 11–14.

Cetron, M.J. (1988). Class of 2000: The good news and the bad news. *The Futurist*, *12*(6), 9–15.

Clark, R.E. (1983). Reconsidering research on learning from media. *Review of Educational Research, 53*, 445–460.

Clark, R.E. (1989). Current progress and future directions for research in instructional technology. *Educational Technology Research and Development*, *37*(1), 57–66.

Colbert, J. (1988, April). *Constraints of computer-based instruction in the Los Angeles Unified School District.* Paper presented at the Annual Meeting of the American Educational Research Association, New Orleans, LA.

Danielson, W.A. (1985, Winter). A report from the barricades of the computer revolution on campus. *EDUCOM Bulletin*, pp. 17–18.

DeLoughry, T.J. (1987, December 2). Videodiscs gain a new role in classrooms as medium to simulate real-life situations. *The Chronicle of Higher Education*, *34*(14), A13, A16–A17.

DeLoughry, T.J. (1988a, January 20). Publishers consider including computer disks in textbooks for a variety of disciplines. *The Chronicle of Higher Education, 34*(19), A11, A18.

DeLoughry, T.J. (1988b, February 17). Plan for scholars to review peer's academic software is announced by college computing consortium. *The Chronicle of Higher Education, 34*(23), A13, A18.

Diamond, R.M., Eickmann, P.E., Kelly, E.F., Holloway, R.E., Vickery, T.R., & Pascarella, E.T. (1975). *Instructional development for individualized learning in higher education.* Englewood Cliffs, NJ: Educational Technology.

Ellis, J., & Wulfeck, W. (1988, April). *Computer-managed instruction for Navy technical training: Why is it failing?* Paper presented at the Annual Meeting of the American Educational Research Association, New Orleans, LA.

Ely, D.P. (1987). Educational technology research: A status report on classroom applications. *EMI, 24*, 74–78.

Estes, W.L. (1978). The information processing approach to cognition: A confluence of metaphors and methods. In W.K. Estes (Ed.), *Handbook of learning and cognitive processes, Vol. 5, Human information processing*. Hillsdale, NJ: Erlbaum.

Farley, F.H. (Ed.). (1982). The future of edcuational research. *Educational Researcher, 11*(8), 11–19.

FIPSE Technology Study Group. (1989). *Ivory towers, silicon basements: Learner-centered computing in postsecondary education*. McKinney, TX: Academic Computing.

Gagné, R.M., Wager, W., & Rojas, A. (1984). Planning and authoring computer-assisted instruction lessons. In D.F. Walker & R.D. Hess (Eds.), *Instructional software: Principles and perspectives for design and use*. Belmont, CA: Wadsworth.

Heermann, B. (1988). *Teaching and learning with computers: A guide for college faculty and administrators*. San Francisco: Jossey-Bass.

Hoelscher, K. (1988, August). *Exploring the use of interactive videodisc in law: A formative evaluation of Harvard Law School students*. Paper presented at the Tenth Annual Conference on Interactive Videodisc in Education and Training, Society for Applied Learning Technology, Washington, DC.

Jacobson, M.J., & Weller, M.H. (1987). A profile of computer use among the University of Illinois faculty. *Journal of Educational Technology Systems, 16*, 83–98.

Jobs, S.P. (1986, Spring). The future of computing in higher education. *EDUCOM Bulletin*, pp. 6–8.

Johnson, J.W. (1987, Winter). Observations on computer-intensive environments. *EDUCOM Bulletin*, pp. 6–8.

Johnson-Laird, P.N. (1988). *The computer and the mind: An introduction to cognitive science*. Cambridge, MA: Harvard University Press.

Klatzky, R.L. (1980). *Human memory: Structures and processes* (2nd ed.). San Francisco: W.H. Freeman.

Kulik, J., Kulik, C., & Cohen, P. (1980). Effectiveness of computer-based college teaching: A meta-analysis of findings. *Review of Educational Research, 50*, 525–544.

Levien, R.E. (1972). *The emerging technology: Instructional uses of the computer in higher education*. New York: McGraw-Hill.

Levine, H., & Rheingold, H. (1987). *The cognitive connection: Thought and language in man and machine*. New York: Prentice-Hall.

Lukes, J.A. (1987). Microcomputer-intensive environments in higher education: An introduction to three policy alternatives. *EMI, 24*, 110–115.

Lukesh, S.S. (1987, Fall). Microcomputer use in higher education: Summary of a survey. *EDUCOM Bulletin*, pp. 13–17.

McClintock, R.O. (1988). Marking the second frontier. *Teachers College Record, 89*, 345–351.

Merrill, M.D. (1985). Where is the authoring in authoring sytems? *Journal of Computer-Based Instruction, 12*, 90–96.

Pagels, H.R. (1988). *The dreams of reason: The computer and the rise of the sciences of complexity*. New York: Simon and Schuster.

Philips, D.C. (1980). What do the researcher and the practitioner have to offer each other? *Educational Researcher, 9*(11), 17–24.

Redish, E.F. (1988, October). *Educational improvement via innovation: How the microcomputer can change the way we teach*. Paper presented at EDUCOM '88, Washington, DC.

Reeves, T.C. (1989). The role, methods, and worth of evaluation in instructional design. In K. Johnson & L. Foa (Eds.), *Instructional design: New strategies for education and training*. New York: MacMillan.

Reeves, T.C. (1988). Effective dimensions of interactive videodisc for training. In T. Bernold & J. Finkelstein (Eds.), *Computer-assisted approaches to training: Foundations of industry's future*. Amsterdam, NR: Elsevier Science.

Reeves, T.C. (1986a). Computer-assisted instruction: Authoring languages. *ERIC Digest*. ERIC Clearinghouse on Information Resources.

Reeves, T.C. (1986b). Research and evaluation models for the study of interactive video. *Journal of Computer-Based Instruction, 13*, 102–106.

Reigeluth, C.M. (1989). Educational technology at the crossroads: New mindsets and new directions. *Educational Technology Research and Development, 37*(1), 67–80.

Roecks, A.L. (1981). How many ways can the computer be used in education? A baker's dozen. *Educational Technology, 21*(9), 16.

Sanders, D.P. (1981). Educational inquiry as developmental research. *Educational Researcher, 10*(3), 8–13.

Sculley, J. (1987, October). *The relationship between business and higher education: A perspective on the twenty-first century*. Paper presented at EDUCOM '87, Dallas, TX.

Semonche, J.E. (1989). *1865: Should the southern states be readmitted to the union?* [computer program]. Chicago, IL: Harcourt, Brace, Jovanovitch.

Shlechter, T., & Kristiansen, D. (1988, April). *Lessons learned in fielding computer-based instruction in an Army training program*. Paper presented at the Annual Meeting of the American Educational Research Association, New Orleans, LA.

Shneiderman, B. (1986). *Designing the user interface: Strategies for effective human-computer interaction*. Reading, MA: Addison-Wesley.

Suppes, P., & Macken, E. (1978). The historical path from research and development to operational use of CAI. *Educational Technology, 18*(4), 9–12.

Taylor, M. (1987). The implementation and evaluation of a computer simulation game in a university course. *The Journal of Experimental Education, 55*, 108–115.

Turner, J.A. (1989, June 21). Projects to measure the effects of computers on campuses make major advances, leave several unsolved problems. *The Chronicle of Higher Education, 35*(41), A9, A12.

Winograd, T., & Flores, F. (1987). *Understanding computers and cognition: A new foundation for design*. Reading, MA: Addison-Wesley.

5
The Status and Challenge of Technology Training for Teachers

Carol Carrier
University of Minnesota

Allen Glenn
University of Washington

Technology has become a part of the American school. Over two million computers are being used for instructional purposes and 95 percent of all schools have a computer in the building. Videotape equipment is also found in almost all schools. To support this ever-expanding use, school districts and state departments of education continue to allocate funds for equipment, training, and educational courseware. School districts are also exploring new ways to integrate technology into new ways of thinking about schools and instruction. As education moves into the 1990s, educators, parents, and society in general appear to have made a long-term commitment to technology's role in education.

What has contributed to this advancement of technology into the classroom? A variety of factors may be identified; however, four general reasons are proposed. First, there is a growing body of research on the positive effects of technology assisted instruction on student performance and attitudes. Heroic statements about what technology can do are being more carefully analyzed, and tentative conclusions support the use of technology. For example, science teachers have found that students can learn as much or more and with less risk from technology based simulations (Glenn & Ehman, 1987) as from more costly lab experiments. Students who have been taught to use word processing systems write more and produce higher quality work than when using more traditional paper-and-pencil practices (Murphy & Appel, 1984). While many questions remain unanswered, positive results like these promote confidence among decision makers at various levels of education.

A second reason for increased use of technology is that technology has expanded beyond the early capabilities of the microcomputer and videotape. New technologies have expanded the capabilities of the microcomputer and linked schools in new and different ways. For example, small, remote schools can now offer an array of academic subjects through two-way interactive television. Or, with the touch of a keypad, teachers or students can access 54,000 still-frame images or up to one hour of motion video on a videodisc. Linking videodiscs and microcomputers can access data heretofore unavailable to most students. CD ROMs now make available entire reference libraries which include encyclopedias, dictionaries, and thesauruses. These and other technologies have expanded the information available for instruction and altered learning experiences for students. Students and teachers alike are able to learn in an information rich environment.

A third reason for technology's availability and use in the schools is teachers' acceptance of the technology as tools to help them perform multiple tasks more efficiently. Technology tools, such as word processing and graphic programs, allow teachers to create higher quality instructional materials more quickly than in the past. Electronic gradebooks help teachers manage student scores and grades. Sophisticated simulations permit teachers to use models that were once too difficult to manage with a group of students. Finally, new technologies offer greater capacity to rationalize the notion of individualized instruction by monitoring student progress, diagnosing student competence, and assigning specific instructional tasks. For more and more teachers, technologies have become integrated into the day-to-day tasks of managing instruction.

The fourth reason for the increased use of technology in the classroom, and the topic of this chapter, is that more teachers are being prepared to use advanced technologies for instruction. During the last decade, teacher preparation institutions, state departments of education, and school districts have made a concerted effort to prepare teachers to use technology. In 1988, 26 states spent $32 million on teacher training (Bruder, 1988). Teacher training institutions also responded by increasing their efforts to prepare beginning teachers.

While the commitment to better prepared teachers has been significant, the number of teachers who need training remains high. For example, the Office of Technology Assessment's study *Power On!* (1988) estimates most teachers have had less than 10 hours of teacher training and that this training ranges from a brief introduction on how to use the computer to more sophisticated instruction on how to integrate technology into instruction.

The variation across districts and institutions is significant and suggests that the vast majority of teachers are not adequately prepared to effectively use technology as a part of the instructional process.

The lack of preparation of teachers to use technology effectively and to integrate it into the instructional process is a serious problem for those interested in technology's role in schools. Effective instructional strategies must be linked to effective use of technology *if* teachers are to become managers of instruction and facilitators of student learning. In the remainder of this chapter we explore this issue. First, we examine the current status of technology training to provide a basis for the discussion of the future training needs of teachers. Much of the information about current preservice and inservice training is derived from a report prepared by the two authors commissioned by the Office of Technology Assessment (OTA) and summarized in their report *Power On!* (1988). Following the discussion of training, the roles that colleges and universities, school districts, state and federal government, business and industry, and professional organizations play in training educators are presented. The chapter concludes with the presentation of a model of technology training that the authors have implemented with teachers to overcome the problems of linking effective instruction with effective use of technology.

TEACHER EDUCATION AND TECHNOLOGY TRAINING

Teacher education programs respond to public opinion, state initiatives, federal directives, and current thinking in the profession. As a consequence, most teacher education programs reflect the mood of the times and allocate resources to critical areas of needs. In order to understand the role of technology training in both today's teacher education environment and the technology training needs of tomorrow's teachers, it is necessary to provide a perspective on the current context in which technology training occurs.

Current issues in teacher education. The 1980s can be characterized as a period in which American schools and teacher education institutions came under severe criticism. A variety of reports were written describing the lack of academic preparation of students (National Commission on Excellence in Education, 1983), the poor quality of instruction in schools (Goodlad, 1984), and the needs to prepare better teachers (Holmes Group, 1986; Carnegie Forum on Education and the Economy, 1986). Each report called for dramatic changes in the curriculum and organization of schools and in the manner in which teachers are prepared.

The impact of these reports was immediate. In almost all 50 states, departments of education or legislatures began reviewing the preparation of teachers. National teachers organizations called for a rethinking of teacher preparation and organizations of professional educators began studies and programs to prepare better teachers. In some cases specific directives were legislated. The state legislature in Texas, for example, mandated a teacher education program of 18 credits including student teaching. The Texas model drastically reduced the academic preparation individuals received in education and placed more emphasis on the liberal arts preparation. Other state legislatures created guidelines for the licensure of teachers. As a result, teacher education programs all across the United States began a careful review of their teacher education curriculum.

This review had a direct impact on the resources and attention given to technology training. While still acknowledging the importance of technology training for teachers, most teacher educators turned their attention to other pressing issues such as liberal arts preparation, clinical experiences, and preparing teachers to work with at-risk students. After investing considerable resources in technology—hardware, laboratories, and software—educators reallocated funds into new programs. Once the centerpiece of many training programs, technology training efforts competed for scarce resources.

Typical technology training programs in teacher licensure programs. Most schools of education in the United States provide prospective teachers with some access to computers. According to a Department of Education survey of teacher education institutions in 1984 (U.S. Department of Education, 1986), two types of courses are most common. The first devotes over 80 percent or more of the class periods to computers as objects of learning or their use as learning or teaching tools. This is the typical introductory course. The second type of course devotes only a small portion of class time to computers and focuses primarily on techniques for using computers to teach subject matter.

At the preservice level the introductory course is the most common. The course is seldom more than one semester or quarter in length and is often listed at the graduate level to accommodate both undergraduate and graduate students. Students are taught how to use the computer, tool applications, and various instructional applications. The most common skill learned is how to use a word processing system. Seldom is the course linked to any other methods of instruction the student may be receiving in the content area.

The second type of course, in which computer technology training is integrated into the methods course, remains unavailable to most students; however, the number of such courses is probably increasing. Integrating technology into methods courses that focus on more traditional instructional techniques is inhibited by the lack of appropriate software and equipment, an already crowded course syllabus, and lack of faculty preparation to use technology (Moore, 1984). Consequently, it is often easier for colleges of education to provide a separate course on using the computer and related technologies than to convince, train, and support methods instructors.

Few institutions offer preservice teachers any training with other technologies such as videodiscs, interactive television, and CD ROM players. Few have easy access to such equipment or to instructors who are prepared to work with beginning teachers.

As a consequence of these decisions, the typical preservice teacher has about 10 to 20 hours of exposure to computers followed by some additional experience during the methods course and student teaching. Some students may, through their own initiative, take additional courses or purchase their own computers. Very little of the instruction the preservice teacher receives focuses on integrating knowledge about effective teaching strategies with effective use of technology. At best most beginning teachers start with their first year with an introductory knowledge of various computer tool applications and very limited knowledge of how to use courseware in an instructional unit.

As colleges and universities look to the future it will be critical that staff consider several important factors. Briefly these may be summarized in the following manner.

1. Teachers must be competent designers of instructional systems which will enable them to assist their students to become critical thinkers and information workers (Bitter, 1989).
2. Tomorrow's technologically oriented schools will call for new teacher roles and knowledge of technology. This means that teachers will need to be proficient, critical users of technology which includes a recognition of technology's limitations and potential.
3. College and university faculty will need to become more knowledgeable and proficient in using technology in order to model effective instructional techniques.
4. Preservice teachers' clinical experiences must be in schools in which teachers and students are actively involved in using technology as a common learning experience.

These will be important challenges for teacher preparation institutions during an era of tight financial resources.

Technology Training as Part of Inservice

Inservice education has a long history in public education. A variety of agencies are involved in the continuing education of classroom teachers.

The most dominant is the school district; however, colleges and universities also have a long history of inservice and graduate education. Other participants include state agencies and businesses. Each will continue to play an increasingly important role in the training of tomorrow's teachers.

School districts. All school districts provide opportunities for teachers to increase their knowledge and skills across a wide range of topics. The amount of resources available for inservice vary significantly across the country and within each state. Typically districts sponsor workshops and give teachers district credit for attending; they cooperate with colleges who in turn provide graduate credit for courses; and districts pay for teachers to attend state and national conferences.

Responding to the call for better technology training, most districts have established district-wide plans to train their teachers. While early efforts focused on programming, current efforts focus on tool and instructional applications. Unfortunately, few workshops are followed with additional training or efforts to insure access to computers and software for teachers.

Inservice technology programs face several critical issues as they seek to prepare teachers to use technology. First, while school districts continue to believe technology helps improve teaching, a National School Boards Association (NSBA) study found most districts to have "weak" long-range plans and not be updating, evaluating, and tracking technology use (Bruder, 1989). While most contend they have written plans, these plans are brief statements that focus on general computer literacy statements. Also, the NSBA survey found district educators' preferring to use technology for direct instruction. This means that most inservice efforts will probably continue to focus on tool and management applications.

Some educators are suggesting that if schools are to be reshaped for the 21st century, important changes must occur in the manner in which teachers are trained. Robert Pearlman (1989) suggests that districts must alter their plans which focus on getting computers in the hands of students and instead put computers in the hands of teachers. They should also encourage teachers to make more decisions related to how technology will be used. Pearlman and others contend that teachers must have an expanded role and assume greater responsibility and authority over the type of technology needed to help them assist students in becoming knowledge workers in tomorrow's society. Not until schools' and districts' plans are reorganized will effective instruction and effective technology use be merged.

Second, the number of teachers who need to receive training will remain significant over the next decade. As of 1987, only about one-third of all teachers had at least 10 hours of training (OTA, 1987). These remaining teachers see training as the number one issue if they are to begin to use technology effectively (Lamon, 1987).

Third, inservice technology training will continue to be confronted with increased demands for other areas of educational needs. AIDS education, teaching students who are at risk, and competency testing all will require financial resources and teacher attention.

To respond to these and other challenges districts must respond with more sophisticated plans and commit resources for an extended period. Two models of such an approach will serve as illustrations of what districts could do.

The Houston Independent School District established a Department of Technology to coordinate the district's technology activities (Sturdivant, 1989). Utilizing a train-the-trainer model, teachers who volunteered for the program were given computers and became involved in the planning for the implementation plan. Using a staff of full-time trainers, 60 to 80 workshops are offered each month to interested teachers and administrators. Teachers receive equipment, training, copies of selected software, and opportunities to observe model teaching via the district's cable TV network. Workshop participants also receive access to district software, technology-related journals, and programs designed to aid in the purchasing of hardware. The key to the program is the district's long-term commitment to implementation.

The Lake Washington (Seattle) School District took an alternative approach. One year prior to expecting teachers to begin using computers in the classroom, teachers were given an opportunity to receive a computer for home use. They were encouraged to use the computer, explore its applications, and become familiar with its potential as a teaching and instructional tool. After one year of personal use, teachers received district training to use computers as part of instruction in their classrooms.

Districts face many difficult challenges as they look to the 21st century. The pressures for change will continue from both within and without the system. The challenge for the district will be to keep technology inservice an integral part of the district's inservice plans.

Colleges and universities. Colleges and universities are responsible for many inservice teacher education programs. The most typical method of inservice is to offer courses for graduate credit or workshops designed to meet the specific needs of a particular district. Courses are taught by faculty whose specialty is technology instruction and by content area faculty who have developed some expertise in technology applications. As a consequence courses range from instructional design of videodisc applicatons to using computer databases in the social studies classroom.

To better meet the demands of improved technology education colleges and universities must make some significant changes. First, faculty development must become a central issue. If public school teachers need access to computers to enable them to gain understanding and confidence in their use, so, too, do college and university faculty. In addition, faculty need training and coaching to integrate technology into their classrooms.

Faculty development programs such as those at the University of Victoria, in which a technology professor teams with a methods instructor, demonstrate how technology can be used to enhance instruction. Or, the program at the University of Delaware, where professor Fred Hofstetter is developing videodisc materials for use in college classrooms, is another example of including technology in the delivery of instruction.

College and university faculty can also make significant contributions to inservice education through research on the use of technology and on effective inservice instruction. Two examples illustrate such contributions. Marker and Ehman (1989) studied over 100 schools in an inservice technology project. The collection and evaluation of the results of the project made significant contributions to the inservice literature related to the implementation of new programs and the impact of these programs on teachers.

Another example of research-related activities is the cooperative partnership between universities and private businesses. The College of Education at the University of Minnesota and the Minnesota Education Computing Corporation have established a Center for the Study of Education Technology. The major goal of the center is to support research and evaluation that will improve the use of technology in the schools, including the training of teachers. Studies to date have examined how databases are used in the social studies and the effects of different follow-up sessions on the retention of workshop information. It is in understanding the relationship between effective instruction and the effective use of technology where college and university faculty may make significant contributions to teacher training. If technology is to become a meaningful part of instruction, teachers must have an integrated model of effective instructional methods that includes technology.

During the next decade technological change will continue at a rapid pace. Colleges and universities will not have the resources and expertise to stay abreast of these changes. It is evident, therefore, they must work cooperatively with school districts and the business community to form partnerships that allow each to utilize its own expertise.

State and federal government. State legislatures and departments of education have played leadership roles in technology development in schools. Their influence on training for teachers is seen in several ways. First, many states have established licensure requirements for teachers that require them to take courses related to technology. California, for example, passed a law that candidates for a clear (permanent) teaching credential in the state must satisfactorily complete computer education coursework that includes "general and specialized skills in the use of computers in educational settings" (Blurton, 1986–87). Included in the law is the charge to develop specific regulations regarding these skills and to disseminate voluntary standards for the training and performance of teachers and resource personnel in computer education. These requirements have immediate impact on the programs offered by colleges and universities at both pre- and inservice levels.

Some states have also created resource, demonstration, or training centers that offer a variety of services to districts. Legislation in Minnesota led to the creation of 17 technology demonstration sites that provided opportunities for teachers from around the state and region to view a variety of technological applications in actual schools and classrooms. New York State has a system of regional centers that provide resources and training for teachers. Teacher organizations have been heavily involved in the setup of these centers.

State funding for teacher training in technology ranges from $20,000 to $15 million annually, according to OTA's 1987 survey as summarized in *Power On!* This report found that 41 states have a technology coordinator or office for technology coordination. Funding for teacher training comes from state sources as well as federal flow-through funds.

One of the most significant roles that states can play in the technology movement is leadership in defining important training objectives as well as coordination to insure that school districts cooperate and learn from each other. Less advanced schools need to learn about what has worked or not worked in other settings.

Policy formation is an appropriate role for the federal government but there has been little progress relative to technology training for teachers. The recently released report by the U.S. Congress' Office of Technology Assessment, *Power On!*, is an excellent summary of the current status of technology in the schools and offers provocative suggestions for new directions. Efforts such as this one can do much to encourage policy discussions at the federal level. Federal block grants to states have been used in some cases for technology training but levels of funding have diminished since the early 1980s.

Agencies like the National Science Foundation have funded training but most of it directed toward math and science teachers. The Fund for the Improvement of Postsecondary Education has listed technology training for educators as a possible funding target in its 1989 call for proposals.

Business and industry. Vendors of both software and hardware have supported teacher training either through direct training or allocations of equipment and software. In fact some of the more comprehensive programs have been funded by groups like IBM, Tandy Corporation, and Apple Corporation. IBM has run workshops and provided resources to establish telecommunication links between students and cooperating teachers and faculty at the University of Virginia and first-year teachers out of Harvard.

Apple Corporation, long concerned with teacher training, has recently teamed with MECC to form the Apple Education Training Consortium. As a pilot project, it consists of school districts, schools of education, service units, and other groups interested in technology in education. Heavy use will be made of audio and teleconferencing as well as the Apple Link system to plan and deliver technology training to groups widely separated by miles. If the consortium works as intended, resources spent on technology training will have a much broader impact than could be realized at the state or local level. Cooperation with multiple institutions such as this one could change how we think about technology training.

Business and industry have much to gain from, and much to offer, the teacher training enterpise. Their natural marketplace perspective is broader than the individual state department of education, school district, or individual university. Their resources can be used to mobilize partnerships with schools and universities. Their distribution systems can be tapped to transmit new information quickly to constituents.

Professional organizations. For the most part professional organizations have had a limited role in technology training. General policy statements advocating the use of technology by teachers have been the characteristic response of these organizations. The National Council for Accreditation of Teacher Education (NCATE), for example, mentions technology in its professional studies standard related to foundations and in its practicum component.

Groups with a strong technology focus, such as the International Council of Computer Education (ICCE) publishes several journals including one directed to teacher educators called *The Journal of Computing and Teacher Education.* It also holds a national conference and sponsors workshops in school districts. Organizations such as this one are likely to have a bigger impact on technology training than most general teacher education organizations that have many other priorities.

SUMMARY OF TEACHER
TECHNOLOGY TRAINING PROBLEMS

Five major problems with typical technology training may be identified. First, technology training remains an "add-on" or additional part of the preservice training of teachers. As a consequence, beginning teachers take a "course" about technology where some linkages are made between effective technology and effective instruction. If the student is fortunate, a methods course may also be available to help him or her apply technology in teaching. Student teaching experiences may also provide opportunities to apply such learning.

Second, inservice programs remain introductory in nature and of limited duration. While districts believe in technology, few have a detailed plan for providing inservice training for teachers. Major efforts are directed toward providing computers for students to use and implementing computer literacy goals in the curriculum, with less attention to linking inservice programs on effective instruction with technology use. Districts with comprehensive plans are constantly confronted with the financial commitments needed to maintain such plans and with an ever-changing teacher population. In addition, increased demands to meet a variety of social issues also detract from training efforts related to technology.

Third, colleges and universities, providers of most inservice and graduate-level training for teachers are struggling to maintain up-to-date technology programs. Faculty development, updating hardware, and establishing cooperative relationships with schools and businesses are all important actions needed to move colleges forward. Research linking effective instruction and technology may provide significant insights into more advanced models of teaching.

Fourth, state and federal agencies will continue to play important roles in determining the role of technology in schools and colleges and universities. State regulations direct activities and both state and federal funding provide resources for inservice activities as well as the purchase of equipment. The federal government remains the most heavily relied-upon source of funding.

Finally, business and industry and professional organizations will continue to play minor roles in the training of teachers. Vendors provide training upon the purchase of equipment; however, the overall impact on the number of teachers needing training will remain small. Professional organizations continue to provide guidelines, conferences, and publications for teachers related to the use of technology in schools.

A PHASED APPROACH TO TECHNOLOGY TRAINING

The preceding paragraphs argue that many groups play a role in technology training for teachers. Most of these groups will, among other tasks, deliver technology instruction through courses, workshops, or seminars. To conclude the chapter we describe a model for technology training that we have developed and implemented. This evolving model attempts to remedy some of the shortcomings of technology training raised in the literature.

To be responsive to the needs of different teachers interested in using technology, we have developed a phased approach. Pieces of this program have been implemented at the University of Minnesota, school districts in

Minnesota, and within U.S. Department of Defense schools in a variety of countries. The first level, which is designed for novices, recognizes the need to help teachers master basic competencies in using technology. This level of the program encourages teachers to become involved in the use of technology by providing them with some basic skills and the necessary confidence to build upon these skills outside of the program.

The next level of the program, the advanced program, addresses the needs of teachers who have the basic competencies, at least some limited experience in using computers with students, and who now are ready to deal with the issues of a more systematic integration of the technology into their classrooms. In implementing both levels, we continuously encourage the linking of content and skills taught in the program to the personal and instructional tasks which these teachers carry out every day.

In the following section, we highlight four aspects of each phase of the program—the characteristics of participants, program content, teaching strategies, and follow-up activities.

The Novice Phase

Characteristics of participants. Teachers enrolling in this program usually share a set of characteristics. To begin with, although most are motivated to learn, the source of this motivation varies. Some report that their own son or daughter is a "computer wiz" and that they feel they should know about computers to avoid total intimidation. Others report that they have observed peers using computers with students and are curious about how they might make use of computing in their own classrooms. Still others have general feelings of anxiety about "being left behind" if they fail to learn about these new technologies. Some teachers have found themselves in the awkward position of acquiring a computer, through no effort of their own, and having no idea what to do with it. Reasons such as these motivate teachers to seek out or take advantage of inservice training on computing.

It is useful to have participants discuss the reasons for their attendance as a means of exposing both their anxieties and expectations. This sharing of ideas is often cathartic and serves to relieve some of the initial tensions so commonplace in the early stages of training. The question "In what ways have computers made life easier or more difficult for you personally?" usually elicits a flood of tales about bank statements, phony personalized form letters, or problems with bills. This provides a way of moving into a discussion of the role of computers in conducting one's personal affairs as well as in the teaching/learning process.

Participants in the novice phase usually anticipate a great deal of hands-on activity at the computer. They tend to be impatient with too much instructor talk; they prefer to act. Many expect to gain specific skills, such as word processing, or the ability to operate specific equipment.

In addition, we have found that participants enjoy an atmosphere in which they are free to work or chat with others as they experience new tasks. Individuals have different preferences, of course, for working alone or with others, but most welcome the opportunity to seek out support from fellow participants.

Content of the program. As time passes, the content in the novice program evolves to meet the changing demands of new technologies. However, certain basic principles continue to govern our choice of content to be covered. One of these principles is that teachers must early on gain some confidence with the equipment itself. Simple *equipment operation* gets addressed early on in our training. Everyone learns how to turn on the computer, manipulate floppy and hard disks, load and save material, and operate the printer and various peripherals. Newer equipment is often easier to operate, but teachers still benefit from careful guidance to insure that they feel comfortable with basic operating tasks.

Along with equipment operation, we integrate a minimal amount of information about the *inner workings of hardware and software.* This allows teachers to understand the basic workings of computers and related technologies so that they can better understand the hows and whys of procedures we ask them to learn. Finding the right balance is important; most teachers are interested in the general workings of the technology but not are interested in long-winded explanations of "computereze."

Building competence in *word processing* has been a successful entrée into the computer world for many teachers. Word processing provides teachers with a flexible tool that can be useful in many aspects of their professional and personal lives. Once a teacher is comfortable with a word processing package, he or she can prepare class materials, write notes to parents, complete assignments for inservice or graduate courses, and communicate with other teachers. We have found that teachers should gain a level of competence and comfort with a single word processing system early on before being introduced to other packages that may offer different features. The specific package is not important; mastering one is important.

Once teachers have become comfortable with word processing, it is relatively easy to move to other *materials generation* packages. Programs that produce overhead transparencies, tests, crossword puzzles, or other games are well received by teachers at all levels. As with word processing, teachers immediately see the benefits of these programs for their own classrooms.

In addition to tools, we introduce teachers to a range of *instructional programs* that are technology-based. They learn about tutorials, simulations, drill-and-practice and testing programs. Along with their exposure to these forms of instruction, we begin to help them develop criteria for making judgments about strong and weak features of programs. This is a "softer" approach to software evaluation in that it grows out of their natural interest in, and criticisms of, other instructional materials.

Teaching strategies. By teaching strategies we refer to the ways in which the content of the novice phase is presented, practiced, and reinforced. The first strategy we employ is that of building a *high degree of structure.* Tobias' research (1987) has shown that learners with little prior knowledge about the content of instruction they are to receive tend to benefit from high levels of structure in the form of instructional support. Our work with teachers who are novices suggests validation of this principle. We create a highly structured environment which consists of cycles of a preinstructional activity, the instructional task itself, and postinstructional activity. A typical sequence would be to introduce a program, give participants a task at which they must work with the program to perform certain operations, and then debrief on their activity. For example, in teaching about how to judge the worth of a software program, we might first present the concept of good documentation. We might list the characteristics, create a checklist of criteria to look for, and then use the checklist as we review one or two examples of strong and weak documentation. The assigned task would be to review the documentation from several programs using the criteria included on the checklist. Once teachers complete this task, either independently or in pairs, we would reconvene to debrief about issues like the dificult of assessing certain criteria or ways to reduce the time it takes to review documentation. This basic cycle, with variations introduced to maintain interest, is repeated at many points in the program.

Another strategy employed is the use of teams. Teachers both enjoy and profit from working together as they learn about technology. Two- or three-person teams are optimal; more members restrict active involvement by everyone. Several guidelines are important in establishing and monitoring team activity. First, it is important that each person interact directly with the computer or other technology. While some people prefer to stay in the background and let others experiment, it is important that all members of the group have the opportunity to operate the equipment. Second, it is usually helpful to have teams move away from the technology for purposes of planning. Too often when a group remains at the computer, one member wants to "play," thus distracting the others and reducing the participation of that individual in the groups's activity.

Third, we monitor the groups to catch any serious problems in group dynamics. To illustrate, if one member appears to dominate or to control the computer, it is important to encourage a change in this pattern. Other members of the group may impose internal sanctions, but if this does not occur, the instructors should intervene. Related to this problem is the need to carefully structure the task to allow about the right amount of time to complete it. If too much time is allowed, the group members will become restless and impatient; on the other hand, too little time invariably causes frustration.

The use of groups can be an effective strategy for teaching many skills related to the computer. A careful balance must be struck, however, between time spent having people working together and independently. Some computer skills, such as word processing, require a good deal of practice. Time must be allowed for each person to struggle with learning these skills individually. If each participant does not have access to his or her own computer during training, it may be important to split the group into two or three subgroups to allow some people to work individually on the available computers while others engage in alternative activities.

Another strategy employed is *supervised individual exploration time.* It allows teachers to experiment, make mistakes, and try again within a sheltered environment. If something "catastrophic" occurs, such as forgetting to save a file before erasing memory, the teacher can get help from the instructor to understand why this occurred. "Teachable moments" arise again and again as the teacher puzzles over the reasons why the technology mysteriously responded in one way or another. This exploration time also allows individuals to work at their own pace, perhaps returning to earlier assignments and seeking clarification on various operations.

Follow-up. This component refers to activities which occur once the formal program is completed. Inservice programs for teachers typically are structured in one of several ways. They may be intensive sessions of short duration, such as workshops. Alternatively, they may consist of a series of sessions held over a period of time. A university course or an in-house program may run for 6 to 15 weeks. If the program is offered over a longer period of time, the teacher can begin to experiment with the use of the computer and report her progress at a subsequent session. Because some of our programs have been of the workshop variety, we have found a need to conduct follow-up activities. Many options are possible; we will report on several that have worked well for us.

Assigning teachers to use the computer within a lesson has been useful. We encourage teachers to do a simple activity at first. For example, they may have their students make posters with "Printshop" or try out a science simulation. By building in a requirement to carry out such an activity, and report on their results, teachers have the incentive to take the first step in using the computer with their own students.

Another follow-up strategy is to send a survey to participants, querying whether and in what ways they have used the computer after the inservice program. Not only do we receive information about usage, but it also serves to remind those who haven't used the computer about possibilities for classroom and personal uses.

The Advanced Phase

Characteristics of participants. The most compelling difference between participants in the two levels of our program is the degree of familiarity with the technology. The effect of having experience manifests itself in several ways with advanced participants. Unlike beginners, these participants are comfortable with the technology. Operation of the equipment has become "automatic" and, as a result, they tend to have much less anxiety about its use.

Advanced participants' expectations for additional training center around needs to expand their current use of the computers as a tool for completing professional and personal tasks. Specifically, they hope to exploit technology to extend their own powers to reach students. These teachers already have experienced both success and failure in working with different technologies and are more willing to take some risks. The novelty of working with computers has lessened, and these participants are ready to deal with more sophisticated issues surrounding applications.

Another expectation shared by most advanced participants is that they will profit from the successes and failures of others in the group. Many expect to learn as much from one another as from the instructor. Because many of these participants regularly consult with other teachers as they experiment with computing in their own buildings, they realize how helpful such shared expertise can be.

One motivator for some participants in the advanced program is the press to train their fellow teachers about computing. Working with other teachers will require knowledge and skill which may be different in fact from that needed to work with their own students. Participants may hope to gain strategies for delivering good inservice instruction.

Some of the advanced participants have begun or hope in the future to create their own software and look to the advanced program as an opportunity to pick up helpful hints for this activity. Some have concluded that little of the existing software meets their needs; others who have programming skills or experience with authoring systems welcome the challenge of creating new material. Although such participants will always represent a minority, their needs can be partially addressed through some aspects of the program.

The content for the advanced program focuses on effective integration of computers into the classroom and the curriculum. Because teachers who attend such sessions frequently serve as resources and leaders to other teachers in their buildings and districts, we are mindful of helping them think about how to help others learn what they are learning in the training.

Classroom management is one area of emphasis within the program. Participants are encouraged to consider how the computer and related technologies can be used for individual, small and large group instruction. Wherever possible, these uses are demonstrated through video or live demonstration. Strategies for designing preinstructional, instructional, and postinstructional activities that involve technology are presented.

We also spend time on the *principles of instructional design.* Our experience has been that most teachers, even those with years of experience, have had little opportunity to study and apply some basic instructional design tasks within their own content areas. By better understanding some of these principles, teachers can create more systematic learning events for students and can better understand the rationale for some of the strategies used in existing technology-based materials.

We spend some time in our advanced training on *lab management* because so many of the teachers in this session acquire, formally or informally, some responsibility for managing the computer lab in their schools. Topics covered include scheduling, maintaining a software library, the physical arrangement of facilities, record keeping, and the acquisition of software and hardware.

A final topic within advanced training is the *development of inservice leadershiop skills.* Teachers in the advanced session often become trainers themselves, both on a one-to-one basis and with groups of colleagues. We give teachers an opportunity to practice some of the skills needed to be good consultants, workshop leaders, or trainers within our sessions. Specifically, this means that they are required to conduct demonstrations, after which they receive feedback on their performance. They are critiqued in role play situations. We ask them to practice certain skills outside of the training and report back on the results of their efforts. These opportunities bolster confidence and add to the investment a district makes in the training time needed for this program.

Teaching strategies. We continue to use many of the methods from the beginners' program but introduce several different ones as well. Since an important goal of the advanced program is to give participants opportunities to practice training other teachers, we use *peer teaching* whenever possible. Teachers may work individually or in small teams to plan, deliver, and evaluate one or more inservice training sessions. Usually, the schedule is arranged so that each practice session can be taught twice. In this way, evaluative feedback from the first session can be used to modify the second one. As instructors, we observe and critique these sessions and, if possible, involve other participants in this process. This activity gives participants an opportunity to follow an instructional design process in which the recipients of the instruction are adults rather than children.

Application of the instructional design principles presented in the program is achieved by the *assignment of a project.* The participating teacher must identify a problem area or topic, select one or more instructional goals, perform an instructional analysis and define performance objectives, create performance measures, decide upon instructional strategies, develop the prototype, pilot it with students, and report the results. Forms of technology must be incorporated into one or more aspects of the design. The project can focus on one mode of operation only, such as individual instruction, or can combine aspects of individual, small, and large group activities. Each phase of the project is shared with other participants to encourage generalization of the principles to a variety of instructional tasks.

A necessary ingredient of this project is a teacher's guide. In order to encourage the designer of the instruction to be explicit about his assumptions, he must document the process so another teacher could teach the lesson or unit and be reasonably confident about its outcomes.

The advanced program requires participants to do more *reading* than the novice program. Chapters and articles about instructional design, effective teacher behavior, and technology-based instruction are assigned.

Follow-up. Follow-up activities for advanced participants often take the form of providing *information about additonal resources.* For example, the teacher may wish to attend a more in-depth seminar on aspects of instructional design or may be receptive to additional readings on this topic or that of effective teaching. Some teachers may select the path of creating their own software. They will need help in the use of authoring systems or programming skills. Further assistance on inservice training activities can be provided in several ways. Advanced program participants can be asked to keep a *log of problems* arising as they conduct such training. Sessions can be held which bring together individuals involved in inservice training to discuss strategies.

CONCLUDING COMMENTS ON THE MODEL AND SOME GENERAL OBSERVATIONS

The model of technology training described here is an attempt to address some of the concerns raised in the earlier part of the chapter about the need for better programs that can help teachers within a broad continuum of experience and interests develop the abilities to integrate technology in the classroom. This program has been largely university-based, drawing personnel from business and industry, the state government, and the schools to deliver aspects of the content. Such collaborative efforts must be pursued if we hope to address the enormous demands of training a large workforce where resources are scarce. No one supplier of training will be adequate. As has been pointed out in this chapter, many groups have entered the technology training effort but the statistics on the number of teachers who receive that training, as well as the amount of training, are depressing.

We conclude our chapter with a few observations and suggestions that bear some consideration. First, there is a dire need for groups interested in supporting the use of technology in the schools to collaborate on the problem of high quality training for teachers. No single organization has the expertise or resources to achieve this goal on its own. University and college faculty must sit down with school district personnel in their locales and decide who can contribute what to the process. Similarly, businesses who are in the training business owe it to their clientele to be certain that the programs they deliver to teachers have integrity and are responsive to the real, not ideal, environments in which teachers operate. School districts must be systematic in planning for training. Who will receive what training? State departments of education should play a role in monitoring the quality of opportunities for teachers and should lead the charge for high standards that must be met by all who would operate in this arena.

A second concern is that districts must be willing to be in the technology training business over the long haul. As previously discussed research has confirmed that the one-shot approach to technology training is ineffective. Teachers must receive training, have the opportunity to take their knowledge back to the classroom, and then be supported as they attempt to make changes in how they teach. The need for follow-up support is essential if we hope to see most teachers make long-term investments in technology usage.

Another concern relates to how we help teachers continue to develop. The program we described here needs some additional phases. How do we support and challenge the competent technology-using teaching to move beyond his or her current level? We can envision these teacher technologists pushing their school districts to new levels. We envision such a teacher experimenting with new classroom configurations, working with businesses to try out some of their products in the schools, creating exciting instructional applications, and so on. Stopping the "brain drain" of excellent teachers out of the nation's classrooms requires that we create an environment that allows teachers to create, to try new ideas, to help their colleagues see new ways of doing things. When teachers with this expertise and interest find that the only way they can experiment is to move out of education and into other lines of work, we lose valuable revolutionaries who could make a difference in our schools.

Another observation is directed toward colleges and universities. Pressures to do a better job of preparing pre- and inservice teachers are felt by most colleges, schools, and departments of education but the resources to get faculty prepared to respond to these pressures are scarce. Currently there are few incentives for education faculty to improve their own knowledge base or skills related to technology. It is convenient to assume that someone down the hall should own that responsibility. Consequently, the vast majority of our college or university level courses are untouched by the dizzying array of technologies available for teachers. Administrators must begin to plan for ways to upgrade the content of courses so that technology is integrated into subject matter and methods courses. Models like the one at the University of Victoria could be employed more universally. Without incentives or opportunities many education faculty will simply assume that it is not their responsibility to worry about the technology training of new or veteran teachers.

Finally, we have observed that there has been little systematic study of the outcomes of teacher technology training efforts. *Power On!* (1988) provided an excellent starting point for additional investigations of the variables that characterize good programs. To build on this excellent effort will require that federal, state, and local resources be tapped so that five years from now, we will have a more sophisticated blueprint to guide our training efforts.

REFERENCES

Bitter, G., & Yohe, R. (1989). Preparing teachers for the information age. [Special Issue.] *Educational Technology, 29*(3), 22–25.

Blurton, C. (1986–87). California's new computer requirements for teachers. *SIG Bulletin of the International Council for Computers in Education, 3*(2,3), 55–58.

Bruder, I. (1988, October). Eighth Annual Survey of the States, 1988. *Electronic Learning, 8*(2), 38–45.

Bruder, I. (1989, March). Industry news: NSBA study says largest districts have weak long-range technology plans. *Electronic Learning, 9,* 10.

Carnegie Forum on Education and the Economy. (1986, May). *A nation prepared: Teachers for the 21st century.* The Report of the Task Force on Teaching as a Profession, New York.

Culp, G. (1986). Do computer-using teachers need programming? *SIG Bulletin of the International Council for Computers in Education, 3,* 25–26.

Glenn, A., & Ehman, L. (1987) *Computer-based education in social studies.* Bloomington, IN: Indiana University, Social Studies Development Center.

Goodlad, J.I. (1984). *A place called school: Prospects for the future.* New York: McGraw-Hill.

Holmes Group, Inc. (1986). *Tomorrow's teachers.* A Report of the Holmes Group, East Lansing, MI.

Lamon, W.E. (1987). Using computers in elementary schools: The 1987 Oregon assessment. *SIGTE Bulletin, 4,* 23–26.

Luehrmann, A. (1985). Why teach programming? Two good reasons. *Electronic Learning, 4,* 10.

Marker, G., & Ehman, L. (1989). Linking teachers to the world of technology. *Educational Technology, 29*(3), 26–30.

Moore, M. (1984, October). Preparing computer-using educators. *The Computing Teacher, 12*(2), 48–52.

Morehouse, D.L., Hoaglund, M., & Schmidt, R. (1987). *Computers in schools: Findings, issues and recommendations: An analysis based on an evaluation of Minnesota's Technology Demonstration Program.* Submitted to The Minnesota State Department of Education, St. Paul, MN.

Moursund, D. (1986). Effective inservice for use of computers as tools. *The Computing Teacher, 13*(5), 58.

Murphy, R.T., & Appel, L.R. (1984). *Evaluation of the writing to read instructional systems, 1982–1984.* Princeton, NJ: Educational Testing Service.

National Commission on Excellence in Education. (1983, April). *A nation at risk: The imperative for educational reform.* Washington, DC: Author.

Nietzke, T. (1985). Wouldn't you really rather have a computer-literate staff? *SIG Bulletin of the International Council for Computers in Education, 2*, 33–34.

Office of Technology Assessment. (1987, March). *Trends and status of computers in schools: Use in Chapter 1 programs and use with limited English proficient students.* Washington, DC: A Staff Paper of the Science Education and Transportation Program.

Pearlman, R. (1989). Technology's role in revitalizing schools. *Electronic Learning, 8*, 8–9, 12, 14–15, 56.

Power On! New tool for teaching and learning. (1988, September). Washington, DC: Congress of the United States Office of Technology Assessment.

Ross, J., & Rochford, T. (1986). New teachers are better prepared for computers. *Electronic Learning, 6*, 23–24.

Sturdivant, P. (1989). Technology Training... Some Lessons Can Be Learned: A School District's Experience. [Special Issue.] *Educational Technology, 29*(3), 31–35.

Tobias, S. (1987). Learner characteristics. In R. Gagné (Ed.), *Instructional technology: Foundations* (pp. 207–225). Hillsdale, NJ: Lawrence Erlbaum Associates, Inc.

U.S. Department of Education. (1986). *Teacher preparation in the use of computers.* Washington, DC: Bulletin Office of Educational Research and Improvement.

6
Issues in the Instructional Design of CBT in Arithmetic

Nira Hativa
Tel Aviv University

Computer-based training (CBT) refers usually to the context of the workplace. In this context, the computer is used for on-the-job training either of novices in the basic skills of the task on-hand or of experts-to-be in achieving professional proficiency and expertise. CBT can be also related to academic learning. Tutorial and drill-and-practice (D&P) programs may serve to improve the basic skills of novices and to increase the proficiency of experts.

Despite the important role that CBT may play in school, there is a dearth of research on planning the most effective strategy for using the CBT system. The design of CBT systems is usually based on educational theories, on intuitive knowledge of effective teaching and learning, and on pedagogical considerations of the specific subject matter involved. In order to fill this gap, I have studied during the last several years the cognitive, sociological, and affective aspects associated with using a CBT system for teaching arithmetic. That research involved four different CBT systems: two widely used in Israel (TOAM, distributed in the U.S. as DEGEM, and SEMEL) and the other two are operated in the US (CCC and WICAT). The central topic of this chapter is largely based on that research, but it also incorporates knowledge accumulated from studies of general issues of teaching and learning.

The discussion here concentrates on CBT in arithmetic at the elementary school level. However, I believe that the issues it presents bear implications for the design of CBT systems for other curriculum topics; for other age levels of students; and for other computer applications, such as microworlds or tools. The chapter discusses first the expectations from this computer application and the related problems that have been identified, and then it analyzes several instructional design issues that were found to affect students' benefits from CBT.

PROMISES AND PROBLEMS IN CBT OF ARITHMETIC

Expectations that computers will improve the learning of curriculum material have flourished since computers were first introduced to schools in the early 1960s. These expectations were based on the computer's unique capability, distinguishing it from all other technology for education, namely, its potential to interact with the individual learner. The potential for computer-student interaction has aroused high hopes for adapting instruction to each student in a more efficient way than is otherwise affordable. High hopes were attached particularly to the application of CBT for improving the learning of arithmetic at the elementary school level. Proficiency in arithmetic is thought of as crucial for learning at higher school levels and for functioning in adult life. Computer-based practice is thought of as a very promising tool for achieving automaticity which is the basis for proficiency in arithmetic. Probably for these reasons, a substantial proportion of all learning software developed for the elementary school level involves drill-and-practice in arithmetic (Becker, 1984).

Have these promises materialized? Indeed, there is research support for the fulfillment of some of these expectations. Summaries of dozens of studies that used quantitative methods to compare CBT with regular classroom teaching (e.g., Hartley, 1977; Burns & Bozeman, 1981; Kulik, Kulik, & Bangert-Drowns, 1985; Niemiec & Walberg, 1985) concluded that students' achievement in learning of arithmetic (as well as of other topics) was larger for those using computer-based practice systems than in control group treatments.

On the other hand, recent studies reveal that in reality, the computer innovation is being ignored at schools without anyone knowing this. The computers are being used only minimally and without apparent focus on educational rationales. Most teachers who do use computers for instruction teach the same things in basically the same ways that they have been teaching, and then on the side they're sticking computers in. Thus, the expectations that the use of second-generation microcomputers in schools will revolutionize the teaching and learning have not been realized (Hativa, Shapira, & Navon, 1989). In addition, several studies that involved qualitative methods of inquiry identified a variety of problems in elementary students' CBT (Hativa, 1988a, 1988b; Hativa & Lesgold, 1990). The major problems were students' difficulties in adjusting to the special learning environment induced by the computer work; the machine's inability to identify what knowledge underlies students' answers (e.g., some answers are judged by the software to be either correct or incorrect on the basis of wrong reasons); affective (e.g., motivational) and sociological factors that inhibit students' learning; and human engineering factors that interfere with students' performance. All these problems caused the computer to incorrectly evaluate students' abilities and consequently the computer has provided these students with learning material that was inappropriate to their real needs.

In order to design better CBT systems that provide solutions to these problems, we need to learn about the factors that cause these problems. We may gain the needed knowledge by studying how current applications of CBT systems in the schools work actually, what are the advantages of using these systems, and what the problems are. Particularly, we should analyze the effects on students' learning of a variety of features related to the hardware, software, and method of operation of these CBT systems. Such features were found in my research to cause the problems with using CBT systems to provide students with practice in arithmetic (Hativa, 1986, 1988a, 1988b). Also, these features had a differential effect on students with low and high aptitudes. Another study (Levin, Leithner, & Meister, 1986) found that even the same CBT system, when operated differently at different sites, produced large differences in student' gains. It is thus important to identify the relationships between a variety of CBT systems' characteristics and students' learning.

This chapter examines several central issues in the instructional design of computer-based practice systems in arithmetic. The CBT systems discussed in this chapter are fully packaged; present material for a full course or even for a multiple class-level curriculum; allow many computers to be in use at one time (in a computer lab) so that all students in a class use them concurrently and individually; and manage students' learning with minimal teacher intervention. Managing the students' learning means that the software makes decisions about the course of instruction based upon an initial diagnosis of the students' abilities or upon the students' past and ongoing performance. The instructional design issues discussed below are related to the characteristics of either the software, or to the method of operation of CBT systems.

ISSUES OF CBT SOFTWARE CHARACTERISTICS

In planning the characteristics of the software of a CBT system, one should consider many alternative decisions. Some of these are whether to present the material as tutorial or as drill and practice; whether to evaluate the students' answer when the student completes typing the full answer and presses a RETURN/ENTER key or to evaluate each digit as typed; whether to limit the time for the student's answer or to provide untimed solutions; whether to present the practice in mixed types of exercises or to present in only one type of exercise at a given unit of time (fixed practice); whether to have the computer make all the evaluations and consequent decisions about what material to present to the student and when to advance him/her in the hierarchical levels of the material presented, or whether to assign some of the decision making and program control to the students.

In this section we discuss three of the issues of software characteristics that may affect students' learning.

Apply a Time Limitation for Entering Answers?

A unique feature of the computer is its capability to count time. This feature allows limiting the time for entering an answer in CAI work. Indeed, many of the computer software programs used in schools today, particularly those designed to provide practice in material already taught in class, limit the time for students' answers. Of the four CBT systems observed, as listed above, two use timing of students' answers to all exercises; one does not limit that time at all; and the fourth uses a combination of both methods so that the first exercises in a sequence are not timed but after the student proves mastery of several types of exercises in this sequence, he/she receives a group of time exercises and is given the option to choose one of three speeds (lengths of the time limit) for typing in the answer.

The rationale for the timing of solutions, as reported in personal communications with designers of two CBT systems, is to avoid students' daydreaming and procrastination; to improve students' concentration; and consequently, to increase students' time-on-task. Increased time-on-task is related to better achievement (Bloom, 1974). Complete lack of pressure to learn caused by the time limitation has been shown to lead to boredom and lack of motivation in task performance (Tarktinsky, 1988). Additional arguments for limiting the time for students' answers are that strict time limitation for an answer reduces the opportunities for students to compare their performance with each other which may affect negatively the learning of low-achieving students (Hativa, Swisa, & Lesgold, 1989). Also, many arithmetic tasks require that the student arrives at a certain degree of automaticity. This means, performance of the task "on the spot." For example, when we present a student with a simple multiplication fact, for example, "$5 \times 4 = ?$" we expect the student to answer promptly, showing that he or she remembers the answer by heart, rather than to compute it by a repeated addition (e.g., $4 + 4 + 4 + 4 + 4$). A short time limit will fail those students who have not memorized their multiplication tables.

On the other hand, timing students' answers may bear some negative effects. There are students who experience negative feelings of pressure and anxiety because of the time limit, or who, when feeling that they do not have enough time to think, merely guess the answer, often incorrectly. Such cases largely annoy students and decrease their self confidence (Hativa, 1986, 1988b). Additional evidence for the negative effects of the time limit, on a larger scale, comes out of an analysis of a questionnaire administered to approximately 250 students using a CBT system in arithmetic that times the answers (Hativa, 1989). Of the 13 optional reasons for disliking to work with the CBT system that are presented in the questionnaire, the item chosen by the largest percentage of students as a reason for disliking the work with the CAI system is related to the time limitation ("The computer doesn't give me enough time to think"). Tarktinsky (1988) also found that extra time pressure decreased students' efficiency in task performance and increased the number of erroneous solutions.

There are some positive effects associated with not timing the students' responses. For one thing, cooperation among peers is developed. Secondly, teachers are able to help students in their lab work more comfortably than in CBT systems that do limit the time of students' answers (Hativa, Swisa, & Lesgold, 1989).

Observations of students involved in computer-based practice in arithmetic (Hativa, 1986) identified aptitude-related differential effects of the timing of exercises. While the better students rarely failed to type in an answer that they knew within the time limit, lower-achieving students missed the time limit for entering an answer that they knew because of boredom, fatigue, difficulties in concentration, slow response time, playing games, or looking at other students' computer display. Hativa, Sarig, and Lesgold (1989) found that 5 percent of students who frequently made time-related errors were high-ability students; 38 percent were average-ability students; and 57 percent were low-ability students. These results reveal that in contrast with our intuition that errors due to time limits are done primarily by low achievers, many medium achievers do these types of errors. However, only few high achievers make time-related errors.

The findings that students with different aptitudes are affected differently by timing the solutions may be explained in terms of differential motivation and persistence. My previous studies (e.g., Hativa, 1986, 1988b) revealed that high achievers were intrinsically motivated to persist in their CBT work and showed a high measure of time-on-task with almost no need for external reinforcement such as time limitation of answers. When these students took a long time to solve a problem, this was because the problem was difficult for them and they did need the extra time to think. In contrast, lower-ability students needed the time limit as an extrinsic motivation in order to use their time-on-task effectively.

On the basis of the discussion above, we may conclude that time limitation bears some advantages and some disadvantages for students' learning. Thus, it is feasible to incorporate into any CGT system the feature of time limitation at least partially. However, the length of this time should be enough for a student to complete the task at hand without too much pressure. The question is—what is the optimal length of time limitation?

The optimal length of time permitted for a solution has rarely been investigated. Research suggests that it is related to the particular task at hand and to the aptitudes of each particular student. The two CBT systems that do limit the time for solutions that I have observed assign different time limits for different types of exercises on the basis of a rough estimation of their difficulty. However, the length of this time limit is fixed for all students. Hativa, Sarig, and Lesgold (1989) show that the time needed for the solution of the same exercise by a certain child may vary on different trials, more so for different tasks or for different children. The more complex the task, the longer the time needed for its solution. Students with low aptitude for arithmetic need more time for solution of a particular exercise than high-aptitude students. Tarktinsky (1988) also found that the more difficult the task at hand, the lower the correlation between speed of solution and accuracy. Because difficult problems require longer time for solution, limiting the time for solution prevents the correct solution of those who need more time to think.

Hativa, Sarig, and Lesgold (1989) showed that tripling the time limit in CBT work had a dramatic initial effect upon the performance of all students. However, after two months, a differential effect vis-á-vis aptitude differences was found. Four months after the time increase, high achievers either increased their benefits or at least kept the initial improvement at the same level as the initial increase in the first two months, whereas low achievers showed a decrease in the benefits. Still, low achievers improved their performance as the result of the increase in the time limit more than the high achievers.

To conclude, I suggest that time limitation should be included as a default feature in the design of a CBT system. However, the length of waiting time for a student's answer should be adjustable to the level of difficulty of the exercise involved and be adaptable to the aptitudes of the individual student. Students of low ability or those identified by the computer as making a large proportion of errors due to the time limit should be assigned a longer time for entering an answer than other students. The question is who will be responsible for the adaptation of the length of the time limit to the individual student—the teacher? the lab operator? or the software? Although the human supervisor can identify behavioral features that affect students' timing-related errors that the computer is not able to detect (e.g., daydreaming, procrastination), our observations in schools showed that teachers only seldom used the option provided by the CBT system to increase the time limit for particular students. Thus, I suggest that the software should include an algorithm which would determine the length of the time limit for each individual based on the number of errors that the student makes due to this time limit. These adaptations require the development of either a teacher-based or a computer-based method for accurately identifying the time limitation that is appropriate for each student.

Tutorials or Drill and Practice?

Traditionally, computerized systems designed to teach curriculum materials were categorized as either tutorials or drill-and-practice programs. Tutorials were those programs designed to replace the regular classroom teaching by providing full instruction of the learning material. Tutorials are usually structured so that the learning material is divided into small units. The material in each unit is presented in small hierarchical steps. The presentation of each step incorporates theoretical explanations as well as practice of the new material. On completion of a unit of study, the student is examined for mastery of that unit.

Computerized drill-and-practice programs were designed to complement classroom instruction, rather than to replace it. The basic idea was that the drill was designed to reinforce skills already learned in class. Under this assumption, students were to receive in the computer lab practice of material either concurrently taught in class or materials that were taught in the past.

However, observations of students using computer-based practice systems in arithmetic (Hativa, 1986, 1988b) revealed an unexpected phenomenon—many students received practice of material before being taught in class. This phenomenon was caused by the individualized pace in the CBT curriculum that enabled students, particularly the fast learners, to advance rapidly in the hierarchical levels of the strands/chains of types of exercises, well beyond the grade-level material. In addition, although the majority of students received practice in material that had already been previously taught, our observations revealed that a sizable number of students forgot how to solve these exercises.

When students encounter CBT exercises that they do not know how to solve, they then use a variety of strategies to discover the correct solutions. The most frequent strategy is to examine carefully the final answers or the full solutions provided by the computer to those exercises that are answered incorrectly. The students try to identify the correct algorithm for solution from these given solutions or from the final answers. This process allows the students to either discover the algorithm for solution or gain full understanding of the concepts involved (Hativa, 1988b). In CBT systems that provide students with the option of receiving on-screen help at the students' request, these "help" facilities are used by the students to learn and understand the new concepts involved. The "help screens" may be of a variety of types. They may provide verbal explanations of a problem or an exercise which is difficult for the student to solve; may serve as a worked-out (guided) examples of problems found in the exercise; may identify the type of error that the student has made and explain the source for error and the correct procedure; and so forth.

The "help screen" or the full solutions provided by the computer serve in these cases as "guided examples" for the students' reference. Zhu and Simon (1987) and Sweller and Cooper (1985) have shown that students learn new concepts in mathematics with a high degree of understanding by referring to worked examples with no additional instruction. This seems to be the case also in CBT. Thus, although computer-based drill-and-practice programs are designed to provide practice of material already studied in class, students do exhibit learning new concepts from the use of guided examples.

On the other hand, computer-based tutorials that are designed to teach new concepts are not confined only to verbal explanations of the concepts or to presentations of worked examples but do include substantial practice of these concepts. This is particularly true for tutorial programs developed in the last several years because there has been in recent years a growing apprehension that students learn arithmetic "by doing," that is, through solving many exercises and problems (e.g., VanLehn, 1986; Zhu & Simon, 1987).

Thus, the categorization of computer-based learning systems into tutorial and drill-and-practice programs is not feasible. This division is artificial as both types of programs teach new material and reinforce it through drill and practice. Thus in both, the practice is an essential part. The principal difference between these two types of programs is in the way in which learning takes place. In tutorials, first the theoretical material is presented and then the practice. In practice programs, the students receive almost all the material in a practice form and only when they face difficulties, they receive theoretical explanations.

Zhu and Simon (1987) have argued that these exercises must be arranged in a carefully planned sequence with increasing order of complexity and difficulty. As they have argued, this arrangement must occur so that students do not make too many errors of induction or require too much trial-and-error search. CBT systems should present exercises in hierarchical fashion so that each one provides practice of a small step forward of the previous type of exercise.

To summarize, I argue here that there is no difference in principle between computerized tutorial and practice CBT programs. Both types include substantial practice. Students demonstrate that they learn new material from practice alone, even with no theoretical explanation. To help students gain knowledge from practice material in an organized way, the exercises and problems of the CBT curriculum should be arranged in a carefully planned sequence with small steps of increasing order of complexity and difficulty. For this aim, I suggest that guided examples are presented at the beginning of each new sequence of exercises and in "help screens." This apparently would allow students to go over these examples and learn the procedures for solving the exercises provided by the computer.

Mixed-type or Fixed-type Practice?

The intended purpose of computer-based practice is to supplement the learning of concepts in the classroom. Pedagogical considerations assume that the teaching of a new concept should be supported by a fixed practice of this concept. "*Fixed practice* is especially good for reinforcement after a specific skill is taught in class. It is helpful to students with specific weak areas. Its specific weakness is that it requires less concentration and tends to be boring for continuous use" (Ragosta, Holland, & Jamison, 1982, p. 41). Other considerations favor mixed practice in CBT. For example, "*Mixed practice* is suitable for most students most of the time to keep interest and attention high. Research has shown it to be effective" (Ragosta et al., 1982, p. 41). The instructions to the CCC system users claim that mixed drill produces longer retention of learning than fixed drill.

Only one of the four CBT systems listed above provides practice which is solely mixed. The other three provide practice at varying levels of mixture as the default, as well as the option for practice which is concentrated on one topic.

As previously explained, when students face in CBT an exercise that they do not know how to solve, they may learn the algorithm for solution from the final answer provided by the software, or through a "help screen." On receiving a second exercise of exactly the same type, the students then apply the rule or algorithm that they have learned from solving the first exercise. In systems that provide mixed practice, students need to remember the method for solution across several exercises of a different type. However, students were observed to forget an algorithm for solution just learned when the second exercise of the same type appeared only after several exercises of a completely different type (Hativa, 1986). Students need high motivation and good memory for mathematical structures in order to remember a new method for solution across several different exercises. Usually, those students with the needed motivation and memory capacity are the high achievers. Thus, in the cases that the practice is in material new to the student, mixed practice seems to favor the high achievers over the other students. Schneider and Detweile (1987, pp. 109–110) have found, on the basis of analysis of context storage for learning to perform a task, that

> Initially it is beneficial to mass practice on a task. . . because the context storage maintains the working memory. In procedural tasks, subjects learn to perform individual procedures quickly during massed practice of single tasks, but then show poor performance when the trial types are intermixed. . . more errors are expected during distributed training than massed training. To be able to perform a variety of procedures in random order, training must progress to distributed practice. The marginal utility of massed practice decreases with time. . . If the subject must randomly execute the procedures at different times, context-based learning may show poor transfer. In sum, the advantages of massing practice early to maintain information in working memory trades off against disadvantages of context learning, showing poor transfer and reducing long-term learning. Procedures which expand the distribution of practice with training are likely to be optimal.

On this basis, I suggest that the presentation of each arithmetic topic start with a fixed practice of particular types of guided examples and "help screens." Only after the student demonstrates mastery of these exercises, should he/she receive another type of exercise. After mastering several types of exercises separately, these particular types of problems will then be presented to the students in a mixed practice mode.

ISSUES IN THE METHOD OF OPERATION OF CBT SYSTEMS

As already described, during the early era of applications of computers for the learning of school material, high expectations were aroused for the improvement of teaching and learning. However, today the educational community expresses disappointment from the results of CBT. Research (e.g., Hativa, 1986) and reality have shown again and again that it is not enough to give a student access to a computer with the appropriate software. Even the best educational software cannot produce substantial beneficial gains to students' learning unless it is operated in a way which provides optimal learning conditions. When planning to operate a CBT system in school, there are many important implementation issues. Several of the major ones are: Should the system be operated for the whole class at the same time or only for a certain group of students? Should a computerized class report be provided? How often should these reports be provided? What information should the report include? Should we enforce strict individualized work on the computer or encourage cooperative work? How many CBT sessions per week should a student attend and how long should each be? How should the system be operated so that it is beneficial to high achievers as well as to low achievers? In what ways should teachers incorporate students' CBT practice into the regular classroom routines? How should teachers respond to the continuous evaluations of students' performance by the computer? The following discussion refers to a few of these issues.

Whom to Operate the System for?

The basic question is whether to operate the CBT system for all students in the class or only for a particular group of students—either high or low achievers. Of course, the computer hardware available in a school is a major factor in a decision of this type. As discussed in the next few pages, I believe that the system should be operated for the whole class concurrently with the system managing the learning situation. However, this type of operation requires either a minicomputer with a sufficient number of terminals to accommodate the maximum number of students in a class, or an equivalent number of microcomputers working through a local network.

Although microcomputers can be operated as stand-alone computers, I argue that this form of operation is inappropriate for a whole class, and that any form of using computers concurrently by only a part of the students in a class is inappropriate. This argument is based upon the following:

1. The use of microcomputers for special groups of students (e.g., for remedial work or for gifted students) when there are not enough terminals for the whole class, requires special logistics. Because these special students leave the classroom at the time that the other students are involved with some particular learning activities, these students miss the regular class activities. The teacher thus needs to make sure that these students receive the classroom material which were presented during their absence, a situation which causes an additional burden on the teacher. Another burden on the school personnel is the need to supervise these students when they are going to and from the computer lab. This supervision cannot be done by the class teacher and is done therefore by another person (usually the lab operator). As a result, the teacher rarely receives complete information about the computer performance of these students. Because the teacher is not fully aware of their performance, it is not very likely that he or she incorporates their computer practice with the regular class learning. This, in turn, reduces the benefits of CBT for these students. For the most beneficial results, the teacher must know and use the students' CBT performance, handle students' difficulties, and assign them appropriate remedial paper-and-pencil work.

2. The logistics of handling concurrently the operation of many micro-computers that are not networked is very complicated. The teacher needs to provide a diskette for each machine, supervise its appropriate loading through the disk drive and its proper operation throughout the computer session. All these activities may cause problems and may result in a substantial burden on the teacher.

    The cited complicated logistics and additional burdens on teachers will have a detrimental effect on the CBT system's effectiveness. In recent years, many studies of CBT applications (e.g., Martin, 1988) have identified teachers' subtle resistance to use computers, at all levels of schools. This resistance is explained in the extra burden that the use of computers puts on teachers' daily work. Cuban (1984) concluded from a study of implementations of school innovations that a necessary condition for extensive teacher adoption of school innovations is the facilitating and improving of what teachers already do without introducing major changes into teachers' work.

3. The importance for availability of computers in a number which is enough for the whole class stems not only from the need to reduce the burden of computer operation on the teacher. Having enough computers for all students also enables the individualization of instruction. Individualized instruction is probably the most promising instructional method for adjusting instruction to students of all ability levels. This instructional method can bring benefits to students' learning that are far beyond what can be gained through regular classroom teaching. Of particular importance in the feasibility of individualized instruction for all the students in a class is the operation of all the computers through a central computer (either a mainframe computer with terminals or locally networked microcomputers). This arrangement enables the management of the CBT program for all students. Because the computer manages the students' work, each student advances through the program units in accordance with his or her level of aptitude and knowledge. The teacher can receive continuous information about the standings and problems of each students. The teacher can also compare each student's standing to a mean level of performance for that class. This information enables the teacher to take care the problems of each individual's problems and to assign students to learning groups on the basis of homogeneous performance.

To conclude, every effort should be made to acquire enough computers that enable all students in a class to attend the lab concurrently and that the computers should be operated through a central computer unit. I recommend this in order to individualize instruction for all students and to reduce the teachers' burden of incorporation of computers into instruction, a burden which may result in the teachers' rejection of the appropriate applications of computers for students' learning. Making the computer work comfortably and beneficially for the teachers will encourage them to use computers appropriately for their students' learning.

WHAT SHOULD THE ROLE OF THE COMPUTER CLASS REPORT BE?

All four CBT systems that I have observed include the facility of providing teachers with a printed report of the class' CBT performance. However, in two of these systems, the report is very difficult to use: It presents the information in a form which is hard to read and not very beneficial for the teacher. Probably for this reason, teachers in these systems rarely ask for and receive the printouts. They use these reports only once in a quarter or a semester as an additional source for information for reporting to parents. The class reports for the third system include more beneficial information for the teacher. However, these reports are hard to read and to store for purposes of comparing students' standings on several consecutive reports. In addition, that system is not used by all students in a class but only by the lower-achieving students for remedial work so that the computer report refers only to these students. The teachers are thus less likely to use the reports to assign individualized work, which is a very important ingredient in the beneficial use of the reports. The fourth system, operated for all the students in a class, provides the most beneficial report and indeed, it proves to make a substantial effect on students' learning. Next is the description of the primary aspects of this report.

Content of a Beneficial Computer Report

Information on the individual student's standings and the identification of particular problems and difficulties in the material practiced. In the particular CBT system that provides the most beneficial class report, the arithmetic curriculum is divided into several different strands, for example, number concepts, decimals, and the like. In each strand, the exercises are arranged in a hierarchy and the student's advancement in the hierarchical steps (named here Levels) in a particular strand is independent of his/her performance in the other strands. The Levels within each strand are numbered consecutively. The computerized class report identifies for each student the Level he/she is currently practicing within a strand, and the mean Level for all strands. If a student makes errors in solving exercises of a particular Level within a certain strand, this information is included in the computer report. The teachers are thus aware of the particular problems that each student faces in completing the CBT program.

Information on other aspects of the individual student's performance. The computerized class report provides a variety of types of information about the individual student's performance during the last CBT session. In addition to the Level of each student's performance in each strand and the mean Level across strands, as mentioned above, the report includes the cumulative number of that session, the number of exercises presented to the student in that session, the number of exercises that the student has solved correctly, and the proportion of incorrect solutions caused because of the time limit. This information helps the teacher to identify students who miss computer sessions; who work too slowly; who make a large proportion of errors in their CBT work; or who face difficulties because the time limit.

Information of the class performance. The computerized reports include information about the mean Level (and standard deviation) of students per strand and across strands. It includes also a histogram showing the frequency of students at each Level (across strands). This report also generates class lists that rank orders students vis-á-vis their mean strand Level.

Effects of Availability of the Class Report on Teachers

Teachers' use of the class report. The report is provided to teachers once a week, and is printed on regular paper. Hativa, Shapira, and Navon (1990) show that teachers use the information included in the computerized class reports in three major ways, for: (a) Students' evaluations: Almost all the teachers who use the CBT system involved use the computer reports as a major source for grading; and (b–c) Individualizing students' work and assigning students into homogeneous learning groups: The computer reports are used for instructional purposes by an extraordinarily high proportion of teachers. Approximately three-quarters of the teachers use the computer reports either to assign individualized work in the classroom or to organize the students into learning groups during the arithmetic class lessions. The individualized work on the basis of the computer reports is done using flashcards, each containing several exercises of the type identified as problematic for the student in the CBT work. The assignment into homogeneous work groups is also done on the basis of the computer reports which enable the teacher to identify those students who are at the same or similar Levels of CBT practice in a particular strand.

Teachers' attitudes towards the class report. Almost all teachers do believe that the computer reports are beneficial both to their work and to their students' learning.

Effects of the CBT work and the class reports on teachers. The individualized CBT work along with the weekly computer report make a substantial impact on teaching methods. A very large proportion of teachers modify their frontal teaching methods in order to adjust to the individualized practice of the CBT work. A questionnaire was given to a representative sample of teachers using the CBT system to investigate their attitudes towards the CBT work of their students (Hativa, Shapira, & Navon, 1990). Of 10 reasons for advantages of work with the CBT system listed in that questionnaire, the two items that were rated the highest by almost all teachers were: "The individualized work and feedback" and "The diagnosis of performance and problems." Teachers thus seemed to appreciate the information provided by the computer reports.

To summarize, the computer class report is a crucial tool for the individualizing of instruction through the CBT work. For this aim, it should contain information about the level of performance of each student and on the particular problems he/she encounters. The report should be printed in a form that makes it easy for teachers to identify the important information and should provide several options for printout (e.g., in alphabetical order, in decreasing or increasing in levels of performance across all strands and for each single strand separately). This type of a report appears to serve as a major tool by teachers for adapting the treatment to the individual student and influences teachers to switch from group instruction to individualized methods of instruction.

HOW TO ENCOURAGE COMPETITION
OR COOPERATION IN CBT?

When planning CBT systems for school curriculum topics, the primary attention is given to cognitive learning. Although social factors such as social comparison and individual competition may substantially affect students' cognitive learning, issues related to these factors are seldom incorporated into the planning of CAI. Competition has positive as well as negative effects on students' learning. On the positive side, competition is a powerful motive for stimulating effort and ambition and it is a source of self-confidence and self-esteem. Because comparative excellence is rewarded in society, students should begin experiencing it at school (Owens, 1985). On the other hand, competition can result in the public humiliation of some students for the benefit of others, which is unethical. It can be a source of insecurity, self-doubt, and personal unhappiness for the large proportion of those who do not win. The positive effects of competition on increasing motivation are those few students who believe they have a chance of winning. For other students, competition induces a continued state of high-level anxiety, which, in turn, significantly interferes with learning and may result in psychological damage (Johnson, Johnson, & Stanne, 1985). Those who experience the negative effects of competition are primarily the low achievers (Michaels, 1977). Prolonged failure experiences of low achievers may result in a sense of worthlessness, inferiority, helplessness, and incompetence; low self-concept; low aspirations; lack of motivation; and more (Lewis & Cooney, 1987; Johnson et al., 1985).

Schools in the Western competitive society often transmit to students the culture of competitive striving as the key for future material success (Owens, 1985). Schools encourage competition through students' evaluations, similarity among tasks in which students are engaged, and similarity of the reference group to the one making the social comparison. Dissatisfaction with competition in school has led to the advocacy of individualistic or cooperative goal structures (Johnson & Johnson, 1975). Individualistic structures produce self-competition rather than competition with others. They eliminate or deemphasize social comparison, encourage a focus on task mastery, and increase motivation. Computer-based individualized instruction was expected to undercut one of the most obvious mechanisms for making social comparisons, that is, attending to the performance of other students. However, Hativa (1986) observed intense competitions among students working individually with a particular CBT system whereas another CBT system was identified as discouraging competition and encouraging cooperative work.

Hativa, Swisa, and Lesgold (1989) examined the software and the method of operating these two CBT systems in order to identify factors that either encourage or discourage competition among students. The factors that were identified to encourage competition consisted primarily of the individualized information printed on the screen. Particularly encouraging competition was the information related to the student's evaluation such as the normative level of the practice that the student receives; the percent of correct responses during the session; and word statements of commendations either after each single exercise or as a summary of the performance throughout the full session. Students compared information that had nothing to do with their cognitive performance, such as the cumulative number of the CBT sessions or the number of exercises presented during the session. Another major factor was the information provided in the weekly computer report. The information that was previously described enabled the comparison of the performance of each student to that of the rest of the students in the class and to the class' mean performance.

These factors were identified to encourage cooperation consisted of those that either reduced or completely eliminated the pressure on students to achieve. These were:

1. The absence of any time limitation. Lack of timing avoids the penalty (if exercises were evaluated as "wrong" because of missing the time limit) to students who have been called upon to help others. Thus, the absence of a time limitation encourages peer cooperation and help.
2. The absence of any numerical evaluation from the screen reduces students' drive to achieve better than other pupils.
3. Computer games incorporated sporadically into the software contribute to decreasing the tension and to the feeling that one does not need to rush to achieve a certain goal.
4. The option to make computations on paper enables the better students to help those who need it by showing on paper how to solve particular exercises.

In a naturalistic study of children's computer behavior, Hativa, Swisa, and Lesgold (1989) have shown that students' competitive or cooperative behaviors in the systems were different from the instructional intentions of the respective systems' designers. The "competitive" system was originally designed to enforce individualized work and the designers of the other system did not entertain any considerations of cooperation versus competition in their planning. However, Hativa et al. found that the first system encourages students to compete in the CAI work, whereas the other system minimizes social comparisons and competition among students, induces a relaxed working environment, and fosters student cooperation.

To summarize, both cooperation and competition can provide powerful motivations for learning and can be employed in ways that have either detrimental or positive effects on student learning. Thus, when designing CBT systems, special attention should be given to factors that either encourage or discourage competition.

CONCLUSION

In this chapter I discuss several central issues in the instructional design of CBT systems for practice in arithmetic. These issues are related to the software, hardware, and method of using the CBT system. The discussion is based on recent research and may contribute to the design of better CBT systems. However, not all aspects of systems' design are covered here. There are still many important and controversial issues which have not been fully investigated. As stated at the beginning of this chapter, I believe that the findings of research presented here apply to CBT systems for curriculum topics other than arithmetic, for age levels of students other than elementary school, and for other computer applications for learning other than drill and practice.

REFERENCES

Becker, H.J. (1984). Computers in schools today: Some basic considerations. *American Journal of Education, 93*(1), 22–39.

Bloom, B. (1974). Time and learning. *American Psychologist, 29*(9), 682–688.

Burns, P.K., & Bozeman, W.C. (1981). Computer-assisted instruction and mathematics achievement. Is there a relationship? *Educational Technology, 21*(10), 32–39.

Cuban, L. (1984). *How teachers taught: Constancy and change in American classrooms 1890–1980.* New York and London: Longman.

Hartley, S.S. (1977). Meta-analysis of the effects of individually paced instruction in mathematics. *Dissertation Abstract International, 38,* 4003A. (University Microfilms No. 77-29, 926).

Hativa, N. (1986). *Computer-based practice in arithmetic (TOAM): Dreams and realities—an ethnographic study.* The Pinhas Sapir Center for Development, Tel Aviv, Israel: Tel Aviv University, Discussion paper number 7–86.

Hativa, N. (1988a). Sigal's ineffective computer-based practice of arithmetic: A case study. *The Journal for Research in Mathematics Education, 19*(3), 195–214.

Hativa, N. (1988b). Computer-based drill and practice in arithmetic—widening the gap between high and low achieving students. *The American Educational Research Journal, 25*(3), 366–397.

Hativa, N. (1989). Students' conceptions of and attitudes towards specific features of a CAI system. *Journal of Computer-Based Instruction, 16*(3), 81–89.

Hativa, N., Sarig, O., & Lesgold, A. (1988). *Timing students' answers in CAI.* Paper presented at the annual meeting of the American Educational Research Association, New Orleans, LA.

Hativa, N., Shapira, R., & Navon, D. (1990). Computer-managed practice—effects on instructional methods and on teacher adoption. *Teaching and Teachers Education, 6*(1), 55–68.

Hativa, N., Swisa, S., & Lesgold, A. (1989). *Competition in individualized CAI.* Paper presented at the annual meeting of the American Educational Research Association, San Francisco, CA.

Hativa, N., & Lesgold, A. (1990). *The computer as a tutor—Can it adapt to the individual learner?* Paper presented at the annual meeting of the American Educational Research Association, Boston, MA.

Johnson, D.W., & Johnson, R.T. (1975). *Learning together and alone.* Englewood Cliffs, NJ: Prentice-Hall.

Johnson, R.T., Johnson, D.W., & Stanne, M.B. (1985). Effects of cooperative, competitive and individualistic goal structures on achievement: Meta-analysis. *Psychological Bulletin, 89*(1), 47–62.

Kulik, J.A., Kulik, C-L.C., & Bangert-Drowns, R.L. (1985). *Effectiveness of computer-based education in elementary schools.* Paper presented at the annual meeting of the American Educational Research Association, Chicago, IL.

Levin, H.M., Leithner, D., & Meister, G.R. (1986). *Cost-effectiveness of alternative approaches to computer-assisted instruction.* Stanford, CA: IFG, School of Education, Stanford University.

Lewis, M.A., & Cooney, J.B. (1987). Attributional and performance effects of competitive and individualistic feedback in computer-assisted mathematics instruction. *Computers in Human Behavior, 3*(1), 1–14.

Martin, C.D. (1988). *Ethnographic methods for studying microcomputer implementation in schools.* Paper presented at the annual meeting of the American Educational Research Association, New Orleans, LA.

Michaels, J.W. (1977). Classroom reward structures and academic performance. *Review of Educational research, 47*(1), 87–98.

Niemiec, R.P., & Walberg, H.J. (1985). Computers and achievement in the elementary schools. *Educational Computing Research, 1*(4), 435–440.

Owens, L. (1985). *Competition in the classroom.* International Encyclopedia of Education. New York: Pergamon Press.

Ragosta, M., Holland, P.W., & Jamison, D.T. (1982). *Computer-assisted instruction and compensatory education: The ETS/LAUSD study.* Princeton, NJ: Educational Testing Service.

Schneider, W., & Detweiler, M. (1987). A connectionist/control architecture for working memory. *The Psychology of Learning and Motivation, 21.* San Diego, DA: Academic Press.

Sweller, J., & Cooper, G.A. (1985). The use of worked examples as a substitute for problem solving in learning algebra. *Cognition and Instruction, 2*(1), 59–89.

Tarktinsky, N. (1988). *Effects of time pressure on speed and accuracy in computerized general-knowledge test* (Report No. 68). Israel: National Institute for Testing and Evaluation.

VanLehn, K. (1986). Arithmetic procedures are induced from examples. In J. Hiebert (Ed.), *Conceptual and procedural knowledge: The case of mathematics* (pp. 133–177). Hillsdale, NJ: Erlbaum.

Zhu, X., & Simon, H.A. (1987). Learning mathematics from examples and by doing. *Cognition and Instruction, 4*(3), 137–166.

7
Self-Paced Instruction: Perceptions, Pitfalls, and Potentials

George B. Semb
University of Kansas
Navy Personnel Research and Development Center

John A. Ellis
William E. Montague
Wallace H. Wulfeck
Navy Personnel Research and Development Center

VIGNETTE—THE STORY OF IMA EXPERT

Ima Expert is an ordinary girl who attends an extraordinary junior high school in Independence, Indiana. She transferred to the school last November. Her greatest fear was that she would be far behind her classmates.

When she arrived at school, however, her fears abated quickly. Her teacher, Dolly Partition, greeted her at the door, "Good morning, Ima, welcome to Independence Junior High School. Let me introduce you to a few of your classmates before we get to work. I also want to show you your desk; actually, we call it a work station and yours is named 'Haley.' As you study your first assignment, Haley will be your tutor and when you're done, she will give you a short quiz to see how well you've learned the material. If you have problems with anything as you go along, come up and ask me or ask one of the other students who has already completed the assignment."

After meeting a few other students, Ima sat down in front of Haley, who was already waiting with a message that read, "Good morning, Ima.

119

My name is Haley. Press any key when you are ready to start your assignment. Don't be afraid. There's not much you can do to hurt me, or my feelings." This was like nothing she had experienced before. She looked around the classroom. The walls were covered with posters of different parts of the world, diagrams for biology assignments, and examples of math problems. Some of the posters even had interactive components and places where you could plug in a headset. In the corner there were three kiosks where students were busily viewing television monitors. Other students were studying the posters, while still others were at work stations solving problems and doing simulations. It looked more like a beehive than a classroom.

At first Ima was confused—she couldn't find the < any key > anywhere. Sensing a long delay with no response, Haley changes his message and asked Ima if she needed help. She said, "Yes," and an instant later Haley was talking to her about basic computer usage. Within a few minutes, Ima had completed the tutorial and was ready for her first assignment.

A new menu appeared with a list of the day's assignments and a short message that told her she could pick up the assignment she wanted to do first. Because she loved to travel, she choose geography, "A Day in the Life of a Midwestern Twister." It was awesome. A 14-year-old girl named Dorothy and her dog Toto were swept across the Midwest on the top of a tornado. The story line sounded strangely familiar. However, every time Dorothy and Toto arrived at a new city, Haley would show Ima an interactive video of the surrounding area, its citizens, and how the city became to be located there. Occasionally, Haley would ask her a question, to which she could type an answer.

Two hours later Ima realized she was getting hungry. "Amazing," she thought, "how time flies when you're having fun." She took a break for lunch with a few other students. Ima was amazed to learn that she could select and schedule her own assignments. There were a few constraints set by her teacher and the results of a battery of tests she had taken before she transferred to Independence had helped place her in the curriculum at her ability level. Classes were nearly all individualized with the exception of group discussions to foster oral communication, debating skills, and problem-solving strategies.

After lunch, Ima took her first quiz. She missed four of the twenty questions, one more than was allowed to "pass" the unit. "Oh, no," she thought, "I failed. I'm in big trouble now."

As Dolly went over Ima's test, she pointed out that Ima had gotten the tough questions right, but it looked as if she had made a few "dumb" mistakes. They discussed the questions she had missed. Dolly was satisfied that Ima knew the material, but suggested that she go back to the work station and review the material on the topography of Kansas that she had missed. Dolly made a few notes on her own computer where class records were stored and instructed Haley to generate another test, this one tailored to the areas Ima had missed the first time. When Ima had finished re-studying the topography of Kansas, and in particular had convinced herself that in fact the highest mountain in Kansas is only 200 feet shorter than the highest mountain in Vermont, Haley gave her the second test.

This time Ima got them all right. "Great," said Dolly, "now you're ready for your next assignment." "But," protested Ima, "what's my grade on the first unit—I missed four the first time." "No big deal," replied Dolly, "you mastered the important stuff. We don't give grades here as such, but if it will make you feel better, you did A-level work."

It quickly became apparent to Ima that grades didn't matter because Ms. Partition was more concerned about her learning the material than assigning a grade. Ima felt good about herself and about her new school.

This hypothetical description of a computer-based, self-paced learning environment is not far from reality. Yet, instructional systems of this kind are not widely used in education and training. This chapter analyzes some of the reasons self-paced learning has not been readily embraced by the educational community. It also suggests some potentials that self-paced learning may have for the future development of instructional models that are more adaptive to individual differences in learning (Glaser, 1978).

In this chapter we will explore several misunderstandings and problems associated with engineering a major change in the learning environment. This discussion will illustrate some of the common and potentially devastating pitfalls of self-paced instruction. It will also illustrate the promises self-pacing has for making instruction more effective, more efficient, more satisfying, and more responsive to individual differences in learning rates and abilities. Finally, we will review the research that has examined the effects of self-pacing on academic achievement, attitudes, and satisfaction.

INTRODUCTION TO SELF-PACED INSTRUCTION

Self-paced instruction is one application of systems design technology to educaton and training. It is frequently compared to more conventional forms of instruction. Common features of conventional instruction include fixed time periods, lock-step progress, lectures, and a teacher-centered environment. In the typical conventional classroom, everyone proceeds through the same material step by step in accordance with a schedule set by the teacher (lock-step). Furthermore, the teacher typically lectures to groups of students in classrooms or laboratories for a fixed period of time. Witness, for example, state laws that mandate a fixed number of instructional hours for a "school year." Conventional instruction is almost always teacher-centered in that the teacher determines not only *when* instruction will occur, but also *what* will be covered. Finally, adaptation to differences in student ability levels and prior knowledge limitations are typically not present.

In contrast to conventional instruction, self-paced instruction gives students the opportunity to determine when instruction will occur and at what pace. That is, students can set the pace of instruction and work through course content at a rate commensurate with their available time, ability, and motivation. Typically the system imposes some constraints such as deadlines by which certain assignments must be completed, a minimum rate of acceptable progress, or a minimum number of completed activities per day. Self-paced learning is not very different from reading a book or watching a movie on a VCR. In both of these instances individuals have the option to start or stop at any time, to repeat portions when necessary or desired, and to change the speed at which they progress through the activity. Notice also that the self-paced learning environment is student-centered, as opposed to teacher-centered. While the teacher or others who prepare the materials may determine what is learned, the student has some degree of control over the rate of learning.

The underlying rationale for self-pacing is that individuals learn at different rates. The whole instructional technology movement has been an attempt to adapt instruction to individual differences thereby gaining efficiency while at the same time ensuring achievement. Self-pacing is one attempt to do this and in almost all cases has been successful. Research has clearly demonstrated that a variety of self-paced formats such as computer-based instruction (Kulik & Kulik, 1987, 1989; Kulik, Kulik, & Bangert-Drowns, 1985; Bangert-Drowns, Kulik, & Kulik, 1985; Orlansky & String, 1981) Bloom's (1968) Learning for Mastery (Kulik, Kulik, & Bangert-Drowns, 1989) and Keller's (1968) Personalized System of Instruction (Kulik, Jaska, & Kulik, 1978) are more effective, more efficient, more highly preferred, and engender more positive attitudes about learning than conventional instruction. Yet, lock-step instruction, and in particular the lecture method, continues to be the predominant method of instructional delivery. With the recent proliferation of low-cost computing, however, self-pacing and other types of individualization are becoming more readily available.

Innovations that have attempted to adjust the learning environment to be more responsive to individual differences in learning rates and abilities have frequently failed. Some have even been criticized. Some of these include teaching machines in the 1950s, programmed instruction in the 1960s, mastery learning approaches in the 1960s and 1970s, and early computer-based systems in the 1970s and 1980s. With each of these innovations, educators have expressed interest in responding to individual differences and giving students more control over the instructional process. However, these innovations failed to become the educational panacea their originators envisioned. Furthermore, in some settings, attempts at self-pacing and individualization have been severely attacked despite empirical demonstrations of their effectiveness. For example, Figure 7.1 illustrates that computer-based instruction in some 40 military training courses is at least as effective as standard lecture courses and students complete them substantially faster (Orlansky & String, 1981; Montague, 1988). Yet, in 1983 the Navy decided to phase out self-paced courses and the software system that managed it (Ellis & Wulfeck, 1988).

Why have attempts at self-paced instruction been so poorly received? First, self-pacing is frequently misunderstood. Misunderstandings exist at several levels from conceptual definition to confusion with other methods and design technologies. For example, it is frequently used as a synonym for individualized instruction, but as we point out later in this chapter, self-paced and individualized instruction are related but somewhat different concepts.

Second, self-paced instruction is frequently accused of delivering poor quality instruction, of stressing lower-level objectives, and of failing to motivate students. However, as we will point out, these criticisms are often the result of "guilt by association" with poorly designed or poorly implemented self-paced courses.

A third reason self-paced instruction has been so poorly received is because it represents a radical departure from how we have come to conceptualized "schooling." "Schooling" typically conjures up images of great scholars lecturing groups of interested students, four-color textbooks, and comprehensive final examinations. It is largely a teacher-centered endeavor. On the other hand, "schooling" in a self-paced environment is quite a different matter. First, the central focus is on allowing students to adjust their study time to ensure their learning. Second, the role of the instructor is different. The instructor in a self-paced setting is not primarily a transmitter of information, but rather a manager of learning who may among other things also be a tutor and a problem solver. It is probably naive to assume that instructors will adopt and accept a new role without training.

In addition to constraints imposed on the instructor, there may also be constaints imposed on the instructional designer. First, a teaching environment that gives content control to the teacher mitigates against using materials prepared by others because the teacher has to study them, like them, and agree to use them. Second, computer-based, self-paced systems require a great deal of advance planning and development, a factor that may serve as a disincentive for many potential developers and users. For example, there are typically start-up costs such as procuring hardware

Self-pacing is a first step in the individualization process, but it is only a step. Individualized instruction typically refers to systems in which the material is designed to accommodate different entry levels and/or different branches or routes through the materials. Students' progress through the material is determined initially by their entry level skills and later by their prior performance. Thus, in individualized instruction, students typically begin at a level commensurate with their ability and then progress, sometimes by alternate paths, through the material. For example in many remedial settings, the instructor administers a pretest and then places the student at the appropriate place in the curriculum.

It is hard to imagine an individualized course that is not also self-paced. But, in some settings, instruction may be delivered to groups of students in different ways (for example, high-, medium-, and low-ability groups). Furthermore, instruction may be given on an individual basis but paced by the instructor. In self-paced instruction, by contrast, the student controls the presence, absence, and pace of contact with the material. A course may, however, be both individualized and self-paced. For example, many computer-assisted instruction packages have both components. A course may be individualized, but not self-paced, as when an instructor gives different feedback to different groups of students. A course may be self-paced, but not individualized, as is the case with many mastery-based courses. Finally, a course may be neither self-paced nor individualized as is the case for most conventional forms of instruction such as the lecture method.

Learning for Mastery, or LFM, developed by Bloom (1968) and the Personalized Systems of Instruction, or PSI, developed by Fred S. Keller (1968) and J. Gilmour Sherman, are two mastery learning programs that are sometimes confused with self-paced instruction. In such learning environments, the student is not allowed to progress to new material until previous material has been "mastered" at some defined criterion level.

Bloom (1968) has implemented successful learning for mastery courses in which students are given two chances to reach the criterion level. According to Bloom, two chances are sufficient for 95 percent of the students. Such mastery-based courses produce performance that is a little more than one-half a standard deviation above the mean when compared to more conventional forms of instruction (Kulik, Kulik, & Bangert-Drowns, 1989). However, these courses are not self-paced.

Keller and Sherman's (1982) Personalized System of Instruction is a mastery-based system that features not only self-pacing but also the use of tutors to enhance both the educational and social/personal aspects of the course. The tutor in PSI performs many functions that are analogous to a computer in a computer-based course from remediation to record keeping. Kulik, Kulik, and Bangert-Drowns' (1989) most recent meta-analysis indicates that PSI student perform about one-half of a standard deviation unit higher than students in conventional courses. Because self-pacing is one component of PSI, it is sometimes confused with it.

Many forms of computer based training and education also have a self-pacing component. Kulik and Kulik (1987), Kulik, Kulik, and Bangert-Drowns (1987), and Orlansky and String (1981) have all reported that when compared to conventional instruction, computer-based delivery systems produce equal achievement with reduced cost. Self-pacing itself, however, is not a defining characteristics of such systems although it is almost always present. For example, it is possible to use computer-based systems with groups of students where screen information is projected to the entire group. It is also important to distinguish between courses in which the material to be learned is *presented* by the computer as compared to systems in which the student's performance is *managed* by the system. Frequently, for example, a computer management system is simply a device for implementing self-paced delivery of instruction (Ellis & Wulfeck, 1988). Again, it is important to note that one must analyze a delivery system closely before concluding that it is self-paced. It is also important to carefully define the function of the self-paced component.

Perception: Self-paced instruction is of poor quality, typically emphasizes low-level skills, and fails to motivate students.

Many attempts at self-pacing, including teaching machines, programmed instruction, and PSI, as well as early versions of computer-based instruction, suffered from all of these maladies. Criticisms about content, however, should be leveled at the instructional developer, not at the method of delivery. Whether self-paced or lock-step instruction is used to deliver poor materials, the result is likely to be the same: poor results! Analogously, if the content stresses lower-level objectives, that will be the educational outcome, regardless of the instructional delivery system. Finally, failure to motivate students is not the result of self-pacing; it is more likely the result of poor course material, poor implementation, or a combination of both.

Because self-pacing is simply a procedure whereby students can control the pace of instruction, it has little to do with the content of what is to be learned (i.e., taught). However, since students can determine when material is to be delivered, it may provide constraints on the selection and design of those materials. The demand for developing quality instructional materials, however, is no different for a conventional course than it is for a self-paced format with the possible exception that if a course is to be self-paced, development must stay ahead of the fastest student. Furthermore, unless course developers receive feedback about the material they have designed, there is little insurance of quality control. In conventional instruction, the instructor is usually in close contact with the consequences of the quality of the instruction being delivered; thus, poor or outdated material can be detected and modified quickly.

Quality materials are essential for creating an effective instructional system. Ironically, one can only imagine that self-paced instruction would also do a better job teaching poor materials than conventional instruction. Our point is that one should not promote or indite a method of delivery like self-pacing until one has analyzed the content and objectives of the material to be taught.

To further explore the relationship between course design and end users, two examples from the Navy's use of computer-based, self-paced instruction will illustrate what should *not* be done (Ellis & Wulfeck, 1988). In 1977 the Navy introduced self-paced instruction in the Radioman Apprentice course. The course had been rewritten the same year using the newly developed Instructional System Development (ISD) methodology. Unfortunately, the way in which the ISD procedure was implemented was to separate the development team from the schoolhouse. In addition, the development team was split into separate groups, each responsible for one phase of the ISD process. A separate analysis group turned its product over to a design team which in turn passed the design to a development team. These actions caused two serious problems. First, because the school felt left out of the process, the developers received very little cooperation from the subject matter experts who were instructors at the school. These were the same instructors who were to teach the new curriculum when it was developed. Second, because of the separation of responsibilities, a great deal of information and knowledge was lost when products moved from group to group. In the end, the instruction was lengthy, not very effective, and not well received by the school or the fleet. Unfortunately, self-paced instruction took much of the blame for the poorly designed and developed instruction. The moral of the story is that unless there is feedback to the developers from those who are going to implement it, the outcome is likely to be a disaster.

In another attempt to implement a large-scale, self-paced CBI course, the Navy redesigned its Basic Electricity and Electronics (BE/E) course in the late 1960s and early 1970s. The course is a "front end," preparatory course for more advanced Navy schools that require basic knowledge of electronics and electricity. It had a history of high academic attrition and complaints from advanced schools that BE/E graduates did not know anything. One reason for this problem is that the course was poorly designed. No job or task analysis was ever performed; instead, materials were adopted from older courses with few ties to what the students would be doing on their jobs or in advanced schools. Most of the material had an academic, engineering orientation rather than one aimed at teaching technical job knowledge and skills. It should not be surprising that many students had difficulty grasping abstract concepts and failed. Evidence that BE/E's problems were curriculum-related and not the result of self-pacing came from a study (Fishburne & Mims, 1975) that compared lock-step instruction and self-pacing with the same objectives, content, and tests. There were no difference in attrition or test performance. However, there was a 50 percent higher training cost for the lock-step course. The moral of the story is that poor course materials produce poor learning, regardless of the method of delivery.

What types of self-paced, computer-based instruction are most effective? The results of several meta-analyses (Kulik, Kulik, & Bangert-Drowns, 1985; Bangert-Drowns, Kulik, & Kulik, 1985; Kulik & Kulik, 1987, 1989) from kindergarten pupils to college students have shown that structured courses taught using computer-based systems raise student examination scores by about one-third of a standard deviation (from approximately the 50th percentile to the 62nd percentile) on the average and they reduce substantially the amount of time needed for reaching criterion. Furthermore, the effectiveness of computer-based instruction appears to increase with time, suggesting that procedures for preparing lesson materials may be becoming more sophisticated. At the precollege level, Kulik and Kulik (1989) report that computer-aided instruction (CAI) and computer-managed instruction (CMI) are moderately effective while computer-enriched instruction (CEI) contributes little to student achievement. CAI appears to have its strongest effects at the elementary level, while CMI appears to be more effective with older students (Kulik, Kulik, & Bangert-Drowns, 1985). While these findings may be suggestive, there is still no conclusive evidence about overall domain-specific effects from computer-based instruction.

Perception: Self-paced instruction requires a great deal of advance planning, development, and organization.

By necessity, material in the typical self-paced environment must be prepared in advance and permanently recorded, such as in the form of a workbook, a videodisc, or a CAI learning package. Only if material is permanently recorded and readily available can students have the opportunity to initiate and terminate interactions with it and to review it when needed. Material preparation, however, represents a disincentive for many developers. The time and cost involved in the design of such materials must be weighed against potential payoffs. These costs, in turn, must also be amortized over the life of the project, a concept that is foreign to many educators, particularly those who are accustomed to conceptualizing education in terms of lectures and class discussions. Furthermore, procedures must be instituted to insure the continued quality of course materials such that poor or outdated material is revised within a reasonable time frame. Finally, a monitoring system must be designed to encourage students to continue to work in self-paced environments.

Monitoring students and motivating them to work in a self-paced environment is not an easy problem to solve. For example, the literature on self-paced instruction frequently refers to a "procrastination" problem, sometimes called a "pacing" problem (Born & Moore, 1978; Glick, 1978). The problem involves how students distribute their work effort. In particular, it is often cast as what to do when students *postpone* a majority of the work to be accomplished until the end of the term or some other arbitrary deadline (thus the term procrastination). If every student had access to a computer and an instructor, the problem might not be acute; however, this is just not how most environments operate. Typically, both hardware and instructional resources are limited and students must be scheduled to make maximum use of those resources.

Scheduling is one component of the problem. Enforcing those schedules is another. Both must be considered in any self-paced environment. Scheduling refers to how equipment and personnel should be allocated to maximize their use. For example, if you have 10 hours of computer-based instruction, one work station, 100 students, and two weeks to complete a training sequence, you have a problem. You may be able to increase the number of work stations, or increase the amount of time allocated, or decrease the number of students. Once you have determined that the instructional task can be completed, the next step is to determine how students are going to pace themselves.

Who will decide the pace? The instructor? The student? Both? In a "self-paced" environment, one would assume that the students sets the pace. However, in most cases, this is rarely done (Glick & Semb, 1978). What happens is that the instructor sets a minimum rate of progress or imposes a series of deadlines. Students are free to work at any rate they choose so long as they stay ahead of the minimum rate or meet the deadlines. One compromise between instructor-set deadlines and no contingency on student progress is to let students set their own deadlines (Roberts, Fulton, & Semb, 1988). In such systems, students typically impose harsher deadlines on themselves than instructors do and complete the instructional sequence at a faster rate.

Enforcing schedules in a self-paced environment almost appears contradictory. If we are going to let students set the pace of instruction, why should they be forced to meet a schedule, no matter who sets it? There are two answers to this question. First, when equipment and instructional resources are limited, as they are in most places, maximizing the use of those resources usually requires some sort of scheduling and enforcement of those schedules. Second, the literature on massed versus distributed practice in which superiority of distributed practice has clearly been demonstrated, or what Dempster (1988) refers to as the spacing effect, clearly argues against letting students procrastinate. Because the typical self-paced environment is divided into a number of units or modules through which students progress, it is in fact an application of distributed practice to learning, one of the few applications of its kind.

There are two general ways to enforce meeting a schedule: (a) reinforce students who are ahead of schedule, and (b) punish students who fall behind. Both work (Glick & Semb, 1978). For example, Semb, Conyers, Spencer, and Sanchez-Sosa (1975) and Powers, Edwards, and Hoehle (1973) awarded students bonus points to maintain progress in self-paced courses. Semb et al. (1975) and Bitgood and Segrave (1975) have used point-loss or decreasing point-values to control the rate of student responding. Philosophically, reinforcing high rate performance seems preferable to punishing slow rate performance. However, both may be necessary to insure maximum utilization of resources.

The major pitfall revealed by all of this research is that there are major policy decisions to be made about implementing a self-paced format, particularly the constraints under which the student will "self-pace." It is clear from these findings that the issues facing self-paced instruction developers and instructors are varied and complex (Van Matre, Pennypacker, Hartman, Brett, & Ward, 1981). The constraints that exist, for example, may dictate whether one uses a negative incentive such as forced compliance with a deadline or minimum rate contingency, or a positive incentive such as bonus pay or the opportunity to proceed to another activity for completion ahead of schedule. The research indicates that both of these procedures work, but the philosophical orientation of the organization may dictate which one is most appropriate.

On a practical note, the first author has managed self-paced courses for over 30,000 students in the past 17 years. He has spent a great deal of time attempting to solve the "pacing" problem. The current solution is both expedient and humane; it uses a minimum rate-of-progress criterion which students must maintain to avoid overtaxing the system as the end-of-course deadline approaches. Students who fall below the minimum rate-of-progress criterion must report to class every session until they catch up. Failure to meet this contingency results in the loss of a letter grade, which the student can earn back by getting ahead of schedule. This is the same solution that will be used when the course is fully converted to a computer-based system.

While self-pacing offers students many options, such as the opportunity to progress at a rate commensurate with their time and ability, it also offers instructors a challenge of how to arrange the learning environment for everyone's maximum benefit. We cannot emphasize enough the importance of determining the nature of that utilization *in advance*. As Glick and Semb (1978) note, in the typical unrestricted self-paced environment, approximately 30 percent of students will work ahead of schedule and finish the course before the end of the term. Another 20 percent will distribute work uniformly across the time allotted and also finish before the end of the term. About 50 percent will postpone work and may or may not finish the instructional sequence; typically there will be a burst of responding near the final deadline. High-rate students and those who adhere to a uniform pace do not impose hardships on the system and may even lead to the initial perception that the system is working fine. However, unless students are monitored at frequent intervals, this may lead to a trap in which (a) there are lulls in resource utilization, and (b) there is a surge at the end when the system does not have the capacity to accommodate the demand. As a consequence, monitoring student progress assumes an important role in self-paced environments (Van Matre et al., 1981).

Monitoring implies a relatively continuous (e.g., daily) assessment of each student's progress relative to the student's goals and schedules. It also involves giving students feedback about their progress. This is not a trivial task in the self-paced environment because students may not be required to report to class every day. Thus, it is important to "flag" students who are not meeting their schedule, regardless of who set it for them. In a computer-managed environment, it is easy to provide "flags." The difficult part is communicating this information to the student and insuring that either the student complies or a new schedule is negotiated. These details require a great deal of advance planning and preparation.

Assuming all contingencies can be reasonably anticipated and that a plan of action can be described, there are many advantages to be derived from a self-paced environment. Students benefit because learning is spaced (as opposed to massed), there is the opportunity to do things over if they are not done right the first time (mastery), and they learn to become more responsible for their own actions and their own learning (self-control). Instructors benefit not only because students benefit as just described, but also because the entire system produces superior results. Finally, the institution benefits because resources are put to maximum use and instructional time per student is minimized.

Perception: Self-paced instruction eliminates the need for instructors.

Nothing could be further from the truth. What changes is the *role* of the instructor, from a transmitter of information to a manager of learning, a tutor, and a problem solver. Many instructors, particularly those who are accustomed to the central, authoritarian nature of conventional education, find the transformation difficult if not impossible to make, not to mention distasteful.

As Ellis and Wulfeck (1988) point out, instructor dissatisfaction was one factor responsible for the Navy's decision to phase out self-paced courses during the 1980s. For example, results from a basic course in propulsion engineering revealed that the advantage of self-pacing was obscured by poor implementation. In particular, there was no training program for instructors to prepare them for how to use the additional instructional time they would gain from computer management. There was also no training on how to deal with students in a computer-managed environment. Subsequent research demonstrated that such training improves both instructor and student attitudes toward computer-managed, self-paced instruction. Furthermore, instructor training resulted in increased student performance and decreased attrition (McCombs, Dobrovolny, & Lockhart, 1983).

Asking an instructor to change his or her way of doing things is certainly a potential pitfall. It requires retraining teachers and instructors not only in how to do things differently in the new environment, but also in how to conceptualize that environment. To conceptualize the learning environment as a place where instructors work with students one on one or in small groups is a far cry from the authoritarian, sometimes adversarial, role of the conventional instructor. Promoting changes in the instructor's view of the learning environment and his or her role in it involves both selection and training.

Selection is important because some instructors are willing to change to accommodate self-paced instruction while others are not. Instructors who view themselves as lecturers may find it difficult to accept a new role in the classroom. Similarly, instructors who are disorganized often find it difficult to operate effectively in a self-paced environment. Before adopting a self-paced format, it is important that the instructors' conceptions of teaching be considered as well as their willingness to adopt the role of manager, tutor, and problem solver.

Training is important because it is necessary for most instructors to rehearse the behaviors required in a self-paced environment: interacting one on one (as opposed to lecturing), prompting students for more information (as opposed to giving it), and providing individual tutoring. During the 1970s when the Personalized System of Instruction reached its zenith, there were hundreds of workshops for instructors to teach them how to organize and operate self-paced learning environments. While no formal evaluations of these workshops were ever made, it was clear from informal sources that most instructors considered training to be an essential part of the successful implementation of self-paced instruction.

Perception: Self-paced instruction lacks an empirical base.

There have been very few empirical studies of self-paced instruction per se. While it is a component of many computer-based, individualized, and mastery-based systems, it has seldom been isolated as an independent variable. This may be the case because in so many delivery systems it is a necessary or logical component. Another contributing factor may be that in many computer-based systems there is too much emphasis on hardware and too little emphasis on human engineering. One notable exception is the literature on the Personalized System of Instruction in which self-pacing has been isolated and experimentally analyzed as a separate component in some 13 studies (Glick & Semb, 1978). While it may not be possible to generalize all of these findings to other self-paced systems, conceptually there is enough similarity among systems to give these findings serious consideration.

As mentioned previously, research on systems that have self-pacing as a component has often shown gains in academic performance. Furthermore, even in studies where little or no differences in performance have been found (e.g., Orlansky & String, 1981), there are significant savings in time in favor of self-paced formats. In addition to gains in performance and time savings, there are also differences in student attitudes and satisfaction. In their meta-analysis of the components of PSI, Kulik, Jaska, and Kulik (1978) report that student attitudes toward self-pacing vary from neutral to favorable. Other reviews of the literature (e.g., Hursh, 1976) indicate that self-pacing is one of the most highly rated features of PSI courses. Ellis and Wulfeck (1988) report that self-paced students are more positive about their instructors and learning experiences than group-paced students. In their study, students in self-paced conditions felt more confident of their ability to perform well in the course and were more satisfied with the amount they had learned than were group-paced students. It seems clear from the data that self-pacing engenders both student satisfaction and confidence.

SUMMARY

The chapter began with a hypothetical description of how an advanced computer-based, self-paced learning environment might work. It then presented a definition of self-pacing as the student's ability to control when and at what rate instruction would occur. Giving students such control over learning can have positive consequences for the student, for the instructor, and for the institution. It also requires a reconceptualization of the learning environment from one that is teacher-centered and in which the instructor *delivers* instruction to one that is focused more on student achievement and where the instructor *facilitates* learning by being a manager, a tutor, and a problem solver. Computers can do much of the transmitting and monitoring, but they cannot replace the classroom instructor.

There are several perceptions surrounding self-paced learning, most of which are not based on fact. Self-paced learning is not the same as individualized instruction, learning for mastery, or the personalized system of instruction. It may be a component of any of those systems, just as it *may* be a component of a computer-based system. Because self-pacing has sometimes been accompanied by poorly designed materials, it has been blamed for inadequacies in the entire system. Poor course outcomes, too much stress on low-level objectives, and a failure to motivate students, all criticisms of self-paced instruction, are almost always the result of poorly designed materials or poor implmentation, not the method of delivery. A well-designed course will work *despite* the method of delivery; it may even work better if it is delivered in a self-paced format.

One perception of self-pacing that has validity, not to mention important consequences for both the instructor and the institution, is the amount of time involved in planning and preparing for a student centered learning environment. Hardware and software must be procured and procedures outlined in advance. As we have pointed out, maintaining correspondence in goals and objectives among course designers and those who will implement it is imperative. Research on self-paced learning indicates that a problem may arise in how students distribute work. In an unrestricted environment, many students will postpone work until a deadline approaches, which may lead to poor utilization of the institution's resources. It is necessary to plan in advance for the constraints that will be placed on the way in which students will be allowed to pace themselves. Both positive and negative consequences can be used and both appear to be effective. What appears to be most important is keeping students in contact with the learning environment so that knowledge of course progress can be communicated.

Another important consideration in the use of a self-paced format is instructor selection and training, no small task given the radical change for most instructors—reconceptualizing the learning environment and changing roles and behavior. To be successful, the potential user must have the knowledge base (both of the content and of the self-paced learning environment), the resources, and the ability to organize and manage students at different phases of learning.

While self-paced learning requires a great deal of advance planning, it can produce significant benefits for everyone involved—the student, the instructor, the course designer, and the institution. Students can schedule work to fit their schedule, they can redo assignments, and they can learn to be responsible for their own actions. Instructors benefit from improved student performance, as do course designer and the institution. Properly implemented, self-paced learning is one of the few systems in education where everyone wins.

REFERENCES

Bangert-Drowns, R.L., Kulik, J.A., & Kulik, C.C. (1985). Effectiveness of computer-based education in secondary schools. *Journal of Computer-Based Instruction, 12*, 59–68.

Bitgood, S.C., & Segrave, K. (1975). A comparison of graduated and fixed point systems of contingency managed instruction. In J.M. Johnston (Ed.), *Behavior Research and Technology in Higher Education* (pp. 202–213). Springfield, IL: Charles C. Thomas.

Bloom, B.S. (1968, May). Mastery learning. *Evaluation Comment* (Vol. 1, No. 2). Los Angeles: University of California at Los Angeles, Center for the Study of Evaluation of Instructional Programs.

Born, D.G., & Moore, M.C. (1978). Some belated thoughts on pacing. *Journal of Personalized Instruction, 3*, 33–36.

Dempster, F.N. (1988). The spacing effect: A case study in the failure to apply the results of psychological research. *American Psychologist, 43*, 627–634.

Ellis, J.A., & Wulfeck, W.H. (1988). *Computer-managed self-paced instruction in Navy technical training: Problems in implementation.* Presented at the American Educational Research Association, New Orleans, LA.

Fishburne, R.P., & Mims, D.M. (1975, March). *Formative evaluation of an experimental BE/E program* (Research Branch Rep. 9-75). Naval Air Station Memphis, Millington, TN: Chief of Naval Technical Training.

Glaser, R. (1978). *Advances in instructional psychology* (Vol. 1). Hillsdale, NJ: Lawrence Erlbaum Associates.

Glick, D.M. (1978). If there is a pacing problem in PSI, will we recognize it when we see it? *Journal of Personalized Instruction, 3*, 42–45.

Glick, D.M., & Semb, G. (1978). Effects of pacing contingencies in personalized instruction: A review of the evidence. *Journal of Personalized Instruction, 3*, 36–42.

Hursh, D.E. (1976). Personalized systems of instruction: What do the data indicate? *Journal of Personalized Instruction, 1*, 91–105.

Keller, F.S. (1968). "Good-bye, teacher..." *Journal of Applied Behavior Analysis, 1*, 79–86.

Keller, F.S., & Sherman, J.G. (1982). *The personalized system of instruction.* Lenexa, KS: Trilogy Systems, Inc.

Kulik, C.C., & Kulik, J.A. (1986). Effectiveness of computer-based education in colleges. *AEDS Journal, X*, 81–108.

Kulik, C.C., & Kulik, J.A. (1989). Effectiveness of computer-based instruction: An updated analysis. *Computers in Human Behavior.*

Kulik, J.A., Jaska, P., & Kulik, C.C. (1978). Research on component features of Keller's personalized system of instruction. *Journal of Personalized Instruction, 3*, 2–14.

Kulik, J.A., & Kulik, C.C. (1987). Review of recent research literature on computer-based instruction. *Contemporary Educational Psychology, 12*, 222–230.

Kulik, J.A., Kulik, C.C., & Bangert-Drowns, R.L. (1985). Effectiveness of computer-based education in elementary schools. *Computers in Human Behavior, 1*, 59–74.

Kulik, J.A., Kulik, C.C., & Bangert-Drowns, R.L. (1989). Effectiveness of mastery learning programs: A meta-analysis. *Review of Educational Research,* in press.

McCombs, B.L., Dobrovolny, J.L., & Lockhart, K.A. (1983). *Evaluation of the CMI instructor role training program in the Navy and Air Force* (NPRDC Tech. Rep. 83-43). San Diego, CA: Navy Personnel Research and Development Center.

Montague, W.E. (1988). *What works: Summary of research findings with implications for Navy instruction and learning* (NAVEDTRA 115-1). San Diego, CA: Navy Personnel Research and Development Center.

Orlansky, J., & String, J. (1981). Computer-based instruction for military training. *Defense Management Journal,* pp. 46–54.

Powers, R.B., Edwards, K.A., & Hoehle, W.F. (1973). Bonus points in a self-paced course facilitates exam taking. *Psychological Record, 23*, 533–538.

Roberts, M.S., Fulton, M., & Semb, G. (1988). Self-pacing in a personalized psychology course: Letting students set the deadlines. *Teaching of Psychology, 15*, 89–92.

Semb, G., Conyers, D., Spencer, R., & Sanchez-Sosa, J.J. (1975). An experimental comparison of four pacing contingencies. In J.M. Johnston (Ed.), *Behavior research and technology in higher education* (pp. 348–368). Springfield, IL: Charles C. Thomas.

Van Matre, N.H., Pennypacker, H.S., Hartman, W.H., Brett, B.E., & Ward, L.Q. (1981). *Computer-managed instruction in the Navy: V. The Effects of charted feedback on rate of progress through a CMI course* (NPRDC Tech. Rep. 82-16). San Diego, CA: Navy Personnel Research and Development Center.

Wulfeck, W.H., Ellis, J.A., & Smith, J. (1988). *Self-paced training: Perceptions and realities.* Presented at the Military Testing Asssociation, Munich, F.R.G.

8
Promising Directions for Computer-Based Training with Gifted Individuals

Michael C. Pyryt
Department of Educational Psychology
The University of Calgary
Calgary, Alberta, Canada

The purpose of this chapter is to examine the potential of computer-based training with gifted individuals. The guiding principle of this chapter is that integration of learner characteristics, software design features, and learner outcomes is essential if computer-based training is to have any substained benefit for gifted individuals. Greene (1985) has suggested that our evaluation of computer-based training is linked to our values and visions. Our affect regarding computer-based training is influenced by the extent to which the current reality mirrors our image of how things should be. In this chapter, I attempt to provide a framework for evaluating the potential of any computer-based training activity for enhancing the lives of gifted individuals. After providing an overview of the nature of giftedness, I focus on software design that incorporates the characteristics of the gifted. I cite some promising applications that illustrate the blending of gifted education and software utilization.

GIFTEDNESS

Although there are many conceptions of giftedness (Sternberg & Davidson, 1986), a useful organizer has been provided by Gallagher and Courtright (1986), who distinguish between giftedness as a psychological construct and giftedness as an educational construct. Psychologists tend to focus on how individuals differ on various traits. Educators focus on designing special educational programs to meet the educational needs of superior students. Differences regarding the construct of giftedness lead to differences regarding the content of educational programming for the gifted.

Trait theorists conceptualize giftedness in terms of the characteristics that gifted individuals possess. Theorists differ on the extent to which the characteristics are perceived as domain-specific. Different conceptualizations also vary in the extent to which cognitive, affective, developmental, and ecological characteristics are included. Sternberg and Davidson (1985) provided five generalizations from the research literature about the cognitive development of gifted individuals, who are perceived as possessing (a) high general ability and exceptional specific ability, (b) exceptional capitalization upon pattern of abilities, (c) exceptional environmental shaping abilities, (d) exceptional problem-finding abilities and (e) exceptional ability to conceive higher-order relations. Foster (1985) described the psychosocial characteristics of productive adults. Gifted adults possess discipline-based knowledge and values, a consistent pattern of productivity, an orientation toward hard work, and an integrated sense of self. Gruber (1985) views the development of giftedness as a lifespan process of self-construction marked by aspiration, mission, attempts to reconcile the discrepancy between the actual and the possible. Since giftedness is manifested in a sociocultural context, examination of cultural belief systems and reinforcements is important (Mistry & Rogoff, 1985).

Educators tend to focus on providing educational experiences for gifted and talented youth. Consistent with Public Law 95-561, programs for gifted students encompass one or more of the following areas: (a) general intellectual ability, (b) specific academic aptitude, (c) creative or productive thinking, (d) leadership ability, and (e) visual and performing arts. Most often, programs for the gifted focus on intellectual ability and operationalize giftedness in terms of scores on intelligence tests (Jenkins-Friedman, 1982). Although the exact score required for placement in a gifted program varies by state, IQ scores in the top 5 percent of the norm group are typically required. Learning characteristics of intellectually gifted students include quick mastery of material, advanced vocabulary, large fund of general information, interest in principles, curiosity, capacity for absorption, boredom with routine tasks, and independence (Renzulli, Smith, White, Callahan, & Hartman, 1976).

Programs for gifted students typically involve some combination of acceleration and enrichment. Acceleration entails permitting a student to master content rapidly, leading to an eventual change in grade placement. An eighth-grade student might complete a computerized precalculus curriculum, then take calculus at a nearby college. Enrichment involves exposing a student to concepts not typically covered in the curriculum. A high school student might complete a computerized tutorial program on the topic of linear regression. The integration of these two components varies according to the philosophic perspective adopted by a given program delivery system/model (Renzulli, 1986). Proponents of acceleration (Stanley, 1980) argue that accelerative practices provide the best opportunity for enhancing content-based knowledge at rates appropriate for a student's level of ability. Proponents of enrichment (Renzulli, 1977) believe that gifted students should be producers of knowledge rather than consumers of knowledge and should be provided training in skills that facilitate future productivity. Proponents of enrichment envision gifted students using computer technology such as data analysis software to facilitate student-generated research that results in new knowledge. Program models that blend acceleration and enrichment provide opportunities for learning material at a rapid rate and applying process skills.

PROBLEMS IN COMPUTER-BASED TRAINING FOR GIFTED INDIVIDUALS

There are four major problems in developing computer-based training for gifted individuals. Two problems are endemic to gifted education while two problems reflect the general status of microcomputer applications in education. Since giftedness is a multidimensional construct with competing educational programming models, teachers will have to select software that is congruent with a particular theory of gifted education. Since instructional designers typically use Gagné and Briggs (1979) as the foundation for software development, it may be difficult for teachers to find software that is congruent with the objectives of a particular programming system.

Another consideration in dealing with gifted students is the importance of ethics and integrity in utilizing computer courseware. Gifted students are capable of computer crimes such as pirating programs, computer alteration of records, unlawful access to classified information, and virus infestation. Teachers of the gifted must model appropriate use of copyrighted material. They need to stress the need for ethical use of computer technology.

Another problem is that most schools have at least 100 students enrolled for each computer owned (Becker, 1984). This situation leads to difficulties in providing significant time on the computer for gifted students. Lack of facilities may force teachers to allocate computer use to small groups in cooperative learning situations. Research by Kanevsky (1985) indicates that gifted elementary students prefer competitive CAI experiences. Finally, teachers may lack the appropriate training in the effective use of microcomputers (Dwyer, 1981; Mittler, 1984). This problem is compounded when higher education faculty lack necessary knowledge and skills to provide instruction in effective microcomputer applications (Blackhurst, MacArthur, & Byrom, 1987) since higher education faculty provide the preservice instruction for elementary and secondary teachers of the gifted.

PROVIDING COMPUTER-BASED TRAINING
FOR GIFTED INDIVIDUALS

The challenge of providing computer-based training to gifted individuals is one of integrating type of giftedness, domain knowledge, learner characteristics, instructional environment, and vision of what gifted individuals should become. Computer-based training should provide opportunities for students to acquire knowledge and to produce knowledge. Knowledge acquisition can be enhanced through well-designed courseware. Knowledge production can be enhanced by developing "tool skills," such as word processing, using spreadsheets, databases, information retrieval with CD-ROM technology, and desktop publishing. In a research project, for example, a student might use a CD-ROM system to locate relevant literature, use databases to locate factual information, use spreadsheets to tabulate results, and use word processing and desktop publishing to generate a research report. Tool skills such as word processing, use of spreadsheets, databases, and desktop publishing also permit gifted students to shape their environment. By using tools to emulate the way professionals operate, gifted individuals are acquiring skills to enhance productivity.

The challenge for educators is to decide what gifted individuals should learn and to select software that is congruent with instructional plans. Sternberg and Davidson (1986) and Renzulli (1986) provide many visions to guide educators. The challenge for software developers is to design software that takes into account the knowledge acquisition capabilities of gifted individuals. The next section will focus on software design/utilization issues.

SOFTWARE DESIGN/UTILIZATION

Although there are many approaches to software/courseware design (Jonassen, 1988a), the key features involve the phases of analysis, design/ synthesis, and evaluation. The analysis phase includes such components as needs assessment, task analysis, statement of objectives, pretest development, and decision about instructional methods. The design/synthesis phase involves the actual development of delivery, motivational, and management strategies. The evaluation phase consists of conducting assessments to provide formative and summative information about the operation of the system. Each phase of the design process has implications for designing computer-based training experiences for gifted individuals.

Needs Assessment

During needs assessment, designers would need to determine what is to be taught. Considerations from this standpoint include a determination of whether the software should promote acceleration or enrichment. Software which promotes acceleration would permit rapid progress through a curricular sequence. Software which provides enrichment would entail opportunities to develop divergent thinking, convergent thinking, and higher-order reasoning skills. Software used for enrichment would also expose gifted students to curricular areas that are not typically covered in the K-12 curriculum. Topics not typically covered include: anthropology, archeology, sociology, psychology, comparative literature, art history, architecture, statistics, zoology, immunology, and biomedical engineering. The educator would need to determine the courseware needed based on an analysis of an individual gifted student's achievement pattern, interests, degree of motivation, learning style and developmental level.

Task Analysis

Task analysis is a key ingredient of most computer-based training instructional designs (Bunderson, 1981; Carrier & Jonassen, 1988; Hannum, 1988; Roblyer, 1988; Scandura & Scandura, 1988; Wager & Gagné, 1988). By ordering skills along a learning hierarchy (Gagné, 1985), it is possible to specify the prerequisite skills needed for future achievement. Software designed for gifted students needs to begin with a content analysis of a discipline (Bruner, 1960). Skills needed to master a discipline should be identified and sequenced. The instructional designer needs to focus on identifying those skills which incorporate other skills. For example, the ability to solve simultaneous equations incorporates the ability to solve simple equations. By including concepts that include multiple skills, it is possible to streamline the number of specific skills that need to be mastered in order to complete a computer-based training course. Educators should choose software that capitalizes on a student's prior learning by involving application of multiple concepts. For example, rather than assess the four arithmetic operations of addition, subtraction, multiplication, and division individually, courseware should assess division, which subsumes the other operations, to determine a student's competence in arithmetic computation. Student success should lead to more complex applications;

student errors should lead to simpler applications. Educators concerned with gifted education should be extremely wary of courseware programs that involve the demonstration of many minute skills in order to complete a course.

Initial assessment procedures should be consistent with the approach to task analysis. Software designers should attempt to develop assessment protocols that start with higher-level concepts involving multiple skills. If an individual can demonstrate mastery of superordinate skills, mastery of subordinate skills is assumed. Multiple regression procedures (McCombs & McDaniel, 1981; Ross & Morrison, 1988), Bayesian procedures (Tennyson & Christensen, 1988), subject matter analysis (Hannum, 1988), and generative learning strategies (Jonassen, 1988b) can be used to determine the most important components for the initial preassessment. Educators should select software that has a definite approach to initial assessment, which provides efficient estimation of a learner's entry skills in the context of a particular approach to assessment.

Preliminary design considerations during the analysis phase will involve decisions about the mechanisms of the delivery system. Such issues as instructional delivery system, the nature of interactivity between the learner and the system, type of feedback, structure of lessons, motivational strategies, and embedding of learning strategies would be determined. Educators of gifted students should look for software programs that permit the learner to have as much control as possible about the information presented and feedback given.

Design/Synthesis

The design/synthesis phase involves the actual development of computer-based training experiences. The key for courseware developers is to remain faithful to the specifications which were developed during the analysis phase. The key for educators is to examine the congruence between program specifications and the actual program designed. In addition, educators need to develop a plan for integrating the software into the curriculum, especially in classrooms that may have only one computer. Rotational strategies, whereby student access to the computer is scheduled in 15-minute blocks might provide an equitable way of coping with the computer shortage problem.

EVALUATION

The evaluation phase involves the implementation of all aspects of the courseware including the assessment of an individual's progress as well as a formative and summative evaluation of the courseware. Gagné and Beard (1978) described the decision-making process in evaluating an individual's progress through specified learning outcomes. Borich and Jemelka (1981) presented a comprehensive overview of evaluation designs that reflect the complexity of assessing the effectiveness of computer-based training programs. Educators should select programs that assess learner outcomes in relation to the design specifications. Educators should also select software that provides information regarding field-tests and empirical evidence regarding program effectiveness. Only 20 percent of the 163 microcomputer courseware programs in Bialo and Erickson's (1985) review provided any evidence of formative evaluation before the product was marketed (Roblyer, 1988).

SELECTED EXAMPLES FROM THE LITERATURE

This section will describe computer-based training experiences with gifted individuals that have appeared in the literature. Commentary regarding perceived appropriateness is also provided.

Suppes (1980) described some experiences in working with gifted students ages 10–15 with IQs mostly above 165 in a home-based setting. Students were given terminals connected to Stanford University's mainframe to utilize in a self-paced mode to master a CAI course such as elementary logic. Results of this "experiment" indicate great variability in student performance. Whereas some students mastered college-level courses rapidly; others failed to make progress. The two most positive aspects of this project were (a) allowing gifted students to accelerate their progress, and (b) providing intellectually-challenging instructional material that is geared to gifted students' abstract reasoning capabilities. On the negative side, the highly-sequential drill and practice nature of the software may have alienated some students (Solomon, 1986). Student motivation clearly affects involvement with the CAI system. This is especially true when students have complete freedom to use the system as often or as infrequently as desired.

An example of the use of tutorial software was provided by Mathias and Storey (1986), who described the implementation of the American Chemical Society's course in polymer chemistry for gifted high school students attending the Mississippi Governor's School. The material is intended for chemists with undergraduate backgrounds in science and mathematics. Supplemental material was needed to fill gaps in the knowledge background of these high school students. The authors were impressed by the graphics and trial-and-error feedback system used in the courseware. The course was supplemented by discussion of the material on the disks and laboratory experiments and demonstrations. The article notes the importance of prerequisite skills for knowledge acquisition. The course would only seem appropriate for students interested in chemistry with well-developed skills in science and mathematics.

Another application of computer-assisted instruction is provided by Barstow (1981) who described the programs at the Talcott Mountain Science Center. Computer simulations are used to supplement courses in astronomy, ecology, and meterology. Statistical programs are also used to analyze data gathered in laboratory experiments. The instructors at the Talcott Mountain Science Center select software tailored to the specific objectives in particular science courses. The software enables gifted students to generate and test hypotheses.

Steele, Battista, and Krockover (1982) examined the effect of drill-and-practice software on the mathematics achievement and cognitive and affective components of computer literacy of high ability fifth graders. They reported gains in computer literacy. There were no differences in mathematics achievement between students in the experimental group receiving computerized drills and the control group receiving traditional drills. Mean pretest and posttest achievement scores are not reported so it is difficult to determine if ceiling effects were operable. Although the authors interpret the results to indicate that computer-assisted drill is just as effective as traditional drill and practice, the findings indicate that the software is probably not worth the expense if cognitive gains are the main criteria.

Kanevsky (1986) examined the use of competitive and cooperative learning environments as compared to flash card drills in mathematics with gifted third and fourth graders. Results indicated that all groups improved their math performance during the study. An analysis of covariance indicated that the three groups were similar on outcome measures when controlling for entry level skills. Gifted students expressed greater preference for competitive versus cooperative structures. This study suggests that gifted elementary students will prefer drill-and-practices activities that have a competitive component.

Other descriptions that appear in the literature (Nazzaro, 1981) typically focus on the use of a programming language such as BASIC or LOGO as a way of training problem-solving skills. Sample programming tasks that are intended to challenge gifted students or examples of programs written by gifted students are provided. Empirical evidence about the effects of such computer literacy training remains anecdotal. There is a critical need for empirical research that examines the extent to which analytic reasoning skills developed while learning a programming language transfer to other situations. The one advantage of having gifted students master programming languages is that it enables those students to gain skills to become producers of knowledge by developing their own software.

GLIMPSES OF THE FUTURE

More sophisticated courseware could become available if courseware designers, domain experts, and gifted specialists would collaborate to design the most effective software for gifted individuals. After field-testing, information about the software could be filed on a database or CD-ROM disk. This information would provide the knowledge base for developing an expert systems software-selection program. Teachers could use the expert systems program to determine the most effective software given a particular type of giftedness, intended learning outcome, knowledge of degree of motivation, learning style, developmental level, and specification of a school system's hardware resources. Advances in computerized educational measurement (Bunderson, Inouye, & Olsen, 1989; Weiss, 1983) will foster the development of courseware that meets the knowledge acquisition capabilities of gifted students. Such courseware will assess student mastery and prescribe instructional sequences based on the student's response to each item. The system will have sufficient capacity to permit students to efficiently demonstrate mastery of the content of a discipline. Opportunities for hypothesis generation and testing will be provided to stimulate gifted students' abstract thinking abilities. Such "intelligent courseware" will also record student performance to document skill acquisition and examine a student's interactions with the courseware. Advances in integrated software combining word processing, spreadsheets, database management, graphics capability, and telecommunications will enable gifted individuals to emulate professionals and produce high-quality work. The utilization of additional hardware such as image scanners, speech synthesizers, and interactive videodisc players will provide opportunities for multisensory experiences. The future possibilities for computer-based training with gifted individuals are limited only by our visions. What happens in the future will depend on our ability to integrate our technological capabilities with our dreams.

REFERENCES

Barstow, D. (1981). The Talcott Mountain Science Center. In J.N. Nazzaro (Ed.), *Computer connections for gifted children and youth* (pp. 49–52). Reston, VA: Council for Exceptional Children. (Reprinted from in *On Computing*, 1979, *1* (3), 34–36)

Becker, H.J. (1984). Computers in schools today: Some basic considerations. *American Journal of Education, 93*, 22–39.

Bialo, E.R., & Erickson, L.B. (1985). Microcomputer courseware: Characteristics and design trends. *AEDS Journal, 18*, 227–236.

Blackhurst, A.E., MacArthur, C.A., & Byrom, E.M. (1987). Microcomputing competencies for special education professors. *Teacher Education and Special Education, 10,* 153–160.

Borich, G.D., & Jemelka, R.P. (1981). Evaluation. In H.F. O'Neil, Jr. (Ed.), *Computer-based instruction* (pp. 161–209). New York: Academic Press.

Bruner, J.S. (1960). *The process of education.* Cambridge, MA: Harvard University Press.

Bunderson, C.V. (1981). Courseware. In H.F. O'Neil, Jr. (Ed.), *Computer-based instruction* (pp. 91–125). New York: Academic Press.

Bunderson, C.V., Inouye, D.K., & Olsen, J.B. (1989). The four generations of computerized educational measurement. In R.L. Linn (Ed.), *Educational measurement* (3rd ed., pp. 367–407). New York: American Council on Education/MacMillan.

Carrier, C.A., & Jonassen, D.H. (1988). Adapting courseware to accommodate individual differences. In D.H. Jonassen (Ed.), *Instructional designs for microcomputer courseware* (pp. 203–226). Hillsdale, NJ: Erlbaum.

Dwyer, T.A. (1981). Some thoughts on computers and greatness in teaching. In J.N. Nazzaro (Ed.), *Computer connections for gifted children and youth* (pp. 71–72). Reston, VA: Council for Exceptional Children.

Foster, W. (1985). Helping a child toward individual excellence. In J.F. Feldhusen (Ed.), *Toward excellence in gifted education* (pp. 135–161). Denver: Love.

Gagné, R.M. (1985). *The conditions of learning* (4th ed.). New York: Holt, Rinehart, and Winston.

Gagné, R.M., & Beard, J.G. (1978). Assessment of learning outcomes. In R. Glaser (Ed.), *Advances in instructional psychology* (Vol. 1, pp. 261–294). Hillsdale, NJ: Erlbaum.

Gagné, R.M., & Briggs, L.J. (1979). *Principles of instructional design* (2nd ed.). New York: Holt, Rinehart, and Winston.

Gallagher, J.J., & Courtright, R.D. (1986). The educational definition of giftedness and its policy implications. In R.J. Sternberg & J.E. Davidson (Eds.), *Conceptions of giftedness* (pp. 93–111). New York: Cambridge University Press.

Greene, M. (1985). Microcomputers: A view from philosophy and the arts. In S. Harlow (Ed.), *Humanistic perspectives on computers in the schools* (pp. 7–17). New York: Haworth.

Gruber, H.E. (1985). The self-construction of the ordinary. In R.J. Sternberg & J.E. Davidson (Eds.), *Conceptions of giftedness* (pp. 247–263). New York: Cambridge University Press.

Hannum, W. (1988). Designing courseware to fit subject matter structure. In D.H. Jonassen (Ed.), *Instructional designs for microcomputer courseware* (pp. 275–296). Hillsdale, NJ: Erlbaum.

Jenkins-Friedman, R. (1982). Myth: Cosmetic use of multiple criteria. *Gifted Child Quarterly, 26,* 24–26.

Jonassen, D.H. (Ed.). (1988a). *Instructional designs for microcomputer courseware.* Hillsdale, NJ: Erlbaum.

Jonassen, D.H. (1988b). Integrating learning strategies into courseware to facilitate deeper processing. In D.J. Jonassen (Ed.), *Instructional designs for microcomputer courseware* (pp. 151–181). Hillsdale, NJ: Erlbaum.

Kanevsky, L. (1985). Computer-based math for gifted students: Comparison of cooperative and competitive strategies. *Journal for the Education of the Gifted, 8*, 239–255.

Mathias, L.J., & Storey, R.F. (1986). Polymer science in a Governor's School. *Journal of Chemical Education, 63*, 424–426.

McCombs, B.L., & McDaniel, M.A. (1981). On the design of adaptive treatments for individualized instructional systems. *Educational Psychologist, 16*, 11–22.

Mistry, J., & Rogoff, B. (1985). A cultural perspective on the development of talent. In F.D. Horowitz & M. O'Brien (Eds.), *The gifted and talented: Developmental perspectives* (pp. 125–144). Washington, DC: American Psychological Association.

Mittler, J.E. (1984). In-service and preservice training. In M.M. Behrmann (Ed.), *Handbook of microcomputers in special education* (pp. 179–192). San Diego: College-Hill Press.

Nazzaro, J.N. (Ed.). (1981). *Computer connections for the gifted children and youth.* Reston, VA: Council for Exceptional Children.

Renzulli, J.S. (1977). *The enrichment triad model: A guide for developing defensible programs for the gifted and talented.* Mansfield, CT: Creative Learning Press.

Renzulli, J.S. (Ed.). (1986). *Systems and models for developing programs for the gifted and talented.* Mansfield Center, CT: Creative Learning Press.

Renzulli, J.S., Smith, L.H., White, A.J., Callahan, C.M., & Hartman, R.K. (1976). *Scales for rating the behavioral characteristics of superior students.* Mansfield Center, CT: Creative Learning Press.

Roblyer, M.D. (1988). Fundamental problems and principles of designing effective courseware. In D.H. Jonassen (Ed.), *Instructional designs for microcomputer courseware* (pp. 7–33). Hillsdale, NJ: Erlbaum.

Ross, S.M., & Morrison, G.R. (1988). Adapting instruction to learner performance and background variables. In D.H. Jonassen (Ed.), *Instructional designs for microcomputer courseware* (pp. 227–245). Hillsdale, NJ: Erlbaum.

Scandura, J.M., & Scandura, A.B. (1988). A structured approach to intelligent tutoring. In D.H. Jonassen (Ed.), *Instructional designs for microcomputer courseware* (pp. 347–379). Hillsdale, NJ: Erlbaum.

Solomon, C. (1986). *Computer environments for children.* Cambridge, MA: The MIT Press.

Stanley, J.C. (1980). On educating the gifted. *Educational Researcher, 9*(3), 8–12.

Steele, K.J., Battista, M.T., & Krockover, G.H. (1982). The effect of microcomputer instruction upon the computer literacy of high ability students. *Gifted Child Quarterly, 26*, 162–164.

Sternberg, R.J., & Davidson, J.E. (1985). Cognitive development in the gifted and talented. In F.D. Horowitz & M. O'Brien (Eds.), *The gifted and talented: Developmental perspectives* (pp. 37–74). Washington, DC: American Psychological Association.

Sternberg, R.J., & Davidson, J.E. (Eds.). (1986). *Conceptions of giftedness*. New York: Cambridge University Press.

Suppes, P. (1980). The future of computers in education. In R.P. Taylor (Ed.), *The computer in the school: Tutor, tool, tutee* (pp. 248–261). New York: Teachers College Press.

Tennyson, R.D., & Christensen, D.L. (1988). MAIS: An intelligent learning system. In D.H. Jonassen (Ed.), *Instructional designs for microcomputer courseware* (pp. 247–274). Hillsdale, NJ: Erlbaum.

Wager, W., & Gagné, R.M. (1988). Designing computer-aided instruction. In D.H. Jonassen (Ed.), *Instructional designs for microcomputer courseware* (pp. 35–60). Hillsdale, NJ: Erlbaum.

Weiss, D.J. (Ed.). (1983). *New horizons in testing: Latent trait theory and computerized adaptive testing*. New York: Academic Press.

9
Future Directions for ICAI

Sharon J. Derry
Department of Psychology
Florida State University

Lois W. Hawkes
Department of Computer Science
Florida State University

In this chapter we advance the argument that development of strategic problem-solving capability is a critical educational goal that can be speeded and enhanced substantially through the application of artificial intelligence to the design of computer-assisted instruction. Specifically, we see the need for intelligent tutoring systems (ITSs) that not only design and present problem-solving tasks compatible with a student's prior knowledge, motivational history, and current instructional goals, but that also can analyze task performance online while the student is solving problems, providing maximally effective guidance, correction, and encouragements directed at improving the problem solving *process*.

In order for an ITS to operate in this sophisticated manner, it must, in some sense, possess all of the following subsystems:

1. An intelligent problem-solving expert that recognizes all feasible plans and strategies possible for any given problem.
2. A sophisticated problem-generation system that can create whatever type of problem the system needs to tutor the student and that matches the student on characteristics such as age, world knowledge, gender, and interests.
3. A multipurpose interface that provides concept-enhancing problem-solving tools for the student to use in solving problems and that also helps make explicit the student's strategies, plans, and misunderstandings.

4. A coaching expert that can recognize and respond not only to correct moves, but also to errors and indicators of motivational breakdowns.
5. A lesson planner that selects problems and instructional routines and assembles them into lessons designed to accomplish instructional goals.
6. A sophisticated student record system for developing and storing student knowledge models and for establishing instructional goals for students.

Machine-based intelligent tutoring systems might eventually achieve remarkable power through integration of all these capabilities. No previous ITS project has yet accomplished this integration, however, and we believe that the primary goal of ITS research in the next five years should be to design a useful microbased intelligent tutor having all subsystems described above. In the sections that follow we share our view of some major issues associated with development and integration of each of these system capabilities.

THE PROBLEM-SOLVING EXPERT

A major part of any ITS is the system expert. The expert "knows" the skills (often expressed as rules) that underlie expert performance in the subject domain, and is able to execute those rules to simulate human expert performance in problem-solving situations.

Within the ITS field, two distinct views to the expert system can be identified. The first is called the *opaque* expert and is one that has expert problem-solving abilities that does not use humanlike reasoning strategies. The other approach, now favored, is the *articulate* expert, that is, one that can explain its problem-solving approach and decisions in a manner comparable to that used by a human expert. It is this latter characteristic that is a necessary knowledge source for tutoring in an ITS and that helps distinguish the ITS expert from the traditional knowledge-based expert system.

Not only must the ITS expert possess a knowledge base that enables both expert performance and articulation of that performance, it also must possess additional domain knowledge that is closely linked to and supportive of any tutoring approach adopted. Since the tutoring strategy (for example, a drill sergeant, cheerleader, collaborator, lecturer, competitor, Socratic tutor, coach [Lepper & Chabay, 1988]) used in an individualized ITS should vary with the student, the curricular goals, and current and past stages in the problem solution, the expert module must contain much additional information needed to support this capability. That is, it must possess those aspects of domain knowledge that enable expert diagnosis of student problems. It is this latter type of knowledge that we propose must be expanded in future ITS experts, which will continue to diverge further and further from the traditional "expert systems" approach. We elaborate on such information briefly below.

All Feasible Solution Plans

ITS researchers have devised various methods for using the expert as a basis for diagnosis and remediation. For example, the expert's execution strategy may be used as a type of template; the model created by the student's execution is "overlayed" onto the expert model to determine those rules that the student did not use and presumably must acquire. Another example approach, stated in general terms, is to compare the student and the expert to determine which skills "deviate" from the expert's.

This diagnostic process is greatly complicated by the fact that different students will approach the same problem in different, although correct, ways. Thus, the expert module must support this versatility in human thinking by being able to produce all acceptable solution paths to any given problem. This is distinct from the traditional expert-system approach, which typically provides one good, if not always optimal, solution.

Evaluation of Various Solution Plans

Associated with each of the solution plans should be some sort of evaluation based on its features, support of curricular goals, and, if possible, the appropriateness for the individual student (an individualization rating). Such information is useful to the tutor when, for example, the student begins to solve a problem in a less than optimal manner. If the student is known to be "very good" at these problems, the tutor may suggest she approach it in another, more efficient way. On the other hand, for a student who previously has had little success with such problems, even a less than optimal approach deserves encouragement.

Metacognitive Data

The term *metacognition* refers to a student's cognitions about the thinking process, as well as the capability to control and evaluate those thinking processes during problem-solving performance. Many metacognitive tasks, such as planning, management of memory overload, and self-checking are performed by human experts without conscious thought and thus have not been captured during the knowledge engineering process that is used to develop the expert system. By the tutor's being able to recognize and prompt when certain metacognitive strategies should be applied, the student can be made aware that such skills could improve her problem solving. In sum, we propose that ITS experts of the future should incorporate metacognitive knowledge.

World Knowledge

Having appropriate world knowledge is often the difference between a correct and incorrect solution. Consider, for example, a word problem that uses the phrase "baker's dozen." Knowing that a "baker's dozen" is 13 rather than 12 would produce a correct (and possibly simple) solution, but lack of this knowledge could confuse the weak student. This type of problem-specific world knowledge should be incorporated into the expert knowledge base. It can allow the tutor to give the proper error diagnosis.

Common Misconceptions

Another type of information is common misconceptions. For example, in word-problem solving, many students believe that particular key words (e.g., "altogether") must always lead to particular operations (e.g., "add"). By incorporating information on common misconceptions, the system expert can help the tutor make faster and more accurate tutoring decisions.

The TAPS Expert

The conceptualization of the ITS expert being advocated is illustrated by the prototype TAPS (Training Arithmetic Problem-solving Skills) Tutor, currently under development in our laboratory. On this system, the student is given a complex word problem and is tutored during the solution process. The role of the expert is to generate, for each problem selected, a problem-specific information source that can be used as a basis for judging and guiding the student's work. The expert receives a problem in parsed form and employs this information to construct a tree of all semantically meaningful solution strategies. Incorporated into the tree for each problem is information concerning what metacognitive skills are needed for successful performance, any world knowledge that might be required, and the common misconceptions known to be associated with particular problem situations.

COMMENTS ON INTERFACE DESIGN

As indicated in Mandl and Lesgold (1988), a major part of an ITS is the interface component that communicates with the student. In many recent

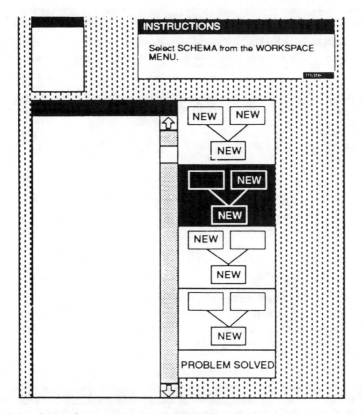

Figure 9.1. **Part of a screen showing TAPS graphics tools for constructing problem trees. Students choose a schema by clicking on it with a mouse and moving it to the workspace.**

systems, such as the TAPS system illustrated in Figures 9.1–9.6, the interface relies heavily on graphics for two reasons. First, recognition of written (typed) and spoken language requires substantial computation and is not yet perfected. Much research remains before natural language processing can become a typical critical addition to ITSs, although this is an important and difficult item on the current research agenda. Second, graphical interfaces are much easier to learn and more user-friendly (Raeder, 1985) than are strictly verbal ones.

Our preference for graphic interface designs is also supported by recent research indicating that a powerful method for helping students reflect upon and analyze problem-solving strategies, both their own and those of experts, is to create systems that allow students and experts to construct graphic representations, or "reifications" of their problem-solving sessions. With this method, computer graphics are used to illuminate the

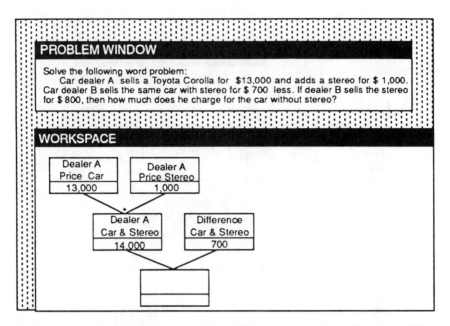

Figure 9.2. Part of TAPS screen showing text presentation of word problems and part of a student solution. The system is performing calculations for the student. The student is labeling sets and selecting operations. (Note that this student appears to be working forward without a plan.)

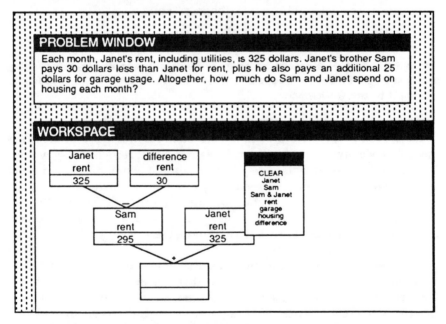

Figure 9.3. Sets are labeled by clicking on a box. A selection of labels appears and the student chooses by pointing with the cursor.

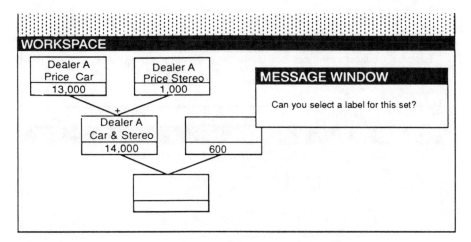

Figure 9.4. Here the system prompts the student to label a set. Labels help the system understand what the student is thinking.

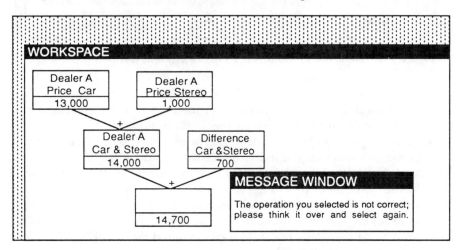

Figure 9.5. Here the system makes a specific correction.

abstract structural relationships implied by different problem-solving strategies, making them visible and physically accessible to students for analysis and manipulation. Graphic tools can be employed by students to aid them in constructing problem representations, or can be used by a system expert as an aid in explaining alternative solution strategies. Graphic reifications also can serve as a basis for helping students pinpoint differences between their own solution approaches and those used by an expert. Anderson, Boyle, and Reiser (1985) have successfully applied this

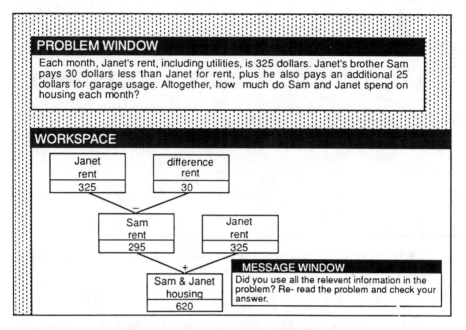

PROBLEM WINDOW

Each month, Janet's rent, including utilities, is 325 dollars. Janet's brother Sam pays 30 dollars less than Janet for rent, plus he also pays an additional 25 dollars for garage usage. Altogether, how much do Sam and Janet spend on housing each month?

WORKSPACE

| Janet rent | difference rent |
| 325 | 30 |

| Sam rent | Janet rent |
| 295 | 325 |

| Sam & Janet housing |
| 620 |

MESSAGE WINDOW

Did you use all the relevent information in the problem? Re- read the problem and check your answer.

Figure 9.6. Here the system "sees" that a student has omitted a step.

method in an intelligent tutoring system for geometry tutoring, and we have implemented a similar idea in the TAPS prototype.

A further enhancement in future interfaces should be the inclusion of intelligence allowing for the individualization of communication. We envision a tutor that will supply generic feedback messages to an interface, which will then deliver those messages in the context vocabulary and syntactic structure appropriate for a particular student. In addition, some history of recent interface messages will be available so that, if a similar prompt is to be repeated, the system can respond more intelligently, for example, "As was mentioned previously,. . . ."

Interface design is an important issue and should be a major focus of future ITS research.

PROBLEM-GENERATION SYSTEM

Part of effective tutoring is the ability to select problems that will support specific curricular goals and motivate individual students. This implies that the problem bank (that part of the system that stores to-be-offered problems) must be much more than simply a problem list.

One way to augment the standard problem bank is to represent classes of structurally isomorphic problems as templates, general schemas that can be instantiated with various objects and numbers, to create many different problems. Not only does this imply significant savings in terms of storage requirements, it helps make the problem bank appropriate for a variety of ability levels; this is accomplished by associating a user dictionary with each class of users and instantiating the problem template from the appropriate dictionary. The tutor can then request a problem with a given degree of structural complexity (for example, in TAPS, a 3-step problem typically solved with two additions and one multiply operation), and with, say, a fifth-grade vocabulary. A college student in a remedial mathematics class could be given the same problem structure but instantiated with a college-level vocabulary.

A problem can further be personalized by matching it to the student's age, sex, and interests, and even including familiar names of friends, family, or pets. And, since each template has the same structure, if the student has difficulty with one type of problem, subsequent problems could be generated from the same template, but with new instantiations.

Incorporated into both templates and user dictionaries could be information supporting the problem-specific knowledge source (PSKS) generated by the expert system. For example, if "baker's dozen" were in the user dictionary, then a definition of the term could be passed to the expert along with the problem parse, for incorporation into the PSKS. The tutor would then have access to this information if the student needed assistance with this point.

COACHING

By what processes do students acquire problem-solving ability and how can this learning be enhanced with particular tutorial strategies? By answering these questions we can determine which instructional methods should be built into an ITS. A thorough treatment of this topic is not possible within the limits of this chapter, but some important principles of tutorial intervention can be overviewed.

Many theories (e.g., Anderson, 1983; Gagné, 1985; Schneider, 1985) acknowledge the extremely important role of practice and experience in acquiring the concepts and skills that underlie complex problem solving performance. According to Anderson (e.g., 1983; Anderson, Boyle, Corkett, & Lewis, 1986), for example, complex bodies of problem-solving knowledge begin as simple, declarative concepts and procedures, as might result from direct didactic instruction. These declarative bits of knowledge gradually evolve through long-term, intensive practice into an integrated system of well-learned concepts and procedures that can be activated accurately and rapidly in response to the cues provided in problem-solving situations.

Complex problem-solving schemas gradually are built up when students repeatedly solve problems in which they combine simpler concepts and procedures. Thus, for instance, many fifth-grade children have acquired a unitized higher-order schema for "buying things." When buying things, one starts with a certain known amount of money from which the total cost of a purchase will be deducted and a certain amount will be left (change schema). The total cost of purchase is determined by adding together the total cost of each item (combine schema). The total cost of each item is determined by multiplying the number of units purchased times the cost of each unit (vary schema).

Of course most problems do not fit neatly into previously learned scripts. Problem representations are seldom handily available, but must be constructed to fit the situation at hand. Nevertheless, schemas are the basic conceptual building blocks of problem-solving activity. We know that experts possess many such schemas, and that this is a major feature that differentiates them from novice performers in all previously studied problem-solving domains (e.g., Simon & Simon, 1978; Larkin, McDermott, Simon, & Simon, 1980).

Unfortunately, building up schema knowledge through practice is known to be a difficult, long-term proposition (e.g., Gagné, 1985). Schneider (e.g., 1985) has demonstrated that literally thousands of practice trials are required to automate even a simple skill, such as responding to a basic relational schema. Considerably more practice is required for development of complex problem-solving approaches.

To promote complex skill acquisition, instructional technologists have long relied on the procedure of offering structured practice with feedback (e.g., R. Gagné, 1985). This classic method, which continues to be widely used, emphasizes the importance of arranging practice exercises to insure that students have mastered elementary prerequisite competencies prior to being presented with the complex problem-solving tasks that employ them. Thus, practice exercises follow an order determined by an instructional analysis that specifies a system of prerequisite competencies and the pedagogical relationships among them. Research in this tradition has shown that mastery-based instructional systems based on task analysis do in fact achieve their objectives.

These are the essential concepts underlying traditional approaches to instructional design, including standard CAI. They are basically sound as far as they go and, as noted by Park, Perez, and Seidel (1987), definitely should not be abandoned. However, recent work in the cognitive science tradition has produced much new knowledge about how problem-solving ability is acquired and many new techniques for facilitating that learning process. As implementation problems associated with these new approaches are worked out and integrated with traditional instructional design theory, substantially more powerful instructional systems will result.

Overview of Some Cognitive Instructional Approaches

One important development is recent research suggesting that traditional practice is not only an inefficient vehicle for learning, but that it may even be detrimental to the acquisition of important problem-solving concepts. For example, in studies by Cooper and Sweller (1987; Sweller & Cooper, 1985), students receiving a modified practice treatment, in which they worked problems after studying an expert's worked examples, acquired and automated more schema knowledge than did students who received traditional problem-solving practice. In explaining their results, these researchers argued that with traditional practice, students tend to employ general problem-solving strategies, such as means-end analysis, to obtain answers to unfamiliar problems. While general strategies may lead to correct solutions, they also tend to exhaust most of a student's available cognitive resources as well as disguise important structural aspects of problems. Thus, they argued, traditional problem-solving exercises can be detrimental to schema acquisition. Worked examples are more successful because this method helps lighten the student's cognitive burden during early learning so that schema acquisition can occur more efficiently.

One problem with the worked examples approach, also pointed out by Chi and Bassok (in press), is that students often do not know what they are supposed to be learning from the worked example. Another problem, particularly acute with less mature students, is that worked examples do not engage the student in activities that focus and motivate attention. Studies in our laboratory demonstrate that a more powerful effect can be obtained if worked examples are supplemented by active tutorial intervention.

Pioneering research on how people think and learn during problem solving (e.g, Anderson, 1983; Anderson et al., 1986; Laird, Newell, & Rosenbloom, 1987; Larkin et al., 1980; Newell & Simon, 1972) has led to development of technologies that permit computers to actually analyze and guide a student's thinking processes during the time that a problem is being solved. Such process-oriented intervention, which can be accomplished on a computer only through the use of AI, is very different from, and much superior to traditional CAI, which provides feedback based on correctness of a student's answer. It is a failing of traditional CAI systems that they must respond to every poor performance with remedial training directed at reviewing all prerequisite concepts and procedures. This is extremely inefficient, since very often the student's primary difficulty is a single troublesome concept, or a self-monitoring or a motivational failure that needs to be addressed in a very specific manner. *Thus, it is a very substantial improvement when an instructional system is able not only to sequence practice exercises with prerequisites in mind, but also to analyze and diagnose specific causes for a student's problem-solving difficulties, and to provide appropriate interventions.*

Pinpointing a student's difficulties, however, does not mean that the tutor should always jump in immediately with explicit corrections and explanations. Rather, many theorists (e.g., Baron, 1981; Baron, Badgio, & Gaskins, 1986; Perkins, 1987; Pressley, Borkowski, & Schneider, 1987) recommended that students be encouraged toward reflective self-evaluation. Reflection is believed not only to improve chances of schema acquisition, but also to encourage the development of general problem-solving strategies and important self-monitoring capabilities. A good method for encouraging reflection is to have a tutor make many general, rather than specific, responses to errors: "Hummmm, are you sure?" "Are you satisfied with that move?" "What is your subgoal here?" "Perhaps you should look at this step again." In our studies with children and adults, general prompting has produced increased sensitivity toward detecting one's own errors.

As previously descried in the section on interface design, another powerful method for helping students reflect upon and analyze problem-solving strategies is to create systems that allow students and experts to construct graphic representaions, or "reifications" of their problem-solving sessions. Graphics tools can be employed by students to aid them in constructing problem representations, or can be used by a system expert as an aid in explaining alternative solution strategies. Graphic reifications also can serve as a basis for helping students pinpoint differences between their own solution approaches and those used by an expert.

Several breakthroughs in instructional technique have been reported by researchers who have studied how self-monitoring skills develop in children through their social interactions with parents, teachers, and other mentors (e.g., Baker & Brown, 1984; Palincsar & Brown, 1983; Palincsar, 1986). One such breakthrough is "cognitive apprenticeship instruction," (Collins, Brown, & Newman, in press), which refers to the sharing of problem-solving experiences between a student and a tutor. The tutor provides overall direction and encouragement, but assumes only that portion of the thinking that currently is too advanced for the student to manage. In early learning, assistance from the tutor enables the student to devote limited working memory to the internalization of critical subskills, while also experiencing the higher-order problem-solving strategies and control processes that are modeled through the tutor's guidance. As the student's problem-solving abilities improve, the tutor gradually fades support, encouraging the student to think independently using strategies and control processes previously modeled. This instructional method has been very successful in improving metacognitive self-monitoring, an important problem-solving capability.

Summary

In the preceding paragraphs we overviewed some representative examples of specific theory-based intervention techniques that have either proved highly effective or that seem highly promising given their sound theoretical support. These include:

1. Structured practice environments that arrange exercises to insure that students have mastered elementary prerequisite competencies prior to being presented with the complex problem-solving tasks that employ them.
2. Cognitive-process technologies whereby a tutor actually analyzes moves and errors made during the time that a probelm is being solved for the purpose of selecting highly specific interventions and corrections.
3. Use of general, rather than specific corrections in cognitive process instruction. This encourages development of self-monitoring skills involved in sensing and locating one's own problem-solving errors.
4. Exposing students to worked examples and models provided by an expert, and encouraging them to reflect upon and attempt to emulate such models.
5. Cognitive apprenticeship, which refers to the sharing of the problem-solving process between a novice and a mentor, such that the mentor removes some of the processing burden from the novice so that a targeted aspect of problem solving can be learned.
6. Graphic reification, which provides a concrete representation of either the expert's or the student's problem-solving session that can be studied, changed and manipulated. Graphic reification can be used as a basis for encouraging the student to reflect upon her own problem solving, to compare personal approaches to those of an expert, and to illustrate the existence of multiple problem-solving strategies for the same problem.

Research by Leinhardt and Greeno (1986) has shown that master human teachers are able to call upon a wide variety of such instructional techniques. We suggest that this idea of multiple teaching strategies will be implemented in future intelligent tutors, giving them the capability of instructing, when appropriate, with all of the techniques described.

LESSON PLANNING

In this section we illustrate how an automated lesson planner might combine multiple instructional strategies to achieve a lesson directed at specific instructional goals. The concept of lesson planning is illustrated with a concrete example based on the TAPS tutor. The type of planning process to be described might actually occur offline. That is, it should be possible to prepare a system for a particular student prior to having that student actually log on, thus significantly reducing waiting time for the student.

A fifth-grade male student is entering the TAPS Tutor for training on how to solve complex arithmetic word problems. Information is passed to a lesson planner by the student record, indicating that he already has achieved two of the system's curriculum goals: Expert level on all 2-step problems representing all possible combinations of the part-whole set relations (combine, change, and compare schemas), and novice mastery on all 2-step problems that include multiplicative structures involving variance (the "vary" schema). Thus, the following currently eligible achievement goals have been posted in the student's record: (a) Achieve novice mastery level for 3-step problems involving part-whole schemas, and (b) achieve expert mastery for 2-step problems involving vary. Since complex problems have not yet been presented, the sytem has not determined the level of the student's skill with planning. However, it has inferred from past performance that the student is "rather poor" in the self-checking department and that the student's motivational level is only "fair."

The lesson planner must now decide which particular goals to work on first. The planner notes from the student record that the last problem-solving session was an expert-mastery drill for 2-step problems involving vary. Employing a variety rule, the planner sets the current lesson goal as achievement of novice mastery on 3-step problems that do not involve vary. The presence of two additional performance goals also are noted: Increase student motivation and promote more self-checking.

The planner seeks to develop a lesson that is compatible with a manageable number of current achievement goals. In this case the planner builds a routine called "Show Me," which requires the student to go through a series of "rounds" that involve (a) observing the expert "think aloud" during a model problem-solving session, and (b) attempting to emulate the expert's performance on a similar problem. By setting performance goals for self-motivation and self-checking, the planner insures that both the think-aloud dialogue during expert demonstrations and the tutorial prompts received during problem solving will focus on self-motivation and self-checking.

Since the student is expected to operate at a novice level in this particular problem-solving routine, the planner sets the coach's initial intervention level at "high," which permits relatively frequent tutorial prompting. To reduce the cognitive burden on the student, the system assumes responsibility for performing all arithmetic calculations and for correcting some types of errors for the student. However, as the coach accumulates information about student performance, the prompting frequency and scaffolding support may be reduced. This would require a capable student to become responsible for more of the problem-solving session.

Both cognitive theories of transfer and common sense suggest that when students are in novice stages of learning, they be given near-transfer problems that are very similar to those demonstrated by the expert. Thus, the lesson planner asks the problem generator to create sets of isomorphically similar 3-step problems. Consulting other information in the student's record, the lesson planner further personalizes the problem request by asking that they be written in the language and context of interest to an elementary-school male.

In sum, the lesson planner first selects from eligible achievement goals (posted in a student record), and establishes a manageable set of instructional goals for the lesson. Goals can be stated in terms of a particular set of skills or ideas that must be acquired (e.g., solving any 3-step problem using backward chaining strategy) at a particular level of expertise (novice or expert). Lesson planning proceeds by devising an instructional routine that is appropriate for the selected goals. An initial level of scaffolding and tutorial intervention is set in accordance with the system's estimate of the student's level of expertise. Based on knowledge of the student available in the student record, a problem set containing problems that the student will practice during the routine is then generated. In general, lessons that aim to promote expertise will employ mostly high-difficulty problems that have great structural variety, while novice problem sets are characterized by less structural variety and lower difficulties.

TUTORIAL DECISION MAKING

We distinguish between two types of instructional decision making and two associated types of student modeling that take place in TAPS and other ITSs in general (Derry, Hawkes, & Ziegler, 1988). One type is global planning, whereby the system selects instructional goals, lesson plans, and problems fitted for a particular student. Global decision making is guided by the student's knowledge model, stored in a student record (the "SR"). The second type is local tutoring, whereby the system coaches the student by responding to errors and other moves made during a lesson's problem-solving exercises. This type of decision is made largely on the basis of the system's model of the student's knowledge model, housed in the SR. In the following paragraphs we will describe how fuzzy representation techniques are being used to enhance both types of diagnostic modeling in the TAPS tutor. Prior to describing these methods, it is necessary to present a brief overview of fuzzy terminology.

Fuzzy Theory: A Brief Overview

In classic set theory an item either belongs totally to a set or it does not belong to that set at all. In other words the membership question is a binary decision with a clear YES/NO answer. An element cannot partially belong to a set. In fuzzy set theory (Zadeh, 1965) an element is allowed to belong only partially to a set. The change from membership in the set to nonmembership becomes gradual rather than strictly binary. Fuzzy set theory is then a generalization of abstract set theory. This is an important concept in capturing the different aspects of vagueness inherent in real world data. There is the inherent vagueness of classification terms referring to a continuous scale, the uncertainty of linguistic terms such as "I almost agree" or the vagueness of terms of concepts due to variability in communication (Zemankova-Leech & Kandel, 1984). Fuzzy set theory is an attempt to provide a systematic and sound basis for the modeling of these types of imprecision which are mainly due to a lack of well-defined boundaries for elements belonging to a set of objects.

Let us consider the problem of determining if a person is intelligent. Someone with an IQ of 85 will not be considered intelligent by most people. Adding one point to his IQ should not have a strong influence on the decision whether the person is intelligent or not. Thus we conclude that a person who has an IQ of 86 is still considered not intelligent. If a system repeats the same idea iteratively, it might conclude incorrectly that a person with an IQ of 100 is not intelligent. Thus there is need for gradual measures of membership of people in the set of *intelligent people*.

In ordinary set theory some arbitrary cut point would have to be found, for example, IQ 100, under which people are unintelligent and over which people are intelligent. A more elegant approach to determining the set of *intelligent people* uses fuzzy set theory. In such a solution one might say that people with an IQ of 100 were fairly intelligent and allow them a grade of membership of 0.8 in our set where membership values are in the range of [0,1]; the boundary values are the crisp values of classical set theory. This intuitively seems to be much more acceptable.

The use of fuzzy terms allows for imprecision and vagueness in the values stored in a database. This provides a flexible and realistic representation that easily captures the way in which the human tutor might evaluate a student. Representing the student as a network of "tick-marks" (Ohlsson, 1986) or discrete yes/no classifications is unrealistic. A human does not, in general, want to deal with numeric values, but prefers to express himself in vague linguistic terms such as "quite high," "possibly," "not likely," and so on. For example, a student could be described as being "very good" at multiplication problems but "rather weak" with division problems. Because many tutoring decisions are not clearcut ones, the capability of dealing with imprecision is a definite enhancement to ITSs. Examples of how the fuzzy approach can be used in future ITSs (in particular in the student record and by the tutor) are given below.

Local Diagnosis in TAPS

Numerous researchers have demonstrated that expert word-problem comprehension is a constructive process that involves recognizing, linking, and operating upon goal-relevant set relations ("schemas") represented in word-problem statements (e.g., Derry, Hawkes, & Tsai, 1987; Marshall, Pribe, & Smith, 1987; Kintsch & Greeno, 1985; Riley, Greeno, & Heller, 1983; Vergnaud, 1982, 1983). During TAPS tutorials, students develop this skill by "constructing" problem solutions on line. The interface is designed so that the student must solve each problem by selecting, labeling, and linking simple relational schemas, thus creating an explicit graphic reification illustrating the problem-solving proces in detail. Our approach uses windows, a mouse, and graphics tools that students can manipulate, because this style of interface requires no natural language processing or keyboard input yet creates an extremely detailed trace of the problem-solving process. Readers are again referred to the screen displays of Figures 9.1–9.6.

The student's performance is monitored through a process of comparing the student's evolving construction to an AND/OR tree of all semantically meaningful solution approaches generated by the system's expert. The monitor builds a trace by identifying the student's strategy (if one is evident), then classifying each of the student's steps as either a good move that matches the tree (good schema), or as a particular type of deviation error. For example, a student may leave out a calculational step (e.g., omit schema), insert a schema for a subgoal not present in the solution tree (e.g., bad schema/subgoal error), or incorrectly label a set (e.g., bad label).

Fuzzy pattern-matching techniques are useful since there are many points in tutoring that can produce imprecise data and since many local decisions are inherently imprecise. We have found 34 specific ways in which a student's move can deviate from what is circumscribed by the expert tree, these error types having been determined from studies of 128 think-aloud protocols obtained from children and young adults (Derry, Hawkes, & Ziegler, 1989). In practice, however, some matching to error types is inexact in the sense that the system may not always be certain when a particular error has occurred.

For example, if a student omits needed schemas from a solution, the tutor may not be able to determine for certain whether the student is exhibiting a lack of planning knowledge, a self-monitoring deficit, or both. However, using fuzzy techniques, the tutor can combine error data with other information to infer the likelihood that this particular performance is a member of certain error categories, such as "bad planning" and "bad self-monitoring." Once any category exceeds a minimum fuzzy value, the tutor can respond with an appropriate message. If during any session the fuzzy value drops below a designated threshold, the tutor no longer responds toward that error category.

To supply another example, suppose a student gives a particular set an imprecise label that is essentially correct (e.g., labeling a set as "Jan's marbles" when what is meant is "Jan's red marbles"). This may not be an error, although our research has shown that imprecise labeling can sometimes indicate overgeneralization, a significant source of difficulty for weaker students. Thus, an imprecise label has some possibility of being a "bad label error," particularly for the weaker student.

In most systems the tutor would have to decide whether the deviation belonged or did not belong to the pattern "bad label." The membership question is necessarily a binary decision with a clear YES/NO answer. Using fuzzy pattern matching, however, elements are allowed to reflect uncertainty by belonging only partially to a set. The grade of membership in a category incorporates a confidence evaluation of the correctness of the classification. Thus, for example, a student move can have a grade of membership of .75 in the set "bad label," where membership values are in the range of $[0,1]$. In fuzzy linguistic terms, this could be expressed as "A bad label error is 'rather likely,' in this case."

Fuzzy decisions can be clarified by the availability of historical data. For example, the tutor often needs to discriminate "slips" from true knowledge deficits, as a less intrusive tutorial response is made for slips. This inference can be made easily when historical performance data are available. A technique for making these data available is incorporated into our method for modeling the student's knowledge, which is discussed next.

STUDENT KNOWLEDGE MODELS AS A CONTEXT FOR TUTORIAL DECISION MAKING

Student knowledge models represents the system's current estimate of the student's abilities within the domain being tutored. Such knowledge models, when housed in a student record, can provide a major source of information for enhancing many decisions made by an ITS. However, most current ITSs still have "generalized" student models which represent a type of student rather than a particular one. None of the current systems (for example, the Lisp Tutor (e.g., Anderson & Skwarecki, 1986), BUGGY (Burton, 1982), WUSOR (Goldstein, 1982) have fully addressed this issue of individualization.

In TAPS, student knowledge models are stored in an intelligent Fuzzy Temporal Relational Database (IFTReD), a tool that provides a structure for incorporating current and historical information on individual students' knowledge, performance capabilities, instructional goals, and so on. This approach to knowledge modeling differs from its predecessors in several significant ways.

First, the approach is based on a relational representation, which has several advantages over other database representation techniques (Rundensteiner, 1987; Tanimoto, 1987). Unlike semantic nets, for example, when the size of a relational database increases, retrieval time does not increase, a significant issue in maintaining response times. Also, the relational model is associated with a set of well-defined operators (a relational algebra) that permit extremely flexible data manipulation and facilitate both high-level retrieval and development of friendly query languages.

Extending the basic relational approach so that the SR can contain fuzzy data entries, the ITS also is able to make good use of the imprecise, incomplete, or vague information that often is acquired through noisy tutoring channels. Furthermore, fuzzy categories can be translated easily into imprecise linguistic terms which can be manipulated with relational operators. This is convenient, since an ITS can be programmed to make judgements similar to that of a human. There are many instances in which human tutors make judgements based on such fuzzy knowledge. For example, a human tutor might say, "Jane usually performs very well on these types of problems, although her last performance was rather poor." In this sense, our system deals with noise in diagnostic data, not by trying to eliminate it entirely, which is impossible, but by creating a system that does not fail when it experiences a realistic degree of fuzziness.

Another enhancement was a temporal extension, which addresses the issue of how to store models representing different phases in student learning and development. This is necessary for effective tutoring at the global level, because the student does not always have a consistent performance. A poor performance may represent a bad day and thus should not unduly bias selection of future instructional goals and problems. Storing information over time also makes a useful research tool, since it allows for comparison and analysis of students' performance changes. Thus the actual effectiveness of the system as a tutor can be verified.

A final enhancement to the SR was incorporation of a fuzzy expert system. The SR houses the system's holistic knowledge about individual students. In reality, the human tutor is not only aware of each student's skills and abilities, but also must constantly form new impressions through analyses of each student's work and through inferences drawn from knowledge about the student. In TAPS, such reasoning is performed by the student record manager, a fuzzy expert system which serves as an interface between the SR and other ITS subsystems.

For example, at the end of each tutoring session (i.e., student is no longer on the system), the ITS sends protocols collected from the tutoring session to the SR manager. The SR manager performs a global diagnosis by matching this information to known performance patterns (fuzzy pattern matching) until a determination is made regarding the student's new knowledge state and the student's new instructional goals. The SR manager determines which items in the SR, including instructional goals, should be updated and makes appropriate changes. Later this information is utilized by the system to plan lessons that meet the student's individual needs. New data are made available for the tutor at the beginning of the student's next tutoring session.

Associating intelligence directly with the student record is an innovation, as most ITSs limit intelligence to the expert model and the instructional modules. Such an improvement is possible since most analyses are conducted off-line and hence do not affect response times.

In sum, TAPS combines the use of fuzzy error categories at the local tutoring level, with fuzzy data entries, temporal enhancement, and a user-friendly retrieval language associated with the student record. These permit a flexible and realistic representation that helps capture the way in which a human teacher might view a student. A human does not, in general, want to deal with numeric values, but prefers to make decisions based on fuzzy, linguistic terms such as "quite good," "possibly will be able to work this," "not likely to be successful," and so on. Our goal is to allow researchers, teachers, programmers, and the ITS itself to communicate and "think" in these humanlike imprecise linguistic terms. Most human tutoring decisions are not clear-cut ones and the capability of being able to model this type of decision making should be a feature of intelligent tutoring sytems.

THE ITS OF THE FUTURE:
SUMMARY AND CONCLUSIONS

The ITS of the near future will be very powerful and will have many capabilities. For example, it will be able to vary the difficulty of its problems and tutoring routines to meet the instructional need of students ranging from grades 4 through remedial college level. Also, like an expert human tutor, the intelligent machine-based tutor will be capable of many different instructional strategies and routines known to enhance learning. For example, one system might support worked examples with expert modeling, graphic reification of problem-solving processes, gradually fading scaffolding, and experimentation with alternative solution strategies.

Future ITSs will be capable of several forms of dialogue. For example, as systems construct problem solutions, they will present dialogue describing and modeling an expert's thinking processes during problem solving. The student will be able to request help if any part of an explanation is unclear. ITSs also will be able to recognize and respond to many categories of student moves, so that personalized coaching will be offered to every student. Coaching will be varied in frequency and detail depending upon the student's abilities, thereby providing different levels of helpful scaffolding.

The ITS of the future also will be capable of requesting from the student information regarding the student's problem-solving plan. That is, the student can be asked to tell the tutor what goals and subgoals it will have for a particular problem. The tutor will be able to recognize incomplete and inaccurate plans, and to correct the student's plan. The system also will be able to use the student's plan to support interpretation of the student's problem-solving moves.

Another aspect of system versatility will be its modularity. That is, researchers will be able to design new instructional routines that make use of other system modules (e.g., system expert, student record, interface), but that do not require reprogramming of those modules. Systems will also permit a number of friendly user queries by the teacher.

The ideas described in this chapter could not be implemented without advanced technology. It would be extremely difficult for any traditional system, including a human tutor, to fully engineer the practice environment so that exactly the right problem-solving exercises are received at precisely the time when the student is ready to learn them. It would be difficult indeed for the traditional system to generate the many hundreds of practice problems that would be required, and much more difficult to provide them in a systematically controlled order. Neither human tutors nor traditional instructional systems can store and query detailed models of each student's current knowledge state for the purpose of instantly tailoring problem-solving exercises designed to remediate missing or weak knowledge components.

Finally, in addition to being able to engineer a complex practice environment that neither the traditional CAI system nor the human tutor can manage, an ITS can support many forms of representation that can be accomplished through other media only with great difficulty. Neither pencil-and-paper, nor concrete tools, nor standard video, nor traditional CAI can approach the usability, versatility, and power of ITS graphics for illustrating the concepts and processes of problem solving, making them visibly and physically accessible to students for reflection, exploration, and manipulation.

REFERENCES

Anderson, J.R. (1983). *The architecture of cognition.* Cambridge, MA: Harvard University Press.

Anderson, J.R., Boyle, C.F., Corbett, A., & Lewis, M. (1986). *Cognitive modelling and intelligent tutoring* (Tech. Rep. No. ONR-86-1). Pittsburgh: Carnegie-Mellon University.

Anderson, J.R., Boyle, C.F., & Reiser, J.F. (1985). Intelligent tutoring systems. *Science, 228,* 456–468.

Anderson, J.R., & Skwarecki, E. (1986). The automated tutoring of introductory computer programming. *Communications of ACM, 19*(9), 842–849.

Baron, J. (1981). Reflective thinking as a goal of education. *Intelligence, 5,* 291–309.

Baker, L., & Brown, A.L. (1984). Metacognitive skills and reading. In D. Pearson, R. Barr, M. Kamil, & P Mosenthal (Eds.), *Handbook of reading research* (pp. 353–394). New York: Longman.

Burton, R.R. (1982). Diagnosing bugs in a simple procedural skill. In D. Sleeman & J.S. Brown (Eds.), *Intelligent tutoring systems* (pp. 157–184). Academic Press.

Chi, M., & Bassok, M. (in press). Learning from examples via self-explanations. In L.B. Resnick (Ed.), *Knowing and learning: Issues for a cognitive psychology of instruction.* Hillsdale, NJ: Erlbaum.

Collins, A., Brown, J.S., & Newman, S.E. (in press). Cognitive apprenticeship: Teaching the craft of reading, writing, and mathematics. In L.B. Resnick (Ed.), *Knowing and learning: Issues for a cognitive psychology of instruction.* Hillsdale, NJ: Erlbaum.

Cooper, G., & Sweller, J. (1987). Effects of schema acquisition and rule automation on mathematical problem-solving transfer. *Journal of Educational Psychology, 79,* 347–362.

Derry, S.J., Hawkes, L., & Ziegler, U. (1988). A plan-based opportunistic architecture for intelligent tutoring. *Proceedings, ITS88* (pp. 116–123). Montreal Canada.

Derry, S.J., Hawkes, L., & Ziegler, U. (1989, March). *Characterizing the problem solver: A system for on-line error detection.* Paper presented at AERA annual meeting, San Francisco, CA.

Derry, S.J., Hawkes, L.W., & Tsai, C. (1987). A theory for remediating problem-solving skills of older children and adults. *Educational Psychologist, 22,* 55–87.

Gagné, E.D. (1985). *The cognitive psychology of school learning.* Boston: Little Brown & Company.

Gagné, R.M. (1985). *The conditions of learning* (4th ed.). New York: Holt, Rinehart, & Winston.

Goldstein, I. (1982). The genetic graph: a representation for the evolution of procedural knowledge. In D. Sleeman & F.S. Brown (Eds.), *Intelligent tutoring systems* (pp. 51–78). London: Academic Press.

Kintsch, W., & Greeno, J.G. (1985). Understanding and solving word arithmetic problems. *Psychological Review, 92,* 109–129.

Laird, J.E., Newell, A., & Rosenbloom, P.S. (1987). Soar: An architecture for general intelligence. *Artificial Intelligence, 22,* 1–64.

Larkin, J.H., McDermott, J., Simon, D.P., & Simon, H.A. (1980). Models of competence in solving physics problems. *Cognitive Science, 4,* 314–345.

Lepper, M.R., & Chabay, R.W. (1988). Socializing the intelligent tutor: Bringing empathy to computer tutors. In H. Mandl & A. Lesgold (Eds.), *Learning issues for intelligent tutoring systems.* New York: Springer-Verlag.

Leinhardt, G., & Greeno, J.G. (1986). The cognitive skill of teaching. *Journal of Educational Psychology, 78*(2), 75–95.

Mandl, H., & Lesgold, A. (Eds.). (1988). *Learning issues for intelligent tutoring systems.* New York: Springer-Verlag.

Marshall, S.P., Pribe, C.A., & Smith, J.D. (1987, March). *Schema knowledge structures for representing and understanding arithmetic story problems* (Contract No. N00014-85-K-0661). San Diego, CA: Center for Research in Mathematics and Science Education.

Newell, A., & Simon, H.A. (1972). *Human problem solving.* Englewood Cliffs, NJ: Prentice-Hall.

Ohlsson, S. (1986). Some principles of intelligent tutoring. *Instructional Science, 14.*

Palincsar, A.S. (1986). The role of dialogue in providing scaffolded instruction. *Educational Psychologist, 21*(1,2), 73–99.

Palincsar, A.S., & Brown, A.L. (1983). *Reciprocal teaching of comprehension monitoring activities* (Tech. Rep. No. 269). Urbana, IL: Center for the Study of Reading, University of Illinois.

Park, O., Perez, R.S., & Seidel, R.J. (1987). Intelligent CAI: Old wine in new bottles, or a new vintage? In G. Kearsley (Ed.), *Artificial intelligence and instruction: Applications and methods.* Reading, MA: Addison-Wesley.

Perkins, D. (1987). *Knowledge as design.* Presented at The Third National Thinking Skills Conference, Cincinnati, OH.

Pressley, M., Borkowski, J.G., & Schneider, W. (1987). Cognitive strategies: Good strategy users coordinate metacognition and knowledge. In R. Vasta & G. Whitehurst (Eds.), *Annals of Child Development, 4,* 80–129. Greenwich, CT: JAI Press.

Raeder, G. (1985, August). A survey of current graphical programming techniques. *IEEE Computer,* pp. 11–25.

Riley, M.S., Greeno, J.G., & Heller, J.I. (1983). Development of children's problem-solving ability in arithmetic. In H.P. Ginsberg (Ed.), *The development of mathematical thinking* (pp. 153–192). New York: Academic Press.

Rundensteiner, E.A. (1987). *The development of a fuzzy temporal relational database (FTRDB): An artificial intelligence application.* Master's thesis, The Florida State University, Tallahassee, FL.

Schneider, W. (1985). Training high performance skills: Fallacies and guidelines. *Human Factors, 27,* 285–300.

Simon, D.P., & Simon, H.A. (1978). Individual differences in solving physics problems. In R. Siegler (Ed.), *Children's thinking: What develops?* Hillsdale, NJ: Erlbaum.

Sweller, J., & Cooper, G.A. (1985). The use of worked examples as a substitute for problem solving in learning algebra. *Cognition and Instruction, 2,* 59–89.

Tanimoto, S.L. (1987). *The elements of artificial intelligence: An introduction using LISP.* Rockville, MD: Computer Science Press.

Vergnaud, G. (1982). A classification of cognitive tasks and operations of thought involved in addition and subtraction problems. In T.P. Carpenter, J.M. Moser, & T.A. Romberg (Eds.), *Addition and subtraction: A cognitive perspective* (pp. 39–59). Hillsdale, NJ: Erlbaum.

Vergnaud, G. (1983). Multiplicative structures. In R. Lesh & M. Landau (Eds.), *Acquisition of mathematics concepts and processes* (pp. 127–172). New York: Academic Press.

Zadeh, L.A. (1965). Fuzzy sets. *Information and Control, 8,* 338–353.

Zemankova-Leech, M., & Kandel, A. (1984). *Fuzzy relational data bases—A key to expert systems.* Koln: Verlag TNV Rheinland.

10
Challenges of Computer-Based Instruction in a Large Urban School District: The Los Angeles Unified School District

Joel A. Colbert
California State University,
Dominguez Hills

INTRODUCTION

There are myriad challenges to designing, implementing, monitoring, and evaluating a computer-based instructional program in any educational setting. However, in a large urban school district, the challenges are compounded by a variety of factors, not the least of which is the sheer size of the district. In addition to size, such factors as assessing needs, planning and organizing instructional programs for a diverse cultural setting, sociopolitics, geography, approval procedures, consistency, and articulation pose unique problems for large school districts. In the present case, the computer-based instructional program in the Los Angeles Unified School District will be examined in light of these and other concerns.

This chapter discusses several important topics: First, the problems with implementing computer-based instruction are identified. Second, the Los Angeles Unified School District is described to provide a context for the reader. Third, relevant literature on computer usage in schools is reviewed. Fourth, the District's computer-based education plan is summarized. Fifth, the constraints of the implementation of computer-based

175

instruction in this large urban school district are discussed. Sixth, further directions and recommendations are offered. Finally, a model for implementing computer-based instruction in a large urban school district is presented.

Statement of the Problem

The problems addressed in this chapter focus on implementing computer-based instruction in a large, urban school district. They include logistical problems, for example, size of the district and procedures associated with the district's bureaucracy; sociopolitical problems, for example, external pressures and school readiness for computers; needs assessment and program planning, especially in such a culturally diverse district as Los Angeles; consistency throughout the district; and, articulation between feeder schools and across the regions into which the district is divided.

Background of the Los Angeles Unified School District

The Los Angeles Unified School District, the second largest public school district in the United States with 644 schools, covers a total area of 708 square miles. There are approximately 600,000 students and over 32,000 teachers. The District is divided into eight geographic regions that include elementary and junior high schools, and four districtwide divisions: the senior high schools, special education, adult education, and child care. The responsibility for computer-based instruction falls into the domain of the Information Services Division (ISD), working collaboratively with the Office of Instruction and the Professional Development Branch. The ISD is charged with integrating computers into all phases of instruction, as well as managing all administrative applications and maintenance of computers.

Although microcomputers have been used in Los Angeles Unified School District classrooms for over 10 years, it wasn't until 1984 that the Computer Education Foundation Program (CEFP), under the auspices of the District's Office of Instruction, implemented a systematic approach to integrating microcomputers into all phases of instruction. This plan resulted from the publication of *Computer Literacy and the Use of Microcomputers in Instruction,* a needs assessment and position statement written by Dr. Robert Baker and Dr. James Taylor (1984). The use of microcomputers in the schools was, for the most part, left up to the individual school or teacher prior to the CEFP.

RELATED LITERATURE
ON COMPUTER USAGE IN SCHOOLS

The number of microcomputers in schools throughout the United States has increased from 292,000 in 1982 to approximately 1.4 million in 1986 (Mothner, 1987). The number of microcomputers has doubled every year since 1984 (Bork, 1987). *Electronic Learning Magazine's* (Mothner, 1987) sixth annual survey of the United States reported that 96 percent of all public schools in the United States had microcomputers. California has been a leader in this growth.

However, not all of the news about computer usage in schools has been good. Data from the National Assessment of Educational Progress (1986), report, *Computer Competence: The First National Assessment,* revealed some interesting, yet dour findings. For example, in their sample of over 24,000 students nationwide, about one-third had *never* used computers in class. At the elementary level (grade three), 47 percent had not used computers in their mathematics class, 75 percent had not used a computer in English, 87 percent had not used one in science, and 88 percent had not used a computer in social studies. At the junior high level (grade seven), over 60 percent had not used a computer in mathematics, over 75 percent had not used one in English, 88 percent had not used one in science, and about 90 percent had not used a computer in social studies. Furthermore, about 70 percent of the 11th graders surveyed had never used a computer in their mathematics class, 85 percent had not used one in their English class, 85 percent had not used a computer in their science class, and over 95 percent had not used one in their social studies class. However, the majority of students had used computers to play games. The NAEP report concluded that computers are used frequently to play games, but infrequently to develop subject matter skills and knowledge.

Rampy, White, and Rockman (1986) presented 21 critical issues for making policy decisions concerning computers in schools. Several of these issues are important in the present case and will be addressed in later sections. For example, what roles do computers have in the school curriculum? Is it necessary for students to become computer literate rather than competent users of computers? How should resources be allocated to ensure equal educational access to computers? How can educational agencies encourage realistic and reasonable plans and expectations related to the use of computers? What computer training should be required for teachers and administrators? What standards should be established for purchasing hardware and software?

Mothner (1987) stated that it is moot to ask in the 1980s whether or not the computer ought to be used in education. The critical question is *how* to use computers effectively in educational programs. The National Council of Teachers in Mathematics (1980) stressed computer literacy as an essential outcome of contemporary education. All students need firsthand experiences with both the capabilities and limitations of computers. Until the 1980s, computer-based instruction focused on teaching about the computer itself, not on how to use the computer in all areas of the curriculum. During the past three years, this focus has shifted so that educators are now perceiving the computer as an important tool for supporting instruction across all content areas.

In *Policy Recommendations for Developing Appropriate Uses of Technology in California Schools,* an unpublished study, Pogrow (1987) discussed several problems with the current direction of technology use in California.

Pogrow first focused on the common practice of "diffusing technology as widely as possible," that is, teaching every grade level and every classroom, sacrificing quality implementation, and minimizing opportunities to enhance student learning. Pogrow focused next on the restriction schools experience on the range of educational practices that can be implemented. Because most instructional strategies related to computer education have not been validated by research, and because the diffusion network throughout California is so broad, the harm done to education is probably equal to the good accomplished in the schools. Pogrow then bemoans "widespread training in widely advocated, but unproven techniques." Many of the instructional strategies in use are not validated by research, yet the training provided in these strategies is widespread and readily available. Finally, Pogrow criticized the lack of interest in the proven technology of distance learning, for example, instructional television, satellite transmissions, and others, which has tremendous educational implications. Computer technology, only one of the many forms of technology with potential educational applications, has received most of the attention.

Pogrow made several recommendations. First, California needs to make more targeted use of pilot projects with careful evaluation procedures. Second, educational leaders should provide technology selectively to teachers who have the desire and ability to use it most effectively. Third, Pogrow advocated emphasizing methodologies for "teaching as a process." Fourth, Pogrow stressed improved curriculum development techniques. Fifth, he believed that California should empower Teacher Education and Computer Centers (TECC) to work with general education evaluators. Sixth, TECC staff should be trained in the importance of avoiding specialization and building on the general use of technology to enhance learning. These two recommendations are moot since the TECCs closed in July 1987 as a result of extensive state budgets cuts. Finally, Pogrow recommended developing stimulating new uses of technology, for example, distance learning and telecommunications.

The explosion of technology in California schools was triggered by Assembly Bill 803 (AB 803), state legislation which provided guidelines and funding for the adoption/adaption of technology across the state. Wulf (1987), in studying the impact of AB 803 funding in Los Angeles County, delineated four major areas of inquiry:

1. To identify factors to explain the variation of success of AB 803 implementation, particularly with regard to the implementation of technology in the classroom.
2. To sample and analyze perceptions about the relative impact of AB 803 on classroom instruction.
3. To identify the range of new technologies now available in school instruction as a result of AB 803.
4. To develop baseline data for making recommendations regarding staff development for teachers and adminstrators in planning and implementing new technology.

Wulf found that:

1. Equipment, mostly computer systems and printers, was introduced to sites that did not have any prior to AB 803.
2. Schools reporting successful implementation of programs funded by AB 803 shared specific characteristics related to student and teacher behavior. These schools reported a high level of teacher motivation, a high level of staff training, improved student test scores, critical thinking/problem solving as the area in which technology is most successfully utilized, and use of technology to teach new concepts.
3. Teacher competence in the use of technology in the classroom situation was an important factor in the implementation of AB 803. Schools reported the following: positive teacher and principal attitudes toward the AB 803 project; a high commitment to AB 803 goals by both teachers and principals; enough funding to achieve stated goals; and, a low level of difficulty in implementation. In addition, students' achievement on criterion referenced tests improved rapidly as the result of AB 803 project implementation because of the change in instructional activities.

Wulf made the following recommendations:

1. Assistance should be provided to local sites to focus proposals on specific instructional objectives for student and teacher outcomes.
2. Local site administration and faculty should be given the opportunity for ownership.
3. Staff development, both in quality and quantity, should be provided.

Another phase of AB 803 was the Technology in the Curriculum Projects, which were implemented in 1986. These projects were designed to:

> help teachers use technology and extend their existing curricula. The primary purpose was to organize information about computer and video programs to serve as a tool for teaching content in mathematics, science, history–social science, and language arts. The projects identified parts of the curriculum best taught electronically or visually and high quality software and video programs available to teach the content. They have designed sample lesson plans that teachers may want to incorporate into their teaching repertoire. (California State Department of Education, 1986)

Every public school in the state of California received a selection of software and resource guides to help teachers integrate technology in the Curriculum Projects into their instructional plans. In Los Angeles, the County Office of Education coordinated the efforts of individual districts to implement the projects. In the Los Angeles Unified School District, advisors for the Computer Education Foundation Program and the Professional Development Center, in collaboration with KLCS Channel 58, the District's instructional television station, produced a 30-minute television program describing the Technology in the Curriculum Projects, with suggestions for implementation, that was shown in every school in the district. In addition, inservice classes were conducted districtwide to disseminate information and training in the appropriate use of Technology in the Curriculum strategies.

THE LOS ANGELES UNIFIED SCHOOL DISTRICT COMPUTER EDUCATION PROGRAM

Computer Education Foundation Program

The District's Computer Education Foundation Program (CEFP), initiated in 1984, is divided into elementary and secondary level components. At the elementary school level, the computer education program begins in the fifth grade and emphasizes mathematical concepts using the computer language, LOGO, and language arts concepts, using the word processor in the commercial software package, *AppleWorks*. In addition, computers are integrated into as many subject areas as possible, and after-school computer clubs provide for enrichment activities. At the secondary level, a District *Continuum of Skills* established a course of study for junior high and senior high students. Included are course outlines for *Introduction to Computers*, a required course at the junior high level, and optional courses in programming and information processing. Additional elective classes include computer programming, Advanced Placement computer science, word processing, data processing, and digital computer technology.

Before the CEFP was implemented, each region established a training center consisting of 16 computers. These sites have served as local training sites for teachers and administrators.

Because of the District's size, each year, beginning in 1984, one-third of the schools were phased into the program, with hardware (one Apple IIc microcomputer and printer) and software (LOGO and *AppleWorks*) provided for every fifth grade classroom, and fully equipped computer laboratories (30 Apple IIc microcomputers, five printers, and software including AppleWorks, BASIC and/or PASCAL) at junior and senior high schools. School selection criteria during 1984–85 included the following: schools willing to participate, recipients of Chapter I funding, largely minority schools, year-round schools, schools with existing but limited hardware, and schools with grade-level continuity between elementary and secondary levels. During 1985–86, another one-third of the District's schools were included, with the final one-third included in 1986–87. Staff development has been provided for both administrators and teachers as part of the implementation. In addition, a District Task Force has monitored and has evaluated all aspects of the program.

There were other factors that facilitated the integration of computers into instruction. First, computer companies such as Apple and IBM initiated "educator buy programs" that reduced the price of hardware and software for classroom and personal use. Second, with the state-funded program, AB 803, discussed previously, it was much easier for schools to apply for and receive, through a competitive proposal process, both technology and the training to initiate its use. As a result, schools that were in the final year of the District's program were able to get a head start and begin integrating technology into the instructional program before receiving their District allocation. In addition, since there were many District-sponsored training programs available, teachers were receiving computer education training before the technology arrived at their schools. These factors greatly accelerated the introduction of computers into the schools from 1985 through 1987.

One of the major concerns with the implementation of the CEFP was equity, that is, did all schools in the District, particularly those in low socioeconomic areas, have equal access to computer-based instruction? This was addressed by the District in several ways. First, schools who received Chapter I funding were given high priority in the implementation process; that is, were phased in sooner than schools who did not receive Chapter I funds. In fact, Chapter I schools had a head start on computer use, using them during the last 1970s and early 1980s for remediation in mathematics and English. Therefore, in these schools, there was most likely a computer literate teacher who had years of experience with using computers in instruction, albeit in a limited capacity, that is, remediation. One example was a large high school in south central Los Angeles in which the author taught. In 1978, there was a complete Chapter I computer lab, with a full-time instructor, for remediation in English and math, with hundreds of students receiving instruction on computers each week. Furthermore, the science department had at least six computers for use in chemistry and physics instruction at that time. Second, with the advent of such state legislated programs as AB 803, all schools, regardless of community socioeconomic level, could receive ample funding to initiate computer-based training. One of the criteria of AB 803 was that equal access be addressed in the proposal and therefore, included in the school's plan.

Phase I of the CEFP was completed at the conclusion of the 1986–87 school year. Implemented during the 1987–88 school year, Phase II sought to broaden the use of microcomputers to support instruction by centering on school level instructional development projects. These projects, in turn, served as models for possible Districtwide expansion of computer use in instruction. At the elementary and secondary levels, additional staff development was provided using a training-of-trainers format. In secondary schools, support continued for all school-based computer teachers. Staff development topics for Phase II stressed infusing all areas of instruction with computers, with emphasis on language arts and mathematics at the elementary level, and with language arts and writing at the secondary level. Phase III, implemented at the beginning of the 1988–89 school year expanded Phase II.

The priorities for instructional development projects were as follows: developing a sixth-grade writing project; an elementary mathematics project; a bilingual/ESL computer-based writing project; the Year 2000 Project, focusing on language arts; IBM's Writing To Read Project (kindergarten and first grade) at selected elementary sites; a secondary writing project; a secondary journalism-graphics arts project; and the Model Technology Schools project that includes an elementary, junior high, senior high cluster and articulates the integration of technology across grade levels and schools. The Los Angeles Unified School District was one of only five Model Technology projects funded statewide. The purpose was to develop an articulated program within a school complex that integrated technology into all areas of instruction. Additional staff development opportunities are being provided for teachers and administrators at participating schools.

Software Evaluation

Software evaluation is conducted by the District's Textbook Services division. Each year, teachers are recruited from each region/division in the

District to serve on a committee to evaluate educational software. There are both elementary and secondary committees. Software vendors supply copies of their software for review.

There is a systematic process involved in the evaluation of educational software. The teachers who serve on the software evaluation committees meet for two or three days. They only review software in the content area that they teach, or in the case of elementary programs, in the subject area that they have the most experience. Training is provided in the criteria for evaluating the software to insure reliability. These criteria include: readability, appropriateness for grade level and subject area, program content, instructional design, ease of use, management, motivation, technical aspects, and ancillary materials.

Descriptions of the software receiving the highest evaluations are then compiled into a publication and distributed to all schools. In addition, there is a software preview lab for individuals to review software on a walk-in basis. The lab operates in conjunction with the District's textbook/instructional materials preview center.

Training-of-Trainers

A comprehensive training-of-trainers program was initiated in 1985 by the staffs at the District's Professional Development Branch and Los Angeles County Teacher Education and Computer Center. This program consisted of three components. The first component reviewed the content and current philosophy of computer use in education as well as methods for conducting effective staff development sessions. To accomplish this, demonstration lessons were taught by the program facilitators and then critiqued by the facilitators and participants. The participants assessed their own leadership style and built a group dynamic by using small group, team-building activities. Building trust among program participants provided the climate for the giving and accepting of feedback and the development of the skills necessary to plan and conduct effective staff development programs. Further, guided lesson preparation with constructive, nonevaluative feedback prepared participants for the second phase of training, the responsibility of designing a two-day workshop focusing on a computer related topic. Teams of three of four were responsible for conducting one component of the two-day workshop. The teams presented their "lessons" to the entire group, with constructive feedback from facilitators and participants. This portion of phase one provided low-risk practice for the participants.

In the second phase of the training, the participants applied their phase one experiences. This was accomplished by having them share training responsibilities in a District inservice workshop on computer applications in instruction. In terms of three or four, participants assumed responsibility for conducting one component of the workshop. Another team served as "coaches," observing the training and providing feedback. Each team served as both trainers and coaches. Thus, maximum learning transfer was achieved with each participant giving and receiving helpful feedback.

Finally, the participants returned to their regions/divisions to deliver training. During the summers of 1987 and 1988 alone, over 80 computer-related inservice classes were held throughout the Los Angeles area with 1600 participants. The facilitators and team members continued to support the new trainers by providing advice, as well as assistance in the preparation of proven instructional materials. The classes that were conducted included: Introduction to Computers in Education, Educational Software Review, Introduction to AppleWorks, Intermediate AppleWorks, Advanced AppleWorks, Database Applications, LOGO in the Elementary Classroom, BASIC Programming, Introduction to the Macintosh Computer, and Desktop Publishing.

Extensive evaluation data were collected during the training-of-trainers program and at the conclusion of inservice classes conducted by these trainers. Where necessary, facilitators provided assistance to the trainers. Using this model, a cadre of computer education inservice class leaders have been trained to conduct a wide variety of successful inservice classes in the District. Furthermore, each region/division throughout the District has conducted its own extensive inservice training in a variety of areas, one of which is computer education. Each year, region/division inservice advisors coordinate with CEFP and Professional Development Branch staff to plan and conduct computer related inservice classes for certified and classified personnel, as well as for teacher aides and parents. Trainers for these classes have been largely those who participated in the training-of-trainers program before its demise due to extensive budget cuts in 1987.

Conclusion

Based on extensive evaluation data collected by the District's Research and Evaluation branch, the Computer Education Foundation Program and related computer education services were found to be very successful. Every school in the District now has uniform hardware and software standard, described previously, with staff development and inservice programs based on these standards. In secondary schools, the program has been particularly effective because there is a teacher available who specializes in computer instruction. Although research has not been done to compare computer-based instruction in the District with the findings from the National Assessment of Educational Progress (1986), at the very least, every fifth-grade teacher in the District uses microcomputers in instruction and every junior high and senior high student takes an introductory computer class. Further research needs to be done to assess the degree to which computers are used in the content areas. Also, there are over 150 different languages spoken in the LAUSD. For example, there is an elementary school where the predominant language is Armenian and many schools where the primary language is Spanish, Korean, Japanese, or Chinese. Research needs to be done on the extent and ease of implementation of CBI at schools where language could be a barrier to the implementation and integration of CBI into the curriculum. To date, this has not been evaluated. The next section discusses the challenges to implementing the computer education program in the District.

CHALLENGES AND CONSTRAINTS

The findings by Wulf (1987), Pogrow (1987), the NAEP (1986), and others, underscore challenges and constraints which surfaced during the past four years of implementation of computer-based education in the Los Angeles Unified School District, suggesting five significant areas that need to be addressed: size and logistics, sociopolitical factors, articulation, consistency, and decision making.

Size and Logistics

The first major constraint concerns the sheer size of the District and the concomitant logistical issues that have resulted. Such constraints include alterations to schools, equipment setup, security, training staff, implementation monitoring, and impact evaluation. Each year one-third of the schools, over 200, participated in the implementation of the CEFP. Schools were chosen, not by geographic region, but on the basis of established criteria described previously. Since the District is so large, that is, over 700 square miles, this created problems since schools selected for implementation were located many miles apart and within very unique geographical and cultural settings. This led to both logistical problems, such as installation of equipment and training, and evaluation concerns, since there wasn't adequate staff to monitor and followup the implementation of the CEFP.

Each secondary school required extensive alterations to the school plant. These alterations involved adjustments in electrical wiring, and installation of security windows, doors, new furniture, and new door locks. The average cost for the room alterations was $5,000.00. There are 72 junior high schools and 49 senior high schools in the LAUSD. Therefore, the approximate cost for room alterations to secondary schools alone was over $600,000. The quality of implementation suffered because of the urgency to equip all of the schools, exemplifying Pogrow's concern about sacrificing quality for quantity. For instance, there were quality control problems with room alterations, installing security windows and doors, and long delays in rewiring. In addition, there were hardware and software problems, for example, partial shipments and delays in purchasing and delivery.

School staffs were given only one 16-hour staff development session initially and were presumed to be competent to use the new technology immediately with their students, contrary to the research findings of Fuller (1969), Hall (1975), and others, that adopting an innovation is a slow process, frequently taking three to five years for full implementation. The initial 16-hour training class consisted of manual operation of the computers, an introduction to *AppleWorks* (an integrated word processor, database, and spreadsheet program), and programming in LOGO for elementary teachers and BASIC for secondary teachers. While there were additional opportunities for staff to receive supplementary training, in many instances they did not. For example, elementary teachers are required to teach 13 different subjects, and many simply did not have the time to sufficiently learn how to integrate computers into their instructional routine. Upon returning to their classrooms, with only 16 hours of training, many teachers did not feel comfortable with the hardware and software. The result was that materials were not used appropriately, frustration resulted, and in some instances, the use of the technology was discontinued, underscoring Pogrow's conclusion that mass diffusion of computer education in schools is a noble idea in concept only.

There was a Phase II training program instituted during 1986 that provided followup to the initial training teachers received. However, while the initial training was required, Phase II was voluntary. Phase II training consisted of several classes: *Intermediate AppleWorks,* with an emphasis on integrating *AppleWorks* into instruction (separate elementary and secondary classes), *Integrating LOGO into Instruction* (elementary), and *Integrating BASIC into Instruction.* Although several hundred teachers participated, Phase II training did not reach the tremendous number of teachers who needed it most, that is, those who lacked confidence and experience in using computers in their classrooms. This was due, in part, to the fact that these classes were only offered after school or on weekends and not on District time.

Each region should have had a staff member who had responsibility for providing support and assistance to teachers by going to schools and doing model lessons, helping teachers develop materials, and conducting miniworkshops. These "advisors" could then have met with central staff regularly to provide formative evaluation data and to consider revising components of the program, where needed.

Sociopolitical Factors

In a District as large and diverse as the LAUSD there are myriad sociopolitical factors influencing policy decisions and implementation of programs. These factors included: lobbying efforts by computer manufacturers; special interest groups external to the District; groups of teachers and administrators within the District; local corporations who "adopt" schools; state legislation; and state department of education policy resulting from legislation.

For example, in the early stages of implementation, there were no official policies concerning program design, hence, groups of teachers with experience in computers wanted to insure that their special interest(s) were addressed, for example, defining the phrase "computer literacy"; deciding which computer language would be used at the elementary and secondary levels; and deciding which hardware and software would be included in the computer education plan. An illustration of this was one particular high school that received funding through one of the state legislated programs and purchased equipment and software that was not compatible with each other—the result being some very frustrating training sessions with incompatible hardware and software and no additional funds to rectify the problem until the next year of funding.

Another illustration, described earlier, was legislation such as AB 803, local adaption/adoption grants to integrate technology into instruction. Schools were strongly encouraged to write AB 803 proposals, even if a particular school felt that there wasn't the need or interest. There were several cycles of AB 803 funding, and towards the end of the program, schools who had not applied were pressured into doing so by region and District level administrators. The result was that faculty and/or administrators were not committed to the program, and if they received funding, the technology was not integrated as it was supposed to be and interest waned quickly. Today, there are schools in the District who still have not committed to using computers in instruction even though they have the hardware and software readily available. What made matters worse was that there was no formative and summative evaluation of AB 803 programs, even though such a plan had to be written in the proposal. With the large turnover of administrators and teachers in the schools, it was common for these projects to be neglected or lowered in priority as changes in staff occurred.

Articulation

The second constraint is articulation, that is, there is often a lack of continuity between the participating secondary schools and their feeder elementary schools. This lack of continuity is not limited to computer-based instruction. Elementary schools, the junior high schools that they send students to, and the senior high schools that complete the cluster rarely articulate with each other, regardless of the content area or program. Furthermore, thousands of students are bussed to other regions in the District as a result of federal mandates and overcrowding, compounding this concern.

Part of the problem centered in the selection process, precluding the selection of a complete set of schools, that is, feeder elementary, junior high, and senior high. With different schools participating in different years, it was apparent that the schools would be at different levels of implementation of computer-based instruction.

Another concern in the area of articulation is the commitment of the administration and faculty to computer-based instruction. For example, if there was strong commitment and a well developed computer-based instructional program at an elementary school, but little to none at the junior high school that the elementary school fed into, both students and parents felt frustrated. The result was pressure applied by parents and region/District administrators to integrate computers into instruction whether or not the school had administrators and faculty who were properly trained or even interested in such innovations.

To illustrate, in one region of the District, there is a school complex with a strong CBI progam in the elementary schools and the high school, but a very weak program at the junior high. This has greatly limited the degree and ease of implementing CBI at the high school because the high school faculty have to cover content that should have been included in the junior high but was not. For example, junior high students would normally be trained in the use of data bases, spreadsheets, and programming BASIC. However, the junior high principal was not computer literate and had a different set of priorities. The consequence was that CBI was given a very low status and did not provide the degree of training necessary to propel students into the high school CBI program.

Additionally, the teacher and administrator turnover rate at schools, which could be quite high at some of the large urban schools, further limited articulation. Thus, the initial program design contributed to the confusion. It may have been advantageous, in each region/division, to identify a small cluster of schools that was relatively stable and to conduct intensive training and development of the computer education program. Working on a smaller scale, with close and systematic articulation between each school cluster, would have provided a much more controlled environment in which to monitor and assess implementation of the program. Currently, the Model Technology Schools Project, which is part of the AB 803 legislation described previously, is addressing this concern. One school complex, consisting of two elementary schools, one junior high school, and one senior high school, is developing and implementing a computer-based instructional program that permeates all areas of instruction and is articulated between grade levels and among schools in the complex.

Consistency

The third constraint is consistency. There are many units within the District that conduct their own distinctive computer education programs. The Computer Education Program conducts staff development sessions. The regions/divisions hold inservice classes to supplement Computer Education Program programs. The Professional Development Center conducts extensive inservice activities on an individual basis and in cooperation with the Computer Education Program and regions/divisions. Outside vendors conduct their own training sessions to familiarize District staff with their hardware and software. The Computer Using Educators organization also offers programs. The list goes on. The result is that, while there is a potpourri of activities available to teachers, there is a lack of consistency districtwide. When the training-of-trainers program, described previously, was in operation, there was consistency in computer education training programs. However, when statewide budget cuts occurred in 1987, the problem of consistency resurfaced. Again, inservice has wide diffusion without equally wide quality implementation. Further exacerbating this concern was the lack of training for administrators. Initially, principals and co-administrators only received a cursory "awareness" session, during which the computer education program was described and a brief "hands-on" introduction to microcomputers was conducted. There simply was not enough training for administrators resulting in limited commitment, and as a result, a lack of consistency within and between schools. It wasn't until 1987–88 that administrator training in computers was initiated, and conducted on a voluntary basis to new site level administrators. There was no training available for experienced administrators. The primary purpose of these training sessions was to introduce the use of computers for administrative functions, so computer-based instruction again was not the priority. Since these training sessions were voluntary, only those who were interested or already knowledgeable participated. The total number of participants during 1987–88 was less than 100 although there are over 3000 administrators in the LAUSD.

The District intended, with the formulation of the policy to provide for the CEFP, quality implementation with mass diffusion. However, in a district as massive as the Los Angeles Unified School District, what has resulted has been more of a focus on quantity rather than quality.

Decision Making

The fourth major constraint is the decision-making process itself. There are many levels of decision-making units within the District. Therefore, before any final decision is made, data are gathered from a wide variety of sources. The data are then assessed, policy is formulated and approved by the Board of Education, and finally, policy is implemented. It can take many weeks from the time data are gathered until the Board acts. The purchasing of a standard hardware package for the schools can provide an example. State law mandates that a bid process be employed when such large scale purchases are made. Vendors such as IBM, Apple, and Tandy submit hardware for evaluation by District staff, including teachers. After evaluation, recommendations are made to the Information Services Division, which reviews, refines, and sends the recommendations to the superintendent, who further refines the report for Board consideration. After careful analysis and many hours of testimony by District staff, the Board makes the final decision. This process, which allows for input by District staff, is comprehensive, thorough, and time consuming.

RECOMMENDATIONS AND CONCLUSIONS

Coordination

There are several recommendations for improving the quality of implementation of computer-based instruction in the Los Angeles Unified School District. First, one unit or branch empowered with the responsibility of administering computer-based instruction throughout the District, with equal representation from instruction, information services, professional development, and region/division staffs, would streamline implementation of computer-based instruction. However, overall administration of the proposed unit would be the responsibility of the instructional branch. Such centralization would provide a coordinated effort from all parties involved and ensure quality implementation, articulation, consistency, and timely decision making. In July, 1988, the responsibility for computer-based instruction was consolidated, with the District's Information Services Division, not the instructional branch, assuming responsibility for instructional applications of computers, management of information systems, and maintenance of all hardware. However, there have been some concerns generated over this shift in responsibility. First, can instruction be adequately addressed by staff from Information Services, without direct input from Office of Instruction staff? While meetings have been conducted to establish a collaborative effort, only time will reveal if such a collegial atmosphere exists. Second, now that the responsibility for computer education has been transferred from the Office of Instruction to Information Services, can collaboration between two administratiave branches be accomplished? Again, only time will tell. Third, the relationship with hardware and software vendors will change. The Computer Education Program has worked with staff from Apple Computer to establish a uniform program utilizing Apple IIc and Apple IIe computers for instruction in all of the schools. Information Services has a longstanding commitment and relationship with IBM. Now that Information Services administers computer-based instruction, how will this change in the relationship between the District and computer vendors affect and impact instruction? In addition, this central unit could address the issues presented by Wulf (1987) and Pogrow (1987). First, this unit could assist schools and regions in focusing on specific instructional objectives by helping schools to conduct an individualized needs assessment. A key element in schools qualifying for an AB 803 grant, the needs assessment, revealed a wide variety of needs, emphasizing the fact that schools differ. In fact, of the schools participating in computer-based instruction, only those schools which applied for AB 803 funding conducted need assessment as part of the grant application process. Second, this centralized unit could address the issue of quality versus quantity, that is, coordinating computer-based educational activities to assure quality implementation instead of mass diffusion.

The second level of coordination would be at the region. Since the schools in each geographic region have unique needs, advisory committees, consisting of faculty, administrators, and parents, should be formed with the responsibility of overseeing computer-based instructional activities within the region. Representatives from these advisory committees would then meet regularly with central office staff for overall program coordination.

Decision Making

The second recommendation relates to the decision-making process. Because hardware and software represent a high-cost area, the purchasing process could be refined to maintain current thoroughness and to reduce time-consuming steps. The central unit charged with administering computer-based instruction, as proposed above, could be charged with establishing committees to evaluate technology-related purchases, calling upon those with expertise to serve as consultants. There is already a precedent for such a system in the District. When Districtwide policies are under consideration, region/division administrators often select representatives to serve on committees. In the past, this was not done for computer-based instructional purchases. The Office of Instruction's CEFP and the Information Services Division were the two administrative branches which scrutinized hardware and software purchase orders and participated in such decision-making capacities. There were teachers and administrators selected to serve on the committees, but input was not districtwide. Although such a committee with members from each geographic region would be cumbersome, considering the diverse nature and size of Los Angeles Unified School District, adequate representation would provide needed thoroughness. Committees such as these serve in other capacities, for example, textbook evaluations, software evaluation, and mentor teacher selection. As a microcosm of the District, such a committee could make important and timely decisions.

Training

The third recommendation focuses on training. Wulf (1987) recommended sufficient staff development, both in quality and in quantity. Again, basing this recommendation on individual school needs would ensure local school implementation of the total program. Computer-based instruction training must be planned, conducted, and evaluated in a collaborative manner, considering the needs of each school, focusing on objectives proposed by the school staff, and coordinated by the unit charged with providing the training. Again, having a central unit charged with such coordination ensures that the needs of each staff member at the school are met. Needs assessment and consistency in the training can thus provide necessary scaffolding for the instructional program at each participating school.

One of the ways to provide the type of training recommended above is to restore the training-of-trainers program that was eliminated in 1987. There can be consistent and quality training only when those charged with computer-based instruction who have expertise in staff development and human resources plan and conduct programs to train inservice leaders.

Articulation

Articulation is the final area of consideration. Continuity between elementary and secondary schools is a critical factor contributing to the success or failure of the total instructional program. A comprehensive approach with workshops, staff development, meetings, and so on, can provide opportunities for staff members to work on articulation. While this has been done on a limited basis in other content areas, such as mathematics, language arts, and social studies, it is even more important with computer-based instruction because of the speed at which technology is developing and permeating instruction in all content areas. Board policy must be adopted and sufficient funds allocated to provide the kind of training imperative for all students in the 1990's. Such training must also focus on other important related areas as well, for example, team building, leadership, and decision making. A total District effort is needed to ensure efficient infusion of technology for instructional purposes and for managing information.

During the past four years, computer-based instruction has been integrated into all areas of the curriculum in the Los Angeles Unified School District. While every school in the District now has computers, printers, and videocassette recorders, the degree of implementation varies not only by region/division, but by school. Wulf (1987) found that such factors as teacher morale, administrator involvement, and training, differentiated schools with a high degree of implementation of computer-based instruction from those that had a low degree of implementation. A coordinated effort to provide consistent, uniform, and efficient integration of computer-based instruction into our schools could provide all students with equal access to quality education.

A MODEL FOR CBT IMPLEMENTATION
IN AN URBAN SETTING

In the preceding pages, one district's attempt to implement computer-based instruction on a widespread basis was discussed. The problems and challenges associated with this endeavor were presented, as well as recommendations for refining the program. In this final section, a model for implementing and disseminating such a program will be described based on the lessons that were learned. While such a program will have different aspects depending on the context in which it is conceived and implemented, there are some generic steps that can be developed, regardless of setting. These steps will be delineated here.

Needs Assessment

Perhaps the most crucial step in any CBI project is to conduct a thorough needs assessment prior to any formulation of policy. Needs assessment data should focus on the unique qualities of each school and region and concentrate on subject areas where computer-based instruction can have the greatest impact, for example, by examining students scores on standardized tests. This investigation should be coordinated by the district's instructional office and research branch, but the data analysis and subsequent program development must be conducted at the school or region level. For a successful implementation, participating schools must demonstrate both commitment and ownership to the program.

Program Development

It is suggested that district-level policy be broad enough to address the unique needs of schools and geographic regions. Rather than mandating the same program districtwide, funds should be made available for each geographic region within the district to design and implement its own computer-based instructional program. A school and regionwide committee, with a majority of teachers, should formulate the region plan and submit it to the central administration for approval, similar to what is done on a state level with grant programs such as AB 803, described earlier. Furthermore, the district's Professional Development Branch can serve in a consultative manner, working with committees and subcommittees to design an effective plan for each school. Plans should be made for at least three to five years to provide enough time for smooth implementation, with ample formative evaluation data collected regularly, and with revisions or refinements made as needed. Summative evaluation should also be an important component of the plan to assess the program's impact.

Hardware and Software

Large school districts must use standard procedures in the procurement of major equipment purchases. However, there should be ample opportunities for teachers to evaluate equipment and provide input into the selection process. The LAUSD did this with both hardware and software and the results have paid off substantially. The software evaluation procedures described earlier are an excellent example of involving teachers in the decision-making process. Similarly, schools should select software to reflect the greatest needs of students. This could be accomplished by reviewing students' scores on standardized tests and selecting software to address the areas where scores are lowest.

What has been frustrating in the Los Angeles Unified School District is the amount of time it takes to repair hardware when it breaks down. Typically, it can take six weeks to two months for technicians to diagnose and remedy a problem. As of 1988, there were only four Apple technicians covering the entire school district. Maintenance logistics is a serious problem that needs to be addressed early in program development. If the commitment is made to implement computer-based instruction districtwide, then there must be efficient and effective maintenance provided.

Training

Effective and appropriate training is a key element to the success of any program. The staff development branch, working collaboratively with instructional units, should design and conduct inservice classes that can best meet the needs of faculty, administrators, staff, and parents. The key here is that training must be based on needs, as expressed by faculty, not mandated by district offices. In addition to learning how to use micro-computers and evaluate software, sufficient time should be spent "role modeling" educational software in the classroom using the district's teacher directed lesson format. The training-of-trainers program, described previously, did just that and was very effective in producing a cadre of trainers who conducted effective inservice classes for their regions/divisions.

There should be training programs for faculty, administrators, parents, and ancillary staff. Microcomputers should be incorporated into the total operation of the school and training programs developed to address key issues in doing so. Principals and co-administrators need to know how to use microcomputers in administrative and instructional settings so that the usefulness of computers in all phases of school operation can be maximized. Likewise, teachers, parents, and ancillary personnel have unique needs that can be met using computers and appropriate inservice classes should be developed to do so. However, it is critical that the design of such programs be done in a *collaborative* manner, incorporating the ideas and strategies of the target audience. Finally, training should take place on district time, not after school and/or on weekends. During the Los Angeles District's initial training, inservice classes were held after work and on Saturdays, which resulted in many negative comments regarding the training schedule.

Mass Diffusion

As described by Pogrow (1987), the common practice of "diffusing technology as widely as possible," while sacrificing quality implementation for quantity, is a critical area that needs to be addressed. Wulf (1987), in her recommendations, stated that CBI assistance should be provided on a local basis focusing on specific needs and objectives with involvement, ownership, and the commitment of the administration, faculty, and community. In any CBI program, sufficient funds and personnel need to be available to provide a focused, quality program with formative evaluation data collected and analysed regularly and revisions made where appropriate and when needed.

Articulation

There needs to be careful attention paid to articulating programs between the elementary and secondary schools within a geographic region, particularly between the elementary, junior high, and senior high schools that comprise a feeder school complex. Committees of teachers, administrators, and parents within a given school cluster, that is, elementary and junior high feeders and high school, need to meet regularly to insure that there is continuity between schools and programs. Responsibility for monitoring articulation should be at the region office, with a reporting procedure to the appropriate district office charged with overall administration. This was not done consistently in the LAUSD. However, where this was done, the implementation of CBI was much more efficiently and effectively accomplished.

Decision Making

The overall responsibility for implementing computer-based instruction should belong to a district's instructional unit, working collaboratively with those offices who impact computer usage in the District, for example, information services. Each geographic region within the district should have a committee charged with designing, implementing, and monitoring computer-based instruction within that region. This committee should be composed of a majority of teachers, but should also include administrators and parents. The research and evaluation branch can also provide input into the design of a diagnostic, formative, and summative evaluation plan to assess the impact of computer-based instruction on the individual schools and region. It is the responsibility of the instructional unit to report to the superintendent and board of education and to facilitate implementation of the program with the regions. In this way, the unique needs of each school/region can be met with a tailor-made program, yet it can be monitored and evaluated by central administrative staff. If teachers, administrators, and parents are equally involved in the decision-making process from beginning to end, the chances of success are greatly enhanced.

REFERENCES

Baker, R., & Taylor, J. (1984). *Computer literacy and the use of microcomputers in instruction.* Unpublished manuscript, Los Angeles Unified School District, Los Angeles, CA.

Bork, A. (1987). *Learning with computers.* New York: Harper and Row.

California State Department of Education. (1986). *Technology in the curriculum resource guide.* Sacramento, CA: California State Department of Education.

Cheever, D.S., Coburn, P., DiGiammarino, F., Kelman, P., Lowd, B.T., Naiman, A., Sayer, G.A., Temkin, K., & Zimmerman, I.K. (1986). *School administrator's guide to computers in education.* Reading, MA: Addison-Wesley.

Fuller, F.F. (1969). Concerns of teachers: A developmental conceptualization. *American Educational Research Journal, 6*(2), 207–226.

Grady, D. (1988, September). Giving teachers their due. *Phi Delta Kappan, 70*(1), 31.

Hall, G. (1975, November). *The effects of "change" on teachers and professors— Theory, research, and implications for decision-makers.* Paper presented at the National Invitational Conference on Research on Teachers Effects: An Examination by Policy-Makers and Researchers, Austin, TX.

Holmes, G. (1982). Computer-assisted instruction: A discussion of some of the issues for the would be implementors. *Educational Technology, 22*(9), 7–13.

LaPointe, A.E. (1988, September). Aims, equity, and access in computer education. *Phi Delta Kappan, 70*(1), 59–61.

Los Angeles Unified School District. (1984, October). *Computer education foundation program.* Unpublished manuscript, Los Angeles Unified School District, Los Angeles, CA.

Los Angeles Unified School District. (1987). *Plan for computer education 1987–88.* Unpublished manuscript, Los Angeles Unified School District, Los Angeles, CA.

Mothner, H.D. (1987). *The perceived effect of educational technology legislation on Los Angeles county school districts.* Unpublished doctoral dissertation, University of Southern California, Los Angeles.

National Assessment of Educational Progress. (1986). *Computer competence: The first national assessment.* Princeton, NJ: National Assessment of Educational Progress, Educational Testing Service.

National Council of Teachers of Mathematics. (1980, May). Position statement. *The Mathematics Teachers,* p. 468.

Pogrow, S. (1987). *Policy recommendations for developing appropriate uses of technology in California schools.* Unpublished manuscript, University of Arizona, Tuscon, AZ.

Rampy, L., White, D.J., & Rockman, S. (1986). Computers in the schools: 21 Critical Issues for Policy Decisions. In T.R. Cannings & S.W. Brown (Eds.), *The information age classroom: Using the computer as a tool* (pp. 26–29). Irvine, CA: Franklin, Beedle, and Associates. (Reprinted from *Educational Technology,* August, 1983)

Wulf, K.M. (1987, September). *An impact study of AB 803 funding in Los Angeles county, 1985–86: Executive summary.* Unpublished document, Region 12 Teacher Education and Computer Center, Downey, CA.

11
Practitioners' Perspectives of Computers in the Classroom

Charles W. Schultz
Nancy Higginbotham-Wheat

The proliferation of computers has changed the focus of education in our schools, and knowledge of computers is no longer superfluous but necessary for someone graduating from high school or college in the 1990s. We as educators have spent millions of dollars on computer equipment only to find many students who have little if any computer experience to show for such a large investment. The problem is best explained by Knupfer (1988) when she said that "computers will not live up to their full potential in the public schools until teachers accept them as a valuable part of the school curriculum, and have enough training and equipment to properly implement them" (p. 30). Furthermore, she points out that most research confirms that teacher perceptions about educational computing are critical to the success of any implementation of innovation or change. Even if change is instituted and heartily endorsed by school administrators, it is bound to fail if the classroom teacher does not perceive it as meaningful to the current classroom environment. Our experience indicates that how teachers perceive their roles as teachers is a critical factor in the success of the implementation process. If teachers can go beyond the role of imparter of information to the role of mentor and guide, successful implementation can be accomplished.

The purpose of this chapter is to examine the implementation process through exploring the problems and frustations experienced by the classroom teacher, by examining the problems of the technology itself (hardware and software), evaluating teacher reactions, and finally offering suggestions to help school systems implement a successful program for using computers in the school. The authors are both former classroom teachers. Charles Schultz taught high school social studies for nine years in inner-city schools, and was chairman of the social studies department for three years. He also taught computer literacy, led faculty workshops on using microcomputers, and organized a program that allowed students free access and support in the computer laboratory after school. Nancy Higginbotham-Wheat taught high school English in inner-city schools for seven years and biology and chemistry in a suburban private school for seven years. She chaired the science department and was instrumental in the implementation of a computer-assisted science program during her tenure.

IMPLEMENTING NEW TECHNOLOGY

Since the early 1970s school systems have spent about $2 billion for 1.7 million computers, and have increased their budgets accordingly each year to try to accommodate the current demand. Last year alone schools spent $153 million on software (Adams, 1989). Although this appears to be an extraordinary amount budgeted for the "latest electronic fad," Richard Adams (1989) maintains that computer expenditures make up only 0.4 percent of a typical state budget. For this investment, however, we cannot show great strides in academic achievement being made for our efforts. The problem begins with implementing state mandates on the local level. Computers arrive at the schools in nice white boxes only to be stored for an indefinite period until they can be assembled. Assembly is often haphazard at best, with parts and equipment mismatched or incorrectly assembled. Further evidence of poor planning is reflected in the fact that as recently as 1983, 37 percent of the elementary schools owning microcomputers did not have disk drives, rendering them useless for instructional purposes (Becker, 1985). Once the machines are up and running, we encountered a lack of professional support for teachers who were interested in using computers in their classrooms. This begins the cycle of teacher/computer problems that leaves many teachers with anger and frustration at the machines (and administrators) before they are ever used the first time! An excellent example of the frustrations experienced by teachers began when the administration implemented the computer education program at Charles' ghetto school. The physical education department was "blessed" with the dubious duty of teaching computer classes. Although the physical education department was to use a state-mandated curriculum (which initially consisted of computer history), there was no one in that department who had any computer experience!

PROBLEMS WITH HARDWARE

After assembly, the question arises of where to place the microcomputers. Computer rooms or laboratories provide maximum protection against theft and vandalism, but problems with scheduling, implementation activities, and easy access for teachers and students alike quickly appear. With centralization there is a tendency for one person to become the resident expert in each school, and the microcomputers will sit idle more often than if a team approach is used to set up and implement a computer program for the school. According to Becker's (1985) survey, the latter method more than doubles the amount of time computers are actively engaged.

Computers can also be placed in school libraries, but this method seems to have had a mixed impact, with elementary schools being least effective (Becker, 1985). Rotating computers from room to room seems to have a positive effect, but security of equipment can quickly become a problem. Due to these same security problems, access to microcomputers was extremely limited at Charles' inner-city junior high school. The only computers in the building were located in the library or computer laboratory, and only two other teachers had keys to provide access. Security was such a constant problem that keeping computers in classrooms could never be considered due to the number of burglaries that occurred every year. Vandalism of hardware was not a major problem, but replacing software (lost or damaged from excessive use) was difficult because of a limited school budget. The most effective method of placement must be one that allows the classroom teacher free access to integrate computer usage into daily activities (Shavelson, Winkler, Stasz, & Robyn, 1983).

Yet fear and apathy can stifle the learning process for teachers as well as students. This fear arose from such teacher misconceptions as "I will be replaced by the machine...this is just more work...too close to retirement to begin learning again...computers are only for the mathematically-oriented student." For example, Charles was asked to teach a computer literacy course for teachers at his school and had rather disappointing results. When the class was mandatory, the teachers were constantly disrupting the class. When it became voluntary, few attended. After surveying the faculty he discovered that few teachers thought computers were important enough to "waste their time" with. After all, it was just another fad, was it not? To be effectively incorporated into daily activities, computers must be viewed by the teacher not as competition, but rather as another instructional tool that is a basic part of modern educational technology used in the classroom (Winkler, Shavelson, Stasz, & Robyn, 1983). With this in mind, however, central districts still find it easiest to implement lab type planning (compared to being placed in libraries or classrooms) at both the junior and senior high levels (Shavel-son et al., 1983).

PROBLEMS WITH SOFTWARE

Technology, it seems, can live up to its promise, but it has outpaced our ability to use it (Foster, 1988). The problem with software appears to center around who is developing it and how well it is being designed. In general, a substantial investment in time and money must be made not only to research and develop a product, but to create the market to support such enormous expenditures. According to Fisher (1982), this new market has two main groups developing software: educational publishers and computer manufacturers.

Publishers seem to think they can easily go into the software market because they supply books and have preestablished avenues for distribution. Much of the software developed, however, ignores the learning process while becoming increasingly more expensive (Knupfer, 1986). According to Fisher (1982), educational publishers "tend to focus on getting their product on the market quickly to meet the demands of a computer-hungry public before they lose their place in the education market. As a result, the publishers frequently end up by just putting their own textbooks on line" (p. 23).

Computer manufacturers must also share part of the blame, for they understand how computers work and are aware of the unique attributes that make them ideal for a variety of educational activties, such as individualization, simulation, and tutoring. Yet these same manufacturers seem to lack the vision necessary to be the pioneers of new innovations for using the computer as an educational tool in the classroom.

In general, commercial software appears to use a rather narrow pedagogy (Knupfer, 1982), which stems from the fact that the best computer minds are in research laboratories and seem totally unconcerned about producing a marketable product (Fisher, 1982). Much of the software that we see on the market today does not apply the principles that these researchers have develboped. Much has been done to add sparkle and make the product marketable, but not enough has been done with the design of the actual instruction. For example, the use of color in screen design of software has been studied extensively (Christ, 1975; Christ & Corso, 1983; Tullis, 1981), and this research indicates that use of color adds no special advantage to human performance (with the exception of search tasks). Yet color-based software is being developed at an ever-increasing rate (Schultz, 1989). Sound and motion may indeed be what is most attractive to the teacher, but it does little to enhance the learning process (Knupfer, 1986).

The major idea that seems to surface from the previous discussion is not new: Computers have many unique attributes and capabilities on which we fail to capitalize (Clark, 1982, 1983). For example, computers are excellent for showing compressed time frames or simulations and have infinite patience to provide individualized drill and practice for slow students. A wonderful example of compressed time is MECC's "Lemonade Stand." This program teaches basic economic concepts by showing how much profit is made each day the lemonade stand is open for business. It is these very characteristics that make computers excellent teaching machines, and it is these strengths that remain untapped.

Another example includes using computer-based instruction (CBI) and computer-assisted instruction (CAI). Although they have had mixed results on achievement (Bangert-Drowns, Kulik, & Kulik, 1985; Burns & Bozeman, 1981; Clariana & Schultz, 1988; Jamison, Suppes, & Welles, 1974), we must remember that all too often the computer is relegated to the unimaginative task of drill and practice (Hativa, 1988). What a tremendous waste of this machine's capabilities and power!

Recently there has been new emphasis in design research and theory that offers hope for the classroom teacher. Current research on media attributes (Morrison, Ross, O'Dell, & Schultz, 1989) and screen design (Hannafin & Peck, 1988; Hartley, 1987) provides numerous suggestions for developing software that capitalizes on sound principles of cognitive theory. Although these are positive ideas for software developers, they are ideas for software that has yet to be developed. We, as classroom teachers, know only too well that what has been developed is of little value in terms of offering immediate solutions. We have seen that there is a wide gap in the time between when software is marketed and when it finally reaches the classroom. Even then excessive costs and stringent copyright laws prevent more than one or two copies of a program being available for students to use.

What can be of greater value to practitioners is expanded research on the software that is currently in the classrooms. Research, such as the work of Rodgers and Bonja (1987), provides new ideas and suggestions for teachers. Taking what is now in the classroom and expanding the program applications are what will be of greatest value and utility for teachers. The quality of research and development of new ideas by students can be greatly improved through the use of programs such as word processors and data bases to which students may have free access both during and after school. One particular teaching method Charles particularly enjoyed involved asking students questions about U.S. presidents and not providing the answers. By his merely saying "I do not know," the students were forced to use the computerized presidential database as a quick resource to answer questions.

Although there are those who suggest that teachers do not program (Manning & Manning, 1984), there are classroom situations where this skill could individualize and enhance the learning process. Who is most sensitive to the needs of students and is best able to understand the limitations of the classroom? The classroom teacher. It is through applications such as authoring software (SUPERPILOT, for example) that a teacher can easily and quickly design and implement programs tailored to fit individual classroom needs. Time, experience, and motivation are another matter. Based on numerous conversations with our peers, we propose that in spite of these positive considerations there will be few teachers who will ever consider writing programs for their classes. Programming is *very* time consuming, and requires a great deal of practice and special knowledge. Teachers are constantly complaining about the lack of time, and programming is just one more burden to add to their frustration.

TEACHER PERCEPTIONS AND THE LITERATURE

We share the belief held by many policy makers, educators, parents, and the public that the computer has the potential to help overcome the perceived mediocrity of American education (National Commission on Excellence in Education, 1983). The Second National Survey of Instructional Uses of School Computers, which gathered information from more than 10,000 teachers and principals in a sample of over 2,300 U.S. elementary and secondary schools during 1985, reveals that, rather than drawing on the computer as a powerful instructional medium or a productivity tool, much computer-related instruction in high schools is most often about the computer (Becker, 1986). As Nancy discovered in her middle-class high school setting, computer "classes" were actually electronics or programming classes foisted on the mathematics department.

As mentioned earlier, all too often we have seen teachers who failed to utilize the tremendous power and benefits of such knowledge, and according to Fisher (1982), some people are indeed skeptical when they first encounter the idea of learning from a computer. The popular press has taken some concerns of the educational establishment to heart in articles with titles such as "Computers in the Classroom: Are They Making the Grade?" (1985). We find, however, that most teachers now perceive the computer as a useful innovation that can add interest, prepare students for the workplace, be used as a reward, and offer variety in instruction. In an article outlining the history of teaching machines, Benjamin (1988) explains teacher resistance to the new technologies of computer-based instruction as a natural reaction to the failure of earlier innovations to significantly revolutionize the educational system. Some of the same fears educators had toward earlier innovations are now directed toward the computer. Papert (1980) contends that critics of the presence of computers in the classroom fear that more interaction with computers will lead to less human interaction and will result in social fragmentation. He differentiates, on the other hand, the reactions of skeptics who conclude that although the computer can produce some improvements in school learning, it cannot lead to fundamental change. The fear of replacement that characterized teacher reactions to the teaching machines of the 1950s (Skinner, 1986) has been replaced by a burgeoning curiosity and eagerness on the part of many classroom teachers to become members of the computer culture.

Knupfer's (1988) survey of classroom teachers in Wisconsin is indicative of how many teachers perceive the problems and promises of computer-based instruction. She found that teacher's complaints focused on the material, managerial, and training problems associated with computer implementation. One such example of implementation problems involved the English teachers at Charles' school. These teachers were told to put all student information on computer disk so that the school board could track student achievement more efficiently. The problem was that only one teacher had any experience with microcomputers. She was overwhelmed with pleas for help, mainly *during the school day!* Secondly, since the computers were located in the library, the English classes spent a disproportionate amount of time in the library so these teachers could work on their computer projects. This situation overwhelmed the English teachers, frustrated the librarians, and angered many of the other teachers in the building who also wanted access to the library.

TIME CONSTRAINTS

Together with time constraints of the daily curriculum, limitations of teachers' schedules make up a large category of general time problems. In Knupfer's (1988) survey, this complaint accounted for the largest (48%) single source of teacher concerns. Teachers need time to prepare applications, evaluate, and learn the software packages and promote curriculum integration. Much of what is expected of teachers in the implementation process is in addition to the demands of the regular school curriculum. Teachers are required to undertake other "extra-curricular" activities such as coaching sports teams, organizing social events, and attending numerous committee meetings. In addition, there is limited time to cover the existing curriculum. There may be ample motivation for the teacher to incorporate the computer into the classroom, but finding the time to accomplish implementation goals is another factor altogether. According to Fulton (1988), most teachers report that using computers makes their job harder, not easier, at least in the initial stages of implementation. Managerial problems include the planning time for scheduling computer use by students, inventories, software check-out procedures, and tracking student progress. Teachers responding to questionnaires by O'Brien (1985) reported that they are invited to innovate, but only if they do so in their spare time. Release time, for both planning and teacher education, is a recurrent issue among teachers. Nancy was told that she could go to the board of education to review software only after school hours. Although this sounds reasonable enough, the school board was across town and closed soon after classes were dismissed, severely limiting the amount of time she could spend there.

The point that we are trying to make is that teachers work within a framework of policies and routines which they must accommodate to any proposed change (Cuban, 1986). If the computer is to become an integral part of the teacher's repertoire, it must fit into the existing environment and routines of the classroom. This accommodation and acclimation takes time to accomplish, and the first year's effort by the implementing teacher may be spent primarily on managerial tasks. An outstanding example of this involved using "Newsroom" at Charles' school. The art teacher directed her ninth grade students to make a student-written, student-generated newspaper. They had limited resources, yet were able to make something they could be proud of. In the process they unknowingly learned the fundamentals of page layout, typing, and grammar, while sharpening their computer skills—all as an art project.

TRAINING

Training both preservice and inservice teachers is another major concern revealed by many researchers (Knupfer, 1988; Becker, 1986; Schimizzi, 1983; Zakariya, 1982). Lack of training was cited as a major problem by 33 percent of the teachers responding to the Wisconsin survey (Knupfer, 1988). A few of those responding (1%) had many hours of inservice training, but the majority reported having none at all. In a survey of 15 of the nation's largest schools of education, Bruder (1988a) discovered that four of the fifteen schools offer a degree in computer education. Computer literacy requirements for graduation and certification are the same as found in Ross and Rochford's 1986 survey, with some 10 of the 15 schools having some computer literacy course requirements for graduation. Three of the 15 schools incorporate units of computer education into general methods classes, and at two of the schools computer literacy must be demonstrated either through coursework, life experience, or work experience. A survey of the same schools in 1981 revealed only one school, Illinois State University, which had a computer literacy requirement for graduation. Bruder (1988b) reported that, as of July 1, 1988, all preservice teachers in California must complete a fifth year of coursework in computer education before they can receive a permanent teaching credential. This fifth year is required of all future teachers in public schools K-12 regardless of discipline. As more and more schools of education require some sort of computer literacy program for graduation, there will be an even greater need for inservice personnel to acquire these same skills.

PRESERVICE EDUCATION

Preservice applications can take many approaches, but we think the primary focus should be on software for two reasons. First, this field is changing so rapidly that it is difficult to keep pace with new products. Secondly, focus on software is vital because it is the software that will make computer applications so flexible in the classroom.

An excellent example of combining computer applications within a teacher training program is provided by Worth and Worth (1984). The major thrust of their suggestions is to incorporate the use of microcomputers in all areas of teacher education, ranging from general and professional education classes to in-depth studies of particular applications in the student's major. Also, they suggest using methods courses to include such topics as software selection, hardware selection, useful applications, and curriculum applications. Of course, these suggestions are made in the context of general curriculum and staff development at the university level.

According to Worth and Worth (1984), a critical step in staff and program development at the university level is circumventing the establishment of a computer mystique with its attendant jargon, acronyms, and polysyllabic buzzwords. They cite the example of just such a situation in the heyday of special education when much of the jargon surrounding the discipline was so alien and incomprehensible that many educators shied away from the whole field. College and university faculty should be involved universally, assessing curriculum and setting priorities for computer usage. Universal faculty involvement would promote "ownership" of the programs developed, thereby lessening the resistance of faculty to their retraining in new ways to teach their preservice teachers. It is emphasized, however, that such sweeping changes at the university level have to be made within the context of the influence of state departments of education and their respective minimum state standards (Worth & Worth, 1984).

INSERVICE EDUCATION

As new teachers reach the field and new requirements for computer literacy are put into place, there will be an even greater need for ongoing inservice education, not only to keep new teachers up to date, but also to recruit veteran teachers into the computer revolution. As Charles found, a pitfall to be avoided in this area is the creation of some sort of computer "priest(ess)" at a particular school, a teacher who has had experience with computers and who becomes responsible for training or performing computer tasks for coworkers. O'Brien (1985) cites one teacher's response to inservice education as just such a priesthood situation: "She took a week's workshop and that put her far above the rest of us. . . . She's reluctant to help us. . . . If we want help, she'll do the work rather than help us do our own." In some cases the better teachers are asked to carry the extra burden of teaching the teachers, pulling their colleagues into the information society. This places an unrealistic burden on the "teaching teacher" and promotes the establishment of a computer priesthood within the school. Too often the veteran teacher shies away from just such a scenario for fear of exposing his/her ignorance, losing status in the eyes of colleagues.

The question that arises is "Do teachers care enough to take the time to be trained?" In Charles' ghetto school few had any desire to become involved with the computer revolution, and those few had little access to computers for individual practice. For example, Charles was flooded with requests for "Print Shop" banners, posters, and cards during every special event or holiday, and long hours were spent after school filling these requests. What became a source of irritation was that these teachers did not want to learn how to use this program (the school board offered workshops for this); rather they wanted someone to do the work for them!

Knupfer (1986) suggests that team training could not only help dispel the computer mystique but also help alleviate problems dealing with access inequities. As teachers work together as a team, they will see their colleagues' initial confusion and fear evolve into later competencies and triumphs.

Not only should the quantity of inservice education be increased, but also the quality of programs should be upgraded, not only for content but for instructional emphasis and instructor attitudes. A case in point: In describing his experiences as an inservice instructor of veteran language arts teachers, Thomas Gandy (1987) relates his introductory remarks in the first workshop as his "standard spiel" (p. 27). After four minutes of this spiel, Gandy describes his audience as an "assortment of glazed eyes, apprehensive stares, and blankly smiling faces" (p. 27). He also condescendingly speaks of "feigned patience" (p. 30). With instructors spouting standard spiels and feigning a patience that they obviously do not possess, is it any wonder that polite learners are smiling blankly? In this ongoing three hour/week workshop conducted for language arts teachers, Gandy (1987) points out that he does not allow printing until the seventh or eighth week. For teachers used to working with a printed text and revising print materials, allowing this much time before a printed copy can be produced is counterproductive to the alleged goals of the workshop!

As Worth and Worth (1984) point out, the word "inservice" for many educators evokes memories of long, boring hours spent listening to some "expert" expound on topics with little relevance to their classroom and professional goals. We think that what is needed is an inservice program that is not only timely but *relevant to the individual teacher.*

Using Orlich's principles for successful inservice education (cited in Worth & Worth, 1984) as a framework, we feel that the following suggestions could help solve many of the problems created by teachers' negative feelings:

1. Teachers should be actively involved in planning their own inservice programs.
2. School-oriented, school-based programs are most successful.
3. The goals of inservice programming should be clear, specific, and well-disseminated.
4. Individualized, small-group training experiences may produce more positive and lasting results than other programs.
5. If inservice training is to improve system operations, then teachers' personal goals must coincide with those of the district.
6. Inservice training is more likely to be effective if adequate time is provided within the teachers' current work schedule.
7. Incentives should be identified and included for participants.
8. Involvement of the building principal in the program is critical for sustained access.
9. Evaluation of any aspect of the inservice training is an important facet to make necessary adjustments.

In summary, these suggestions require active teacher participation and inservice programs targeted to specific audiences. Teachers also maintain that the best inservice programs should have strong emphasis on software applications. It is possible to present software demonstrations that target both the level and subject area at any particular school.

Black and Mishler (1988) provide an overview of one district's approach to inservice education. The Portland Public School District, through the services of the Instructional Technology Services Unit of the Curriculum Department, provides some 20 different instructional technology inservice courses, many beginning in one classroom with a teacher who has an idea that develops into a successful teaching technique. As these teachers are identified, they are encouraged to share their techniques and develop a syllabus for a college-level course. The syllabus and resume are submitted to Portland State University for accreditation. Courses are offered on a cooperative basis through that university and the Portland Public Schools. The district sponsors the courses and budgets the instructors' salaries, allowing personnel to attend classes without cost or to receive college credits for a minimum fee. Members of the Instructional Technology Services Unit attribute the success of the program to several factors. Teachers enrolled in these courses are confident that, since material presented to them has been tried and proven successful in district classrooms, what they learn will be relevant and usable in their own classes. Topics for courses include instructional management tools, materials selection and development, computers as a curriculum area resource, and computer application software uses for students. Since instructors are themselves classroom teachers there is a feeling of common ground and comraderie, and teachers are encouraged to contact the instructor between classes if there are questions. Labs used are housed in district schools and the majority of class time is spent with hands-on activities. Many of the materials used or created in class are taken home at the end of the sessions, while other materials are available in a demonstration center in the district administrative offices. Since there is a wide range of computer experience levels among district teachers, classes are rated as beginning, intermediate, and advanced on advertising posters distributed among area schools. Teachers are directed into appropriate classes when they register. The number of course offerings for each year exceeds the budget; therefore, those classes with consistently high enrollment receive priority. Classes are offered immediately after school, late afternoons and evenings, and weekend classes begin on Friday and run all day Saturday. These accommodations to the needs and wants of area teachers have resulted in dramatic increases in enrollment each year (Black & Mishler, 1988).

SUMMARY

Computers are now common in our society. What was once confined to the business office is now in the home as well. There is increased demand by both parents and legislators to accelerate implementation and integration of computers in the schools. Teachers are also eager to incorporate the new technologies of instruction into their classroom activities. They are concerned, however, about hardware and software problems and the lack of teacher training before implementation takes place. Practitioners have been bombarded with the promise of computers in the classroom. But what is needed is not more *hyperbole* about the promise of the computer as a teaching tool, but more *help* for the problems encountered by the practitioner.

Based on numerous discussions with other classroom teachers and a synthesis of current research in implementation of computer-based instruction, we offer the following list of recommendations:

1. There should be a stronger emphasis on long-range planning with more teacher input. With teacher participation from the beginning, practical problems and limitations might more easily be identified.
2. Develop software capable of adapting to its environment. We feel that software that does not conform to the existing curriculum/text is of little value. Here it is important to note that schools should adapt rather than adopt.
3. The term "computer literacy" needs to be redefined. Rather than maintaining the current emphasis on programming skills, teachers want the definition to encompass effective utilization of existing programs for classroom application.
4. Provide more and better teacher training at both the inservice and preservice levels. Teachers believe that state certification should be divided into two parts: *computer science* to encompass the history of computing and more technical aspects such as programming, and *computer literacy* to include the application aspects of computer knowledge.
5. School systems need to provide motivation (i.e., release time, reimbursement, college credit) to encourage current teachers to develop computer skills. Release time is especially important to help teachers review and investigate new software and technology.
6. Make the technology simple. According to Papert (1980), engineers, hardware developers, and software programmers comprise a computer culture that speaks a language unique to their industry. It is imperative that both software and hardware manufacturers create documentation so the neophyte computer user can use this technology.
7. Teachers and developers must better utilize available software. New efforts must be undertaken to increase the usefulness of what is already in the classrooms. New ideas need to be encouraged and shared among schools and school systems.
8. Make computers available to the teacher in the classroom. There are indeed problems with security, but teachers feel that relegating the computer to the safety of a locked laboratory will only discourage frequent use.
9. Computers must be effectively integrated into the curriculum. Too often computer classes are scheduled more as an afterthought than a forethought.

10.   Classroom use of the computer should not be based on conduct or merit, but should be a regular part of the school day for all children. It is neither a reward nor a punishment but a normal part of the educational environment.

11.   Regular evaluation of the implementation plan is essential. Planners must consult with teachers to identify what works and what does not, and modify accordingly.

12.   There should be frequent feedback from teachers as implementation takes place. Teachers can identify problems before they become disasters.

It is hoped that with thoughtful planning and encouragement from the beginning, computers will become commonplace in the classroom. We can no longer afford to take a "do not touch" approach to technology that is now an everyday part of our society.

REFERENCES

Adams, R.C. (1989, January). Computers in school: What's the real use? *NEA Today, 7*(6), 26–31.

Bangert-Drowns, R.L., Kulik, J.A., & Kulik, C.-L.C. (1985, April). *Effectiveness of computer-based education in secondary schools.* Paper presented at the annual meeting of the American Education Research Association, Chicago, IL.

Becker, H.J. (1985). *How schools use microcomputers—summary of the first national survey* (ERIC Document Reproduction Service No. ED 257448). Baltimore, MD: The Johns Hopkins University, Center for Social Organization of Schools.

Becker, H.J. (1986). *Instructional uses of school computers: Report from the 1985 national survey, Issue no. 1* (ERIC Document Reproduction Service No. ED 274319). Baltimore, MD: The Johns Hopkins University, Center for Social Organization of Schools.

Benjamin, L.T. (1988). A history of teaching machines. *American Psychologist, 43*(9), 703–712.

Black, T., & Mishler, T. (1988). How one district handles technology in-service education. *Electronic Learning, 8*(91), 32–34.

Bruder, I. (1988a). ED schools: Literacy requirements stagnant, but more offer degrees. *Electronic Learning, 7*(7), 18–19.

Bruder, I. (1988b). California teachers need extra course in computer literacy for credential. *Electronic Learning, 7*(7), 16–17.

Burns, P.K., & Bozeman, W.C. (1981). Computer-assisted instruction and mathematics achievement: Is there a relationship? *Educational Technology, 21,* 32–39.

Christ, R.E. (1975). Review and analysis of color coding research for visual displays. *Human Factors, 17,* 542–570.

Christ, R.E., & Corso, G.M. (1983). The effects of extended practice on the evaluation of visual display codes. *Human Factors, 25*, 71–84.

Clark, R.E. (1982). Antagonism between achievement and enjoyment in ati studies. *The Educational Psychologist, 17*(2), 445–459.

Clariana, R., & Schultz, C.W. (1988, November). *Computer-assisted instruction at St. Anne's School*. Paper presented at the Annual Meeting of the Mid-South Educational Research Association, Louisville, KY.

Computers in the classroom: Are they making the grade? (1985, November). *Better Homes and Gardens*, pp. 38–43.

Cuban, L. (1986). *Teachers and machines: The classroom use of technology since 1920*. New York: Teacher's College Press.

Fisher, F.D. (1982). Computer-assisted education: What's not happening? *Journal of Computer-Based Instruction, 9*(1), 19–27.

Foster, D. (1988). Technology: Implications for long-range planning. *Educational Technology, 28*(4), 7–14.

Fulton, K. (1988). Preservice and inservice: What must be done in both. *Electronic Learning, 8*(2), 32–36.

Gandy, T. (1987). The inservice workshop: When you're responsible for introducing other teachers to the mysteries of micros. *Classroom Computer Learning, 7*(8), 27–31.

Hannafin, M.J., & Peck, K.L. (1988). *The design, development, and evaluation of instructional software*. New York: Macmillan.

Hartley, J. (1987). Designing electronic text: The role of print-based research. *Educational Communication and Technology Journal, 35*(1), 3–17.

Hativa, N. (1988). Computer-based drill and practice in arithmetic: Widening the gap between high- and low-achieving students. *American Educational Research Journal, 25*(3), 366–398.

Jamison, D., Suppes, P., & Welles, S. (1974). The effectiveness of alternative instructional media: A survey. *Review of Educational Research, 44*, 1–67.

Knupfer, N.N. (1986). *Implementation of microcomputers into the current k-12 curriculum: a critical discussion of issues*. (ERIC Document Reproduction Service No. ED 275292). Madison, WS: University of Wisconsin.

Knupfer, N.N. (1986). *Implementation of microcomputers into the current k-12 curriculum: a critical discussion of issues* (ERIC Document Reproduction Service No. ED 275292). Madison, WS: University of Wisconsin.

Manning, M., & Manning, M. (1984). Teachers don't need to be software developers. In R.A. Camuse (Ed.), *Microcomputers in education: Literacy plus +* (pp. 326–329). Rockville, MD: Computer Science Press.

Morrison, G.R., Ross, S.M., O'Dell, J.K., & Schultz, C.W. (1988). Adapting text presentations to media attributes: Getting more out of less in cbi. *Computers in Human Behavior, 4*, 65–75.

National Commission on Excellence in Education. (1983). *A nation at risk: The imperative for educational reform*. Washington, DC: U.S. Government Printing Office.

O'Brien, T.C. (1985, February). *Teachers talk—The failure of computers in education* (ERIC Document Reproduction Service No. ED 260702). Paper presented at the Fifth Annual Conference on "The Role of the Computer in Education", Arlington Heights, IL.

Papert, S. (1980). *Mindstorms: Children, computers, and powerful ideas.* New York: Basic Books.

Postman, N. (1982). *The disappearance of childhood.* New York: Delacorte Press.

Rodgers, R.J., & Bonja, R.P. (1987). *Computer utilization training in staff development* (ERIC Document Reproduction Service No. ED 291 374). Paper presented at the National Conference of the National Council of States on Inservice Education, San Diego, CA.

Ross, J., & Rochford, T. (1986). New teachers better prepared for computers. *Electronic Learning, 6*(1), 23–24.

Skinner, B.F. (1986, October). Programmed instruction revisited. *Phi Delta Kappan, 68*(2), 103–110.

Schimizzi, N.V. (183). *Microcomputers in the schools* (ERIC Document Reproduction Service No. ED 247904). Albany, NY: State University of New York Research Foundation.

Schultz, C.W. (1989). *Results of a pilot study of text density preference using the paired comparison technique.* Paper presented at the Annual Meeting of the Association for Educational Communication and Technology, Dallas, TX.

Shavelson, R., Winkler, J., Stasz, C., & Robyn, A. (1983, April). *Teachers instructional uses of microcomputers* (ERIC Document Reproduction Service No. ED 246888). Santa Monica, CA: Rand Corporation.

Tullis, T.S. (1981). An evaluation of alphanumeric, graphic, and color information displays. *Human Factors, 23,* 541–550.

Winkler, J., Shavelson, R., Stasz, C., & Robyn, A. (1983). *Successful" use of microcomputers in classroom instruction* (ERIC Document Reproduction Service No. ED 247911). Santa Monica, CA: Rand Corporation.

Worth, M.M., & Worth, C.E. (1984). Teacher training and competencies in the area of microcomputer technology. In R.A. Camuse (Ed.), *Microcomputers in education: Literacy plus +* (pp. 452–462). Rockville, MD: Computer Science Press.

Zakariya, S.B. (1982, May). The computer goes to school. *Principal, 61*(5), 16–20, 52–54.

12
CBT and Higher Education: Issues, Barriers, and Solutions

William L. Deaton
Auburn University

By identifying and discussing issues and concerns related to the use of computers in the preparation of teachers, managers of colleges of education can prepare for the decisions which face them. This chapter will examine the implications of various courses of action available to college administrators regarding the use of computers in their programs as well as describe an approach for college administrators and faculty to use as a tool for decision making. Barriers to the implementation of CBT and the solutions to overcoming these barriers will be discussed from my perspective as an associate dean of graduate studies and research in the College of Education at Auburn University. In this position I have assumed major responsibility for the support of computer applications in the College's instructional and research areas.

The College of Education at Auburn University has six academic departments and two research units. It maintains two microcomputer laboratories and adjoining classrooms. One laboratory is equipped with IBM PS/2 model 30 microcomputers and the other contains Apple IIGS microcomputers. Courses in computer applications are offered through the Department of Educational Foundations, Leadership, and Technology with content-related courses taught in the other five departments.

Examples of how computers could be integrated into teacher preparation programs will be described. Implications of computer-based instruction on the preparation of teachers will be examined in detail.

A CONCEPTUAL MODEL OF CBT IN HIGHER EDUCATION

Theories of cognitive development (Piaget), moral development (Kohlberg), and human needs (Maslow) have enabled us to consider such complex phenomena as stages of growth and development. Stage theories are useful because they identify ideal discrete steps and behaviors associated with levels of development.

If CBT is viewed as a developing phenomenon, a theory of development may be postulated to explain past, current, and probable future stages of computer-based training in higher education. Insight may be gained from such an exercise and it may be possible to predict future events associated with the use of CBT. Predicting the future may be of value as we pursue CBT today.

Stage one of CBT may be likened to infancy. Tremendous potential exists for infants but their behaviors begin as somewhat haphazardous and serendipitous. One major desire is to apply CBT to everything, everywhere, and for everyone. The adage "Give a child a hammer. . ." is transformed into views about all situations. Examples of infantile applications of computers to education include the use of computers as electronic page turners for text presentation, linear branching for programmed learning material, electronic grading procedures, poetry generators that created certain lines of a simple poem, banner or sign maker programs, and drill sheet printers for students' use in mathematics, spelling, and science. Similar outlooks are seen with college students who have completed one course in statistics. These students look at the world with "t-test eyes." Every research activity is molded to fit a t-test.

Egocentrism is a characteristic of infants. Stage one of CBT was concerned with the computer itself. Hexadecimal addition, binary operations, Boolean algebra, multivibrators, nand and nor gates, full and half adders, punched paper tape, and wiring boards were of primary interest. Assemblers were high-level languages. The task was to get the computers to *do* something related to education or training, thus ignoring questions of utility and validity. The research and development phase of phase one seemed to have practical applications of computers as the goal.

Stage two may be likened to adolescence. Hormones drive teenagers; technology determines the problem. Computers have been described as solutions awaiting problems. "The use of computers should increase test scores." "The use of computers should make training more efficient, more cost-effective." Integrated circuits signaled the entry into computer adolescence. Mainframe computers handled all computer-based training. Foreign language requirements for advanced degrees were replaced by computer programming skills, graduate students were introduced to mainframe computers as "number crunchers," and word processing was available on mainframe computers.

Young adulthood was entered at stage three; the young and restless. Reasoned approaches to problems are rarely used by young adults. Instead, results count; immediate results are better than later ones. As the old saying goes, if it's bigger and faster, it must be better. The appearance of the personal computer heralded CBT young adulthood. Power came with microcomputers as memory increased from 1K to 16K to 32K and then to 64K. Disk drives replaced cassette players. BASIC came with the machine. Fluency with different operating systems was viewed with the same awe as were people who spoke three, five, or seven different languages.

Spreadsheets entered the classroom at stage three along with collections of software developed by teachers. The Minnesota Educational Computing Consortium (MECC) offered software for Apple computers for use in the classroom. Until the mechanics for using it became overwhelming, our College of Education maintained membership in MECC. Approximately 200 diskettes had to be prepared to receive the software. Backup copies and copies for circulation had to be made. This resulted in an investment of over $1,000 just in diskettes. Many of the programs required user manuals and teacher manuals. These print materials had to be copied and made available to users. Thus, more money was required to support the MECC system. The membership was terminated when it was realized that only an extremely small number of faculty and few students used the MECC software.

Auburn University was selected as the site of the communications committee of the Alabama Council for Computer Education (ACCE). A microcomputer system was purchased, including a modem and dedicated phone line, to install and support an electronic bulletin board for computer users in the state. A graduate assistant was hired to implement the system and function as the system operator. After over one year of operation, only three teachers had used the services of the bulletin board. This level of use could not justify the continuation of the financial support necessary to maintain the bulletin board. Although the bulletin board was a great idea somehow, it remained just that.

Faster chips, fewer manufacturers of microcomputers, similarities of operating systems, and user friendliness marked the fourth stage of adulthood. Differences in cultures and ethnic origins are accepted by most adults. There seems to be a place for variety and differences in computer systems. Networks are used for communications and sharing of computer facilities. Computers schedule meetings and classes. Simulations of complex problems are possible. Interactive hardware and software are available.

Problems are present, too. *A Nation at Risk* (1983) recognized computers as the "fourth R" of education. Kent (1988) observed that students' computer skills outdistanced those of faculty. Future teachers receive training on today's (or yesterday's) computers, yet they will be teaching in the schools of tomorrow. We are told that tomorrow's leaders must be able to use new technology. Yet tomorrow's leaders are in the schools and colleges of today where little new technology is used to prepare the majority of tomorrow's leaders.

Many classroom teachers have not received formal education in computer-based teaching. Yet their students have grown up with television, digital watches, calculators, video arcades, microcomputers, robots, and talking automobiles. As a result, students in elementary schools may have computer skills which are very well developed.

School systems invest thousands of dollars in computer hardware and software. Buildings require major renovations to handle the demands of the equipment and associated security devices. Libraries and media centers are transformed into computer centers. Computer teachers are required to become experts in copyright law.

Parents feel the changes. Television advertisements arouse feelings of guilt unless children are provided spelling checkers, word processors, spreadsheets, and modems for school work. Some parents may even receive phone calls from a computer at school if a son or daughter is absent.

SOLUTIONS

The basic management process model developed by Kaufman (1972) can be used as a framework for explaining some of the problems and barriers identified in this chapter. The model specifies five essential steps:

1. Identify and clarify the problem
2. Determine solution requirements and alternatives
3. Select solution strategy
4. Implement strategy
5. Determine performance effectiveness

Revisions are made, as required, during each step and during the progressions from one step to the next.

Step 1 of the model is of particular importance because it requires the clarification of the problem. The assertion that computers should be used in schools is insufficient for identifying the problem. Statements of opinion (teachers should use computers, colleges should instruct teachers in ways to use computers, etc.) do not identify the problem and, therefore, do not contribute to problem resolution.

Steps 2, 3, and 4 have been taken by many Colleges of Education. Microcomputers have been purchased and faculty have been encouraged to incorporate the microcomputers into more courses. The interesting point is that solutions have been selected and implemented prior to problem identification and clarification. As a result, actions already taken by Colleges of Education may have erected additional barriers to effective management. The examples given for the first three stages of CBT development illustrate the results of skipping Step 1 of the model. Successful approaches to the use of computers in instruction seem to have concentrated on one or two problems and have not tried to solve all problems.

Faculty who teach methods courses (Methods of Teaching Science, Methods of Teaching Mathematics, etc.) have been reluctant to incorporate the use of computers in content courses. Students generally teach as they were taught. If faculty do not use computers as they teach methods courses, it is less likely that their students will use computers when they enter the classrooms. Similar problems were observed by Bitter and Scherer (see Office of Technology Assessment, 1988, p. 101). All university faculty, not just faculty in Education, must demonstrate the use of computers in courses. Future teachers complete more course work outside the School, College, or Department of Education than from within. The entire baccalaureate and master's programs must reinforce the use of computers if future teachers are to be expected to use computers in all subjects taught.

Collis (1988) noted that resistance to computer use may be explained by an awareness of concern regarding the implementation of *any* innovation. Collis (1988) recommends training of school staff through the use of an approach based upon the seven levels of use of an innovation (Hall, Loucks, Rutherford, & Newlove, 1975). A similar approach can be used to prepare faculty to use computers in methods courses.

Faculty may be considered to be at one of the seven stages of concern. Better yet, faculty can place themselves in one of the seven stages. Activities can then be tailored to the particular level of the faculty with progression to the next level(s) dependent upon designing goals to prepare faculty to further incorporate computers into content courses.

Computers are often used to teach about computers. Faculty with specialized preparation or extensive experience are assigned to teach those courses which teach about computers. What future teachers need are faculty who have knowledge and skill in using the computer to teach other subjects. Classroom teachers seldom teach about computers. Exchange programs that place classroom teachers in university courses as instructors and university faculty in classrooms as teachers offer promise. A classroom teacher proficient in the use of computers in instruction can assist a faculty member in teaching a methods course or in determining how to use a computer in a content course.

USING CBT IN A COLLEGE OF EDUCATION

Colleges of Education have as a primary mission the preparation of teachers. This mission includes the preparation of professionals who will assume positions related to, but not necessarily limited to, educational institutions. Faculty are expected to contribute by preparing students to be professional educators. Administrators are expected to support the faculty and students in this effort.

Calls for reform in teacher education include making a distinction between teacher education at major research institutions and other teacher education programs (The Holmes Group, 1986). Reform agendas refer to the need to produce future teachers who have broad preparations in the liberal arts (The Holmes Group, 1986). The need for economic security is given as a priority by the Carnegie Forum on Education and the Economy (1986), *A nation prepared: Teachers for the 21st century.* Some reform statements include increased preparation in the subject areas to be taught. Most reform agendas recognize the need to prepare teachers who can prepare their students to engage in higher-order thinking and who can manage abstract thinking. Most calls for reform note the need for future teachers to spend increased amounts of time in the school setting. Almost all statements of reform refer to the need for teacher education faculty to model effective teaching behaviors.

As noted earlier, most teachers teach as they were taught. If education students do not see faculty teaching with computers, using computers in instructional tasks, or using computers to manage information, that they will not likely incorporate computers in instructional and management tasks.

Certain individuals are goal- or task-oriented. These individuals are punctual; they expect meetings to start and finish on time. When task-oriented people are placed on committees, other committee members tend to adapt their behavior in order to become more task-oriented. Similarly, if faculty and administrators who use computers are placed with faculty and administrators who do not use computers, behavior changes may be predicted. To insure that the changes are in the desired direction (to the use of computers), computer-using faculty and administrators must be seen as more productive, more task-oriented, and more effective.

It may be helpful to describe some uses and potential applications of computers by faculty in a College of Education. To completely computerize the operation of a College of Education is probably not a worthwhile goal. However, many activities of a College can be improved through the use of computers. Faculty in most Colleges are expected to publish. Faculty are expected to engage in research and scholarly activities which will result in publications. Although data are not available to support the assertion that faculty with word processors are more productive researchers and publishers, observation of over 100 faculty seems to verify the assertion. Word processing may be accomplished with dedicated word processors, microcomputers, or mainframes.

INSTRUCTIONAL USES OF COMPUTERS

One of the biggest challenges facing Colleges of Education is how to use computers to teach about subjects other than computers. A related concern is what future teachers should know about the instructional and non-instructional uses of computers in schools. Colleges of Education are preparing tomorrow's teachers but those teachers are entering the schools of today. A survey of 502 newly certified teachers for 1987–88 in Alabama found that approximately 50 percent of the teachers reported that they possessed less than adequate skill in using computers in instruction (Baird & Ost, 1988).

What do future teachers need to know about computers? An introductory course on how to use computers may sound appealing. However, if computers were used in *all* education courses, the need for an introductory course would be diminished, if not eliminated. Teaching with computers should consist of more than demonstrating the use of particular software in methods courses.

Some content-related uses of computers are obvious. Courses in the teaching of language arts can use word processors to assist in the teaching of writing. Mathematics methods courses can use computers as calculation devices. Software simulation programs can be incorporated into social sciences courses. Gorrell, Cuevas, and Downing (1988) reported that students using computer simulations of actual classroom problems had increased confidence in applying techniques of behavior modification and the students felt they had more knowledge about computers as a result of using the computer simulations. The teaching of music can be expanded by using computers as music synthesizers.

Perhaps the question of what future teachers need to know about computers should be rephrased: What do teacher education *faculty* need to know about computers? This question, in turn, can be viewed as: What are the best current and potential uses of computers in education?

The Office of Technology Assessment (OTA) identified the most promising current uses and demonstrations of computers in education (Office of Technology Assessment, 1988). These uses and the associated implications for Colleges of Education follow.

Drill and practice to master basic skills. Computer assisted instruction (CAI) has proven to be an effective supplement to traditional classroom instruction. Faculty should be able to demonstrate the use of different types of drill and practice software in each content area, particularly at the elementary and middle school grade levels. Faculty should be able to prepare drill and practice exercises for students. Some software packages can be modified to match individual needs of students. Authoring systems are available to allow teachers to construct drill and practice exercises for individual students or for groups of students in need of particular types of drill exercises. These approaches allow teachers to personalize the computer delivered items or exercises. In addition, these packages can be tailored to individuals by using city names, friends' names, names of pets, hobbies, or sports enjoyed by students, and other "personalized" terms suggested by the student or selected by the teacher.

Development of writing skills. Although word processing by itself does not create better writers, it has helped ease the physical burden of writing and reading. Both faculty and future students should be able to use word processing. Faculty should use word processing packages for preparing manuscripts for publication. Students should prepare class assignments and reports with word processing packages. Electronic dictionaries, spelling checkers, and thesauruses should be used in writing assignments. Faculty should be using word processors to prepare student examinations and assignments. Faculty should consider using packages which allow comments to be inserted on disks containing student assignments.

Problem solving. There is some evidence that teachers can use computer simulations, educational games, databases, and other software to train students to break problems down into their component parts and set strategies for their solution. Faculty can pose "What if . . ." questions to themselves and to students. Brainstorming related to potential uses of computers may be helpful to generate new ideas and new approaches to problems. An interesting question might be "What if each student had a computer?"

Understanding abstract mathematics and science concepts. Microcomputer-based laboratories (MBLs) combine microcomputers with probes to measure phenomena such as light, heat, and temperature. With specially designed software, students can produce almost instant graphs of the data and explore effects of different variables. Faculty can prepare computer programs to demonstrate or to solve mathematical and scientific problems. Faculty could explore the uses of computers to demonstrate concepts and to permit manipulations of the demonstrations. Solutions to different applications or concepts can be prepared that will allow step-by-step examination of problem-solving approaches.

Simulation in science, mathematics, and social studies. Simulations provide science students with self-contained worlds. Consider a frictionless world where the laws of Newtonian physics are apparent and in which experiments can occur quickly and results are seen immediately. Students can test abstract concepts and experiment with scientific processes that are not feasible or are too dangerous for actual classroom work. By playing the role of world leaders or citizens in other countries, for example, students engage in higher levels of critical thinking, gain a better understanding of political affairs, and appreciate different perspectives of an issue. Faculty can design and conduct simulations in various content areas.

Manipulation of data. Database management systems encourage students to define a problem in specific terms and break it into component parts. Students must then identify the data needed, extract them from the database, put the data in a useful order, use the data, and then communicate findings to others. Faculty conducting research projects and analyzing research data could use computers to collect and analyze information.

Acquisition of computer skills for general purposes, and for business and vocational training. The most obvious use of computers and related tools in the classroom is to prepare students for the increasingly technological world they will face. The early emphasis on programming for all students is being replaced by keyboarding and skill in using generic computer programs. Faculty and students who did not have adequate keyboarding or typing training could use software packages to improve their skills. Faculty with interests and responsibilities in the arts could use computer packages for drawing, designing, and composing. Obviously, faculty in business education programs could use computers to supplement their activities and instruction. Some faculty may have interests in computer-assisted or -aided design.

Access and communication for traditionally unserved populations of students. Some classroom teachers have described the computer as "the freedom machine" because it has made the very act of communication possible for some special needs students. Word processors allow students who could not hold a pencil to write; speech synthesizers provide some students with a means to communicate orally for the first time. Faculty can prepare student assignments related to the use of computers in serving students with special needs. Computers equipped with touch-sensitive screens can be used to demonstrate unique applications of computers. Research can be conducted to determine the effectiveness of different delivery systems for students with physical handicaps.

Access and communication for teachers and students in remote locations. Electronic networks allow students and teachers to share information and experience across cities, states, or continents, thus ending the isolation of the classroom. Students engaged in internships could be provided with computers and modems to communicate with similarly equipped faculty. Colleges that provide "student warranties" could use the computers and modems as communication devices for delivering advice and assistance to recent graduates. Electronic bulletin boards could be operated by faculty in the College so students and teachers could request assistance with particular problems encountered in classrooms.

Individualized learning. The increasing capacity of computer-based technology makes it possible to develop instruction that adjusts to each student's prior knowledge, rate of learning, and the nature and style of the students' responses. For example, technology offers some very promising applications for strengthening reading comprehension through analysis of the students' understanding of the text. Similarly, intelligent tutoring systems in areas such as geometry can provide the learner with an expert tutor. Still another example is that "hypertext" systems allow students to manipulate text, graphics, and different levels of information. The computer can also help teachers to determine individual student needs by keeping exact records of student progress. Faculty could use computers to diagnose students' knowledge at course entry and prescribe activities appropriate for each student based upon the diagnoses. Software that identifies specific areas of strengths and weaknesses could be used to individualize student assignments and projects. The same software could be used by the faculty to identify their specific strengths and weaknesses and to prepare individualized activities for professional growth.

Cooperative learning. Using an electronic network, students in many locations can gather information from many sources. Students of mixed abilities can be grouped in small or large teams to wrestle with tasks that cannot be performed individually. Faculty could work together to solve problems involving computers in instruction. Teams of faculty with varying degrees of computer experience and knowledge could be formed to address specific problems by content areas, grade levels, or groups of students.

Management of classroom activities and record keeping. Computer programs such as spreadsheets, database managers, and desktop publishing can streamline record keeping and material preparation. In addition, computers make it easier to record the progress and determine the needs of individual students. Faculty should use computers for class attendance, student evaluations, and student test scores. Of course, a most important use of computers could be to maintain records of computer use by students.

ADMINISTRATIVE USES OF COMPUTERS

The College can equip a central word processing center with microcomputers, letter quality and graphics printers, and word processing packages. Faculty can prepare draft manuscripts and then take the disks containing their manuscripts to the word processing center for final editing and printing. Local area networks can be installed which enable faculty to electronically transfer the draft manuscript to the word processing center for final editing, formatting, and printing. This approach has been used successfully in our College of Education. Faculty appreciate the ease of transferring manuscript files electronically. They also like the option of selecting from a variety of word processing packages for their writing. The word processing center can transfer files from one format to another without faculty involvement. More time is garnered for faculty to write by transferring the responsibility for formatting, referencing, spelling checks, and pagination from faculty to trained word processing operators.

Local area networks offer security for tests prepared by faculty. Item banks can be prepared and used to produce tests as required by faculty. It is also possible for test scoring and item analyses to be performed as part of the network functions.

College administrators (deans, department heads, directors, and coordinators) attend many meetings. Scheduling meetings can be time consuming and, at times, very frustrating. The computers can schedule meetings with minimum conflicts if the administrators maintain a calendar of appointments on a network. Insuring that individuals maintain calendars on the network does not have to create problems. Let the Dean schedule a meeting of all administrators with the computer just one time. Be assured that those administrators who do not attend will keep a calendar of appointments from then on.

Electronic mail and electronic communications between and among faculty in the College reduce the amount of time required of faculty and staff to deal with paperwork. Distribution lists can be prepared once and used thereafter to direct messages and notices.

Student advisement can be improved by having student information available on the College network. Some deans and department heads may have access to student information through university mainframe computers but this does not guarantee that the College network has access. Security concerns must be addressed if student information is placed on a network. Network users should be able to view student information but they should *not* have the capabilities to change student information. Network managers can designate files as read only and should do so on files containing student information. It may be helpful to create at least two different student databases. One database could contain information on undergraduate students and the other on graduate students. Departments may find it beneficial to have data bases of students enrolled in different departmental programs. Networks offer these capabilities.

Information related to faculty and staff can be maintained on the College network. Administrators must keep track of faculty who are eligible for promotion and tenure, and computers are ideally suited for managing such information. Each year, or each term if necessary, deans and department heads can produce a list of the faculty who are eligible for promotion or who should be considered for tenure. Keeping track of faculty accomplishments is made easier with a computer network. Requests for faculty information are often made by university officials or representatives of other agencies. These requests can be fulfilled through the use of faculty databases. Accrediting agencies require faculty resumes; the word processing center can maintain current resumes in different formats to meet these requirements. In addition to faculty information, accrediting agencies demand course outlines; these, too, can be maintained by the word processing center for immediate access.

Program management and tracking require different types of information. Computer application packages are available to assist both administrators and faculty to manage programs. As an example, an accrediting visit requires the planning and coordination of many College faculty, staff, and resources. Timelines for completion of tasks can be prepared with computers as well as assignments of who is responsible for what aspect of the activities. These assignments and target dates can be integrated with the individual calendars of faculty and administrators, and status reports can be produced on short notice.

Program management software can also be used to track proposals submitted for external support. Tickler files can be created to notify administrators of due dates and other project requirements. If information related to external funding opportunities is maintained in the College, reports can be generated to show funding received by departments and other units within the College. These reports may be useful as goals are established for departments and for the College.

Budget information can be placed on the College network. As might be expected, department heads prefer information on departmental accounts be subject to strict policies of access. Again, the network manager can designate that department accounts be available only to the department head or other individuals deemed appropriate.

If information on student enrollment is maintained on the College network, trends may be identified and plans may be made to respond to program or course enrollment changes. Graphic presentations of enrollments are helpful as decisions are made. Relational databases allow for the preparation of reports showing cost vs. enrollment, full-time equivalents vs. external support received, annual projections of department maintenance expenditures, and other college-wide summaries.

Information related to faculty assignments will be available on the network as it is entered into the databases. Department heads can tell at a glance which faculty assignments may have to be changed due to last minute student enrollment in courses.

OTHER USES OF COMPUTERS

The Alabama State Department of Education (SDE) has installed a computer network with microcomputers placed in each of the 130 local school systems. Similar initiatives are occurring in other states as well. Reports required by the SDE can be electronically transmitted by the school systems. Updates on legislative action are placed on the network to keep local school superintendents informed of possible actions and local impact. A teacher job bank is maintained which allows school systems to advertise position openings across the state and to provide teachers seeking positions with information about openings.

It is anticipated that the SDE will allow colleges and universities to access the statewide network in the near future. Such access will provide more information exchange among educators. Colleges of Education could announce special courses, seminars, or workshops on the network. Local school systems could request special services or assistance from colleges to address immediate concerns.

If appropriate licensing agreements are in effect, software could be exchanged. Public domain software could be made available as well as user evaluations, suggestions, and examples of innovative uses of the software. Student entries to computer fairs could be placed on the network for other students or teachers to use as examples of student solutions to assigned problems.

The SDE could use the network to announce changes in certification requirements to all schools and colleges. Requests for proposals could be broadcast to all schools and colleges. Comments about proposed changes in programs could be requested from local school systems and Colleges of Education. Questions addressed to SDE personnel could be answered on the network so all Schools and Colleges of Education could have identical and timely responses. Perliminary budget requests could be presented on the network for comments and suggestions. Recent federal and state rulings on education matters could be placed on the network to keep local personnel and College faculty informed of court decisions. Press releases could be sent to local school systems and education personnel. Minutes of the State Board of Education meetings, other State committees, and SDE task forces could be distributed on the network.

BARRIERS TO THE INSTRUCTIONAL USES OF COMPUTERS IN COLLEGES OF EDUCATION

Selection of equipment. Colleges of Education must select the type of computers to be used in teacher preparation programs. One method is to select the computer systems that are currently being used in the schools that will employ the largest percentage of graduating teachers. This approach will maintain the status quo but it will not enable the College of Education to exert leadership in shaping the instructional practices for tomorrow's schools. Another approach is for the College of Education to identify the computer systems which *should* be used in the classrooms of the future. Teachers prepared through this approach will then be able to influence the decisions which will be made at the local level to select computers for use in classrooms. Yet a third method is to consider school superintendents as "buyers" of the Colleges' "products." This situation suggests that superintendents should be polled to determine the type of computer experiences desired of new teachers.

Availability of appropriate instructional software must also be considered as hardware is selected. Many schools and classroom teachers have software for the Apple series of computers. Although not all of the software is of high quality, the current base is quite large and cannot be ignored as hardware is selected. Computer manufacturers and third-party vendors are offering software and associated hardware that will enable some programs written for the Apple microcomputers to run on IBM or IBM compatible microcomputers and vice versa. This approach may offer a solution to Colleges of Education that have invested in IBM or Apple computer systems.

Placement of computer applications experiences in the teacher education program. The question of "territory" must be faced by Colleges of Education. Should future teachers receive instruction on computer applications from one course or sequence of courses, or should future teachers be taught the use of computers in all teacher education courses?

If computers are placed in special rooms or labs, this is another contraindication that computers will be isolated from instruction in other subjects. Place the machines, even one or two, in methods' faculty classrooms. These computers can be physically secured and serve as stations on the local area network. Security of files and application programs can be provided through the network administrator.

Internships with computer-using classroom teachers should increase the number of future teachers capable of applying computers to content areas.

Caporael (1985) studied the use of computers by undergraduate students in a technical setting. Caporeal concluded: "Learning to use a computer has two important components: the opportunity for trial-and-error and the social transfer of information" (p. 187). Undergraduate students described their learning strategies as "playing around," "experimenting," and "tinkering." The students said they relied heavily on other, more knowledgeable students. Microcomputers were seen as shared resources.

Future teachers can be expected to use the same approach to learning to use a computer. Faculty may be more reluctant to rely on others unless the others are close friends and colleagues.

Selection of faculty to deliver instruction. Current faculty may have to be prepared or retrained to deliver the instruction to future teachers. It may not be appropriate to expect all faculty to use computers in all courses.

Curriculum development and revision. Courses in existing teacher education programs may or may not contain material dealing with computer applications. Will one or more computer application courses be required of all future teachers or will such courses be offered as electives? This concern also relates to the question of "territory" or ownership of courses.

Incorporating other high technology applications in teacher preparation programs. Interactive video, CD-rom applications, electronic communication, networks of computers, artificial intelligence, computer-managed instruction, tailored testing, and data retrieval services will impact upon programs aimed at preparing teachers for tomorrow's schools. Provisions for incorporating these and other developments in technological applications must be recognized as Colleges of Education redesign programs for preparing teachers.

Evidence of effectiveness. Research on the effective use of computers in classrooms must continue. Computers may or may not be the delivery system of choice for different areas of classroom instruction. Our knowledge of the value of computers for student learning is growing but it is far from complete. Colleges of Education may need to reorganize teacher preparation programs to insure the continued investigation of questions related to effective uses of computers.

Money. Acquiring computers for faculty and students requires a large financial expenditure. Some colleges may secure equipment from donations from computer companies or other vendors. College administrators can set an example by preparing successful proposals to external funding agencies for the purchase of computers and related equipment. Grants received for research projects may allow purchases of computer equipment which can also be used for instructional purposes.

Many faculty travel to professional meetings to present results of research. Perhaps some faculty would consider foregoing one trip in exchange for some assistance in purchasing a computer for their use.

Incentives. University faculty generally are rewarded for excellent teaching, scholarly publishing, conducting research, and securing external support for research. Incorporating computers in instruction has not been viewed as a priority by university administrators. Restrictions are usually placed on rewards faculty may receive for developing software with university resources. Software development has not been viewed as a legitimate or highly valued counterpart to publishing. Salary increases may or may not be influenced by faculty preparation of instructional software. Promotions traditionally are based upon teaching effectiveness, research activities, and publications. Unless these perceptions (and realities) are changed, faculty have few incentives for devoting tremendous amounts of time and effort to implementing computers in the instructional program.

CONCLUSIONS

The analogy of CBT in higher education and a stage theory of development enables some past and future applications of CBT to be explained.

However, as with many analogies, not all events can be explained. Human growth and development occurs in spurts and different functions of humans develop at varying rates. Development also seems to occur in a spiral fashion. That is, while general cognitive functions may advance with increased chronological age, specific cognitive functions may recede prior to advancement. People may be at an advanced level of development while still functioning at lower levels. It has been said that there is a child in each of us. Likewise, CBT may maintain some infant or adolescent characteristics as it progresses to more advanced levels of development.

The fifth stage of CBT in higher education will be entered as the move from adulthood to wisdom occurs. Wisdom requires experience, patience, trust, and vision. As we reflect upon past experiences with CBT, we will be able to face future decisions with more confidence. New possibilities and solutions will be discovered by those who may be in the stage of infancy now or those who are mature, fifth stagers. Computer-based training in higher education will continue to grow and develop.

Future teachers will benefit from the use of computers in education to the extent that individual Colleges of Education focus on solutions to fewer problems. The University of Virginia concentrated on linking student teachers with University faculty via computers equipped with modems; Florida State University and the University of Illinois maintained systems approaches to computer-assisted instruction; and the Massachusetts Institute of Technology developed and extended LOGO as an education tool. These notable successes reflect the consequences of selecting one aspect of the "computer problem" and developing innovative approaches to selected areas of CBT. The stage theory of development applies in this situation: Adults select one career or one specialty and concentrate their efforts in this one area. Careers may be changed but significant accomplishments are usually realized by adults who have narrowed their areas of primary interest. Colleges of Education may expect to make lasting contributions as faculty select a few key areas on which to concentrate.

REFERENCES

Baird, W.E., & Ost, D.H. (1988). *The Alabama teacher: 1987*. Auburn, AL: Truman Pierce Institute.

Caporeal, L.R. (1985). College students' computer use. *The Journal of Higher Education, 56*(2), 172–188.

Carnegie Forum on Education and the Economy. (1986). *A nation prepared: Teachers for the 21st century*. New York: Carnegie Corporation.

Collis, B. (1988). *Computers, curriculum, and whole-class instruction: Issues and ideas*. Belmont, CA: Wadsworth.

Hall, G.E., Loucks, S.F., Rutherford, W.L., & Newlove, B.W. (1975). Levels of use of the innovation: A framework for analyzing innovation adoption. *Journal of Teacher Education, 26*(1), 54–55.

Gorrell, J., Cuevas, A., & Downing, H. (1988). Computer simulations of classroom behavior problems. *Journal of Computers and Education, 12*(2), 283–287.

The Holmes Group. (1986). *Tomorrow's teachers.* East Lansing, MI: The Holmes Group.

Kaufman, R.A. (1972). *Educational system planning.* Englewood Cliffs, NJ: Prentice-Hall.

Kent, P. (1988). The evolution of a computing assistance program for faculty. *Academic Computing, 3*(2), 28–29, 51–53.

National Commission on Excellence in Education. (1983). *A nation at risk.* Washington, DC: U.S. Department of Education.

Office of Technology Assessment (1988). *Power on! New tools for teaching and learning* (OTA-SET-379). Washington, DC: U.S. Government Printing Office.

13
Implementing Computer-Based Instruction in Community Colleges

Lois S. Wilson
Ford Aerospace Corporation
Reston, VA

BACKGROUND

During the late 1960s, the community college system in the United States began to expand both in student enrollment and in number of colleges. At the same time, interest in computer-based instruction was beginning to stir in the research communities in industry and universities.

In 1971, the National Science Foundation (NSF) through its Office of Technological Innovations, awarded the MITRE Corporation, a not-for-profit systems research firm, a multimillion dollar grant to develop a computer-based instructional (CBI) system and demonstrate its impact upon education.

Under the NSF grant, the first application of the system was to provide English and mathematics instruction at two community colleges. NSF chose the community college environment for the initial demonstration because of its many unique characteristics in the academic community, including such characteristics as the growing enrollment, the need for more efficient use of instructors, the emphasis upon teaching rather than research, the willingness to apply innovative teaching techniques, and the diversity of student backgrounds and entrance abilities.

Because of those fortunate combinations of characteristics, community colleges were among the early seats of CBI innovations. Phoenix College of the Maricopa County (Arizona) Community College District and the Alexandria campus of Northern Virginia Community College were chosen as the demonstration sites for the NSF program. Remedial and freshman mathematics and English composition were selected as the initial demonstration courses. These two courses were chosen not because of any sophisticated media selection algorithm or because they were especially suited to CBI presentation. Instead, they were selected for the very practical reason that all students were required to take mathematics and English and, therefore, the program would be assured of a very large target population. That, indeed, proved to be the case.

CBI as Mainline Instruction

Computer-based instruction, when used at all in the 1960s or early 1970s, had generally been considered as an adjunctive resource to supplement conventional classroom instruction or as remedial instruction. (It should be noted that these are still the most frequent uses today.) Very often, CBI applications were not instruction at all; they consisted of short programs of practice or test questions given to the students on a computer. The most frequent application of CBI was in drill or practice exercises given to students after they had been taught about a topic in a conventional classroom by a teacher. In certain other cases, CBI was used as short-term enrichment programs for the students who were progressing faster than their average classmates.

The instruction for the NSF program, however, was very different. It was designed as complete, mainline instruction. The computer would be the primary method of delivering instruction, and the classroom instructor would serve as a facilitator-manager-advisor for the classroom rather than as the primary deliverer of the instruction. The built-in testing program required the students to reach specified levels of mastery, spending as little or as much time online as it took them to master each objective. Large blocks of instruction at several difficulty levels were included for each objective to allow students at many entry levels to achieve mastery. Students not only proceeded at their own pace, but they also had control over the sequence of their instruction and the strategies they used to learn an objective.

Complete courses were developed by subject matter experts, instructional designers, and graphics designers working in conjunction with faculty members from the two community colleges. Students began using the mathematics course during the 1974–75 academic year; the English courses were begun a year later.

Independent Evaluations

NSF contracted with the Educational Testing Service (ETS) to conduct an independent evaluation of the educational impact of the English and mathematics CBI courses at the two community colleges. The evaluation was a two-year study conducted from 1974 through 1976. The results demonstrated that in both English and mathematics, the students who completed the CBI courses scored significantly higher on objective posttests than comparable students who completed equivalent courses in conventional classes. English students also scored significantly higher on an essay posttest (Alderman, 1978). Similar positive results also occurred in a concurrent evaluation conducted by Brigham Young University (BYU) using remedial English students (Bunderson, 1977).

The ETS report for English compared only those community college students in both the CBI and the conventional courses who completed the courses in the academic term. In those courses in which CBI was used as it was designed to be used, that is, as mainline instruction, there were consistent and statistically significant differences favoring the CBI course over conventional instruction on the objective tests of writing skills. Student performance on the essay tests was also higher in the CBI sections, except in one section in which the instructor in the CBI class was not familiar with CBI.

When the CBI course was not used as mainline instruction (despite its design as such), the achievement results for students were mixed. When the CBI course was used as adjunctive instruction, only students of relatively high academic ability experienced gains on the posttests. Those CBI students of low academic ability scored lower on posttests than similar students in conventional classrooms. Use of the CBI course, in this case for supplemental instruction with low ability students, did not produce the positive gains found in mainline CBI applications, nor was it designed for that purpose.

The ETS report for mathematics was not limited to students who completed the CBI course within the academic term because the completion rates were too low. It must be noted here that the CBI courses were entirely self-paced, and no external pressures were exerted upon students to complete the course within the academic term. To expand the population that was being analyzed, ETS included all students who completed the mathematics courses during the academic year. In that analysis, students in five of the six CBI courses achieved significantly better than students in the conventional classes.

ETS also examined subscores of the mathematics posttests to determine whether CBI was more effective in teaching certain areas of mathematics. Results in two areas showed statistically significant differences, and both

favored the CBI instruction. The two areas were solution of routine problems and equations. The effects are most likely attributable to the depth
of coverage of the two topics in the CBI course and the extensive opportunities for practice on the system. In those areas of mathematics considered to be most difficult, the CBI course showed consistently positive
effects.

Completion Rates

One key phrase in the study that should be noted was "students who completed the CBI courses." The percentage of students who completed the
CBI courses within one academic term varied widely among the different
applications of the courses. Completion rate is clearly dependent upon the
environment in which CBI is used. What is more, completion rate is an effect of self-pacing rather than of CBI and must be managed in self-paced
classes in any medium. Research indicates that unless there is some sort of
external management effort, fewer students will complete a self-paced
course than an instructor-led course (Atkins & Lockhart, 1976; Lloyd,
McMullin, & Fox, 1974).

The initial community college implementations of the mathematics
period is built into the course in the form of scheduled classes, assignments, and tests. Motivation must be built into a self-paced course also,
particularly in a CBI course in which students may be studying at many
different times of the day rather than during a scheduled class time. The
CBI instructor must assume the role of course manager, giving each individual student specific progress goals and periodically evaluating the student's performance in relation to those assigned goals. Completion rates
within a CBI course will often depend upon the extent to which an instructor serves as the course manager. More will be said about the instructor's role in CBI later in this chapter.

The initial community college implementations of the mathematics
and English courses placed no emphasis upon course completion. Early in
the evaluation period, it became obvious that high completion rates could
not be expected unless there was a more structured environment. Therefore, when BYU set up their CBI program using the same instructional
materials as the community colleges, the CBI classes included weekly
scheduled class meetings, periodic small-group discussions, student and
instructor meetings, and scheduled tests. These interactive periods were
designed to motivate students to complete the courses within the academic term.

The result of this approach to CBI completion was that it produced
completion rates generally higher than those for comparable conventional
classes at BYU.

The average completion rates for the CBI English classes were extremely high, ranging from 88 percent to 96 percent. The CBI completion rates exceeded the conventional class completion rate of 82 percent even though the latter was calculated very much more liberally than the CBI rates. (The conventional classes' rate calculations did not include any of the large number of students who withdrew before the third week of class although the CBI rate calculations did include those students. The CBI calculations included all students who began the online instruction.)

The average completion rate in BYU conventional mathematics classes was 65 percent. All classes taught by instructors who were trained in CBI produced higher completion rates. Two classes were taught by instructors who were not familiar with CBI, and they produced mixed completion rates. One had a completion rate of 72 percent, and the other had a completion rate of 33 percent.

It is apparent that, when specific efforts are taken to encourage students to complete their CBI courses and their progress is monitored at regular intervals, it is possible to increase completion rates substantially and still work within the self-paced environment. Although the community college CBI implementation did not have completion rate as a criterion for evaluation, the community college English instructors held class meetings and group discussions. The community college mathematics courses were totally self-paced, had no class meetings, and imposed no penalty for reenrolling for the same course in subsequent terms. As a result, the community college English competition rate was significantly higher than the community college mathematics completion rate.

Following the evaluations and as a result of the completion data collected during the studies, more rigorous management strategies were put in place at the community colleges. As a result, course completion rates since the initial evaluation have met or exceeded those of conventional classes. In fact, at one of the community colleges students were for several years permitted to select either the CBI course or the conventional course. In the last few years, enrollment in the conventional class declined to the point that it is no longer offered. All freshman mathematics is delivered through CBI.

It should be noted that even in the first year of implementation of a radically new approach to instruction, nearly as many English students finished the course using CBI as did those using the conventional approach to instruction, and the CBI students performed significantly better on achievement tests.

CBI in community colleges is a very powerful instructional tool and will continue to have substantial impact on educational approaches to instruction. The two demonstration sites for the NSF project have been using CBI without interruption for more than fourteen years. These sites have been joined by several new community colleges during the last several years.

The new sites have used the original mathematics and English courseware and have developed additional courseware by themselves. The community colleges have also developed a policy of sharing courseware among one another so as to enlarge their body of instructional materials without having to produce it all by themselves.

COURSEWARE FOR CBI

The preceding dicussion of an early implementation of CBI in community colleges clearly indicates that CBI can be highly effective and can succeed as an instructional tool if careful planning precedes its implementation. Radical changes in the educational process can occur only with detailed and full planning. That is especially true when the change is a major change to the existing system, and CBI is a major change to the instructional environment in most community colleges.

As will be discussed in detail in the next section of this chapter, developing courseware for CBI is not a trivial pursuit. Furthermore, implementing CBI in a community college requires planning, preparations, training, and funding. Therefore, as a first step, let us examine the kinds of courseware that are appropriate for CBI so that appropriate implementation is more likely to occur from the beginning.

Certain types of instruction lend themselves well to CBI, but others do not. It may be obvious that teaching most motor skills, such as driving, with CBI will not work very well. It is perfectly acceptable to teach the theory behind driving or the rules of the road using CBI, but the actual motor skills of driving must be taught on actual or simulated vehicles. However, teaching other motor skills, such as typing, will work very nicely. Students can use the computer keyboard as easily as a typewriter keyboard to learn typing skills.

A somewhat less obvious difficulty is attempting to teach skills that require analysis of text passages. Computers do not analyze large text passages well. A CBI program can be developed to teach and analyze grammar rules or spelling rules or punctuation rules, but it cannot determine the literary or analytical quality of an original text passage. In the community college English program described above, all essays were graded by instructors offline. Students learned rules and theories online, the applications were performed offline, and the grades were entered onto the computer to be managed online.

A third consideration when selecting CBI courses is the peripheral equipment that may or may not be available with the computer system that will be used and the expenses involved in using peripheral equipment. For example, the conversational part of language instruction can only be taught when audio is available with the system. Videotapes, videodiscs, audiotapes, and audiodiscs are available as peripheral devices for certain CBI systems, but not for all. And they increase the price of any system. If the goal is to teach second-language conversation courses, one or more of those devices will be necessary in the CBI program. When teaching what is often called "soft skills," such as salesmanship or interviewing techniques, video is generally necessary. Video will raise the cost of the system, and it will raise the cost of the courseware.

To determine the courses that will work well as community college CBI courses, let us consider the community college environment and the reasons for changing a course from conventional instruction to CBI. Each community college environment will be different, but some typical examples will illustrate the concept.

Suppose the community college wishes to teach a course in basic chemistry, but very little laboratory space and equipment are available for the students. CBI can simulate science experiments very well and give the students a lot of opportunity to investigate chemical principles. One computer laboratory with no other equipment will serve as the science laboratory. In this case, the laboratory portion of the course may be online and the remainder of the course may be taught conventionally.

Next, suppose that a particular community college finds that it has a large population of students who require remedial instruction in basic mathematics. First, much of the mathematics faculty dislikes teaching the basic course, so it is difficult to staff. Second, the students need a lot of drill with basic mathematics operations. Third, the students are often embarrassed in a classroom situation that exposes their lack of knowledge of basic mathematics skills in front of their peers. CBI will handle each of these problems very nicely. It will reduce the number of instructors who must teach this basic mathematics course, since one instructor can manage many more students in a CBI classroom than in a conventional classroom. Students can pace themselves and take the number of drill exercises that they need to master the basic operations. Students will also be working independently for the most part and, therefore, will not reveal their errors to their peers.

Finally, suppose that the community college is in a large city, and three-quarters of the student body is composed of working adults who are trying to get a college education in many different fields. First, they must take classes and study at odd hours of the day. Very often, these odd hours are after work, and scheduling the classes they need to complete a program can be difficult. Second, because they are interested in many different fields, there may not be sufficient students in one term to justify a regular class. In this situation, CBI can solve both problems with mainline instruction, as described earlier. If the course is computer-based, students may have open entry to and open exit from the course. They can also be permitted access to the system 24 hours a day for studying. CBI is also especially useful for courses that have limited enrollment, but are still necessary to offer. An instructor need not be dedicated to teaching a section of the course each academic term. Instead, the material is online whenever a student wishes to register for the course, and an instructor can be assigned to monitor and manage students in several different courses at one time.

A few of the possible scenarios that might support a community college CBI effort have been described above. The scenarios are not intended to be exhaustive. There are, for example, a great many reasons that CBI is particularly beneficial to adult learners, including the following.

First, many community college students are students who have not performed particularly well in conventional classrooms. CBI offers a novel way to learn, removing them from the environment in which they did not perform well earlier.

Second, CBI is motivating and infinitely patient with students. It will allow the student to try a problem repeatedly without becoming annoyed with the student.

Third, feedback on student progress can be given to the students and instructors immediately. Adult learners want to know how they have progressed. They often cannot wait weeks for a paper to be returned to find out what they do not know.

Fourth, instruction is self-paced. Since the knowledge that adults have varies much more widely than with children, students can stay in lessons until they are sure they have mastered them, and they can move quickly through lessons that contain materials they already know. Adults are much less tolerant of "busy work" than are children.

Fifth, instruction is individualized to meet the student's needs. Most adults are intrinsically motivated to learn materials they need to know and intolerant of learning materials they feel they will never need.

Sixth, peer pressure and embarrassment can be reduced or eliminated by CBI. Adults have great difficulty exposing a lack of knowledge to others and often have learned to compensate for limitations that can keep them from learning.

Seventh, student performance can be evaluated immediately and accurately by the computer and standardized records can be produced automatically.

Eighth, highly trained instructors can use their time counseling students and helping those who are having difficulty rather than spending their time grading papers or delivering the same primary instruction hour after hour.

There are clearly many reasons to use CBI in community colleges, and there are some reasons not to use it. The particular circumstances in the community college should determine whether it is used or not. If the administration of a community college makes the decision to use CBI, extensive planning must occur before any program is undertaken and many groups of people must be included in that planning process. The programs that succeed are those that are preceded by proper planning based on the specifically identified needs of the community college.

PLANNING FOR CBI IMPLEMENTATION

The years of experience since the initial implementation of CBI in the two community colleges described earlier in this chapter have produced many lessons learned. From these lessons, a checklist has been developed to assist others in the process of implementation. The checklist is reasonably comprehensive and will put the potential implementation program on the right path for success.

Off-the-Shelf Courseware

Developing courseware is by far the most expensive and time-consuming part of implementing CBI. Equipment costs are a small fraction of the costs of implementing CBI. The better approach for an initial CBI implementation is to use courseware that already exists. Some of the courseware may even be public domain materials and, therefore, available for reproduction costs. That is the case with the English and mathematics courseware developed under the NSF grant for the community college program. Courseware can be reviewed before it is purchased, and instructors should always take the opportunity to evaluate the courseware for their own applications before any commitment is made to purchase it.

One warning should be given about off-the-shelf courseware. Instructors are notorious for voicing the position that "if it was not invented here, it cannot be good." When they evaluate off-the-shelf courseware, instructors must consider ways they can fit it into their own environment just as they would do with a textbook. If they think of the courseware as a tool to use in the classroom, they will consider effective ways to use the materials. They should also be aware that many courseware programs can be modified or customized in some ways before it is implemented. That is far less costly than starting from scratch to develop new courseware.

If the decision is made that courseware will be locally developed, plans must be put in place for that development to occur. Instructors must be given extensive release time if they are to assist in producing the courseware. It is reasonable to figure that one hour of CBI instruction will take between 50 and 300 hours to develop, depending upon its complexity, the quality of the authoring language used, and the experience of the staff doing the development.

The best courseware is developed by a team that includes a subject matter expert, an instructional designer, an instructional programmer, and a computer graphics designers. Such teams can usually be assembled at a university that has grant funding, research budgets, and graduate assistants. It is much harder to do that at a community college. If a team such as that cannot be put together, the community college should either dismiss the idea of new development and purchase the courseware or plan for extremely slow development of the new materials. That may mean that the computer system will not be used for anything except courseware development for several years, and students will have to wait for the system to become an instructional tool.

If the instructors are to develop the courseware alone, they must be taught to program the lessons and they must be taught basic principles of instructional design. Instructors are excellent subject matter experts, but few of them have the other skills that are crucial to effective courseware development.

When instructors have a part in selecting the materials, revising the materials, or developing new materials, they are much more likely to want the program to succeed. That is a first step in having a successful CBI program. The administration must involve the classroom instructor in the process.

Computer Operations and Maintenance

Someone must operate the computer systems that run the CBI courseware. Although this is generally not a difficult or time-consuming job, it is an essential job and time must be set aside to perform system operations.

The operator must first be trained to run the system. Most CBI systems have procedures to bring up and take down the system, to back up student data each day, and to load new materials when they become available. These procedures must be learned.

As essential as system operations is system hardware and software maintenance. CBI systems are often sold with 90-day or one-year hardware warranties and one-year software subscriptions. There should be provisions in the budget to renew hardware and software maintenance contracts when they expire.

The Federal Government estimates the life of a computer system to be eight years, but most CBI systems will last much longer if they are properly cared for. Parts of the CBI systems used in the community college programs described earlier are more than 14 years old and are still functioning. Preventive, or periodic, maintenance should be conducted regularly.

These tasks may be the job of the operator or the classroom instructor. The important thing is that someone must take the responsibility for system operations and maintenance and perform the tasks that must be done to keep the system running properly.

Instructor Training

Classroom instructors must be trained to use CBI. Most important, they must know thoroughly the CBI materials that they will be using in the classroom, just as they would know thoroughly a new textbook that was being introduced in their program. They must go through the online materials themselves as if they were the student. They must try all the different branches and paths included in the materials. They must know how the materials can be adapted to individual student use and when it is appropriate to remove students from online materials and help them with other instruction.

CBI is considerably different from conventional instruction in many ways. If the CBI program is to be used as supplemental materials or enrichment materials, the instructor must determine the appropriate places to offer it to the students and the appropriate students to offer it to. The instructors must develop a curriculum that fits the various media into a total package of instruction.

If the CBI program is to be used as mainline instruction, the role of the instructor changes in the CBI classroom. Instructors must be trained to handle this new role, which will be new to most of them. Instructors must be taught key features of managing an individualized and self-paced classroom, in which each student will be at a different place in the course and no two students will be studying the same materials.

The classroom instructor becomes the tutor-manager-advisor rather than the primary deliverer of instruction. In the role of tutor, the instructor works one-on-one with individual students who need more help than they get from the CBI materials. Instructors no longer have to grade the student or produce reports for the administration; these tedious jobs are done by the computer automatically. The instructors' time is spent with the students.

As the experience of the early community college programs illustrated, the instructor must also assume the role of manager-advisor. The instructor becomes more critical to the students in helping the students to manage their progress. The instructor must help students by setting reasonable completion goals for them and then monitoring their progress towards those goals. The instructor has the benefit of computer-generated reports that will track the students, but these reports must be used by the instructors to determine who is falling behind or not attending the CBI sessions of the class. When students are taking one CBI class among many conventional classes and they are told there is no penalty for delayed course completion, they will set the CBI class as their last priority. A study conducted by the Alexandria campus of the Northern Virginia Community College indicated that the average usage of CBI workstations for students not completing the CBI courses was approximately 30 hours. The conventional classes, however, met for 50 hours each term in addition to homework time (Sasscer, 1977). Clearly, students who do not take their online instruction will not complete the course.

Although mainline CBI courses can be conducted entirely as self-paced programs, early community college experience has indicated that occasional group meetings are useful for course continuity and as vehicles for encouraging and tracking progress. In certain courses, group sessions can be used to develop specialized skills such as speaking to the class or conducting specific team projects. Interpersonal skills developed in a collegial atmosphere can benefit all students.

Instructor training is indeed key to all successful CBI implementations. Planning for instructor training must begin early and must be thorough. Instructors chosen to conduct CBI classes must approve of this medium of instruction and must be willing to adapt to the changes required of self-pacing and individualization. Instructors who enjoy most the classroom role of delivering information will find CBI mainline instruction inappropriate for them. Instructors who enjoy most the role of working with the individual student to correct his or her immediate problems will be the best CBI instructors.

Student Training

Students must also be trained to use the CBI system and the courseware for their program. The classroom instructor can generally train students to work online very quickly. The community college instructors in the two pilot programs developed a short course that taught their students to use the CBI mathematics and English courses in about 30 minutes. Students do not have to have keyboard skills to use the computer keyboards for most programs, since typing time does not matter in most programs. Use of the system can be taught in a group session at the beginning of the course, using either a short workbook with online exercises or a fully online course. The instructor can then observe any students having problems and handle those problems immediately. By the end of the first class session, all students should be able to begin their CBI course and work comfortably at their workstations.

Students must be assured during the orientation session that they cannot damage or destroy the system no matter what they type or touch on the display. The greatest fear that most students have when they first encounter CBI is that touching certain keys will destroy all of the courseware or cause them to lose all of their work. Since students are not working with the internal system software when they are using CBI programs, it is very unlikely that they can do any damage to the software or courseware. Good CBI courseware will always warn the student on the display when an action can cause the student to lose work he or she has completed.

During the orientation session, students should also be taught to care for the CBI equipment. Most CBI hardware is not fragile, but, like any equipment, it can be damaged. The most common hardware problem is with keyboards. If students are permitted to eat or drink near the keyboards, there is always risk that liquids can be spilled on the keyboards or food dropped on the keys. The spills and crumbs can cause the keyboards to fail.

A word must be said about CBI course materials that permit learner control. Many individualized programs, including the mathematics and English programs used in the early community college pilot study, permit the students to control their own learning paths. They can skip materials that they feel they do not need, they can do as many practice exercises as they feel necessary, they can skip whole pieces of instruction by passing a pretest, and they can spend long periods in certain sections of the materials. The learning theory behind permitting the students to control their own paths of instruction is sound and is based on the fact that only the students know at any given moment exactly what they do or do not know. The instructor can assess a student's knowledge only immediately after that student has completed a test.

However, it is important to note that many students will not use learner control effectively and efficiently unless they are explicitly taught to do so. The most frequent pattern that students will follow is the pattern that they use with textbooks in conventional classes; that is, they will study everything carefully, answer every practice exercise, and access each part of the program even when they already know the materials. Students must be guided to use various sensible paths through the CBI materials by showing them the different approaches they can follow in studying the materials. They should be encouraged to skip materials they already know and to take only as many practice exercises as they need to be sure they can pass the lesson test. They must be told that exhausting the pool of practice items does not raise their grade as it might with workbook assignments.

The New Community College Environment

If CBI is to succeed in the community college, certain things in the environment must change to accommodate the different approach to instruction. One of these is a change in the times students can be in the classroom. CBI students often want to work online at off hours, particularly in the evenings. To get the greatest cost benefit from the CBI equipment, the college administration should arrange to have the system available for student use many more hours of the day than classes are in session. If the system is available to them, students can work for long hours alone to catch up with work they missed or to move ahead on lessons. The classroom instructor need not be always available when the students are online. Certain scheduled hours can be announced to let students know when the instructor is available. Student assistants or classroom proctors can monitor the CBI room when instructors are not available.

Depending upon the individual community college's facilities and regulations, a computer laboratory can be set up to provide open access to the system, or the system might be installed in the library, which often operates for extended hours. The important thing is that facility planning occur early in the program.

Budgets must also be planned well ahead of a CBI implementation. Budgets must be for the life span of the program, not just for the equipment. Budgets should be planned for continuing maintenance, for instructor and proctor time, for the purchase of additional software and courseware as new programs become available, for telephone lines if the system requires telephone hookups, and perhaps for release time to develop or revise courseware programs. When budgets are planned to cover only initial purchase of the equipment, administrators suddenly discover that much more is needed to run the CBI program effectively. Thus, the full budget planning should be done well ahead of time and cover the entire anticipated length of the program.

Another environmental change that is necessary but sometimes difficult to make in the community college is redefinitions of staff roles and full-time equivalencies (FTEs). A role should be defined that permits the use of proctors or students assistants in off hours rather than using instructor time. If mainline CBI courses are planned, class sizes can generally be considerably larger than they are in conventional classes. At Northern Virginia and Phoenix Community Colleges, a hundred or more workstations are available for students to use. A plan for accounting equitably for these large classes must be developed so that instructors are not unduly rewarded or penalized for the CBI program.

One other environmental change is crucial to the success of a CBI implementation. Most community colleges that are considering a CBI implementation already have computers in use in administrative functions. It is possible for many CBI systems to be used for both academic and administrative computing purposes, but there is great risk in combining the two functions on a single system. Computer systems, when they are first purchased, are seen as having enormous capacity. But just like filing cabinets or closets, they are quickly filled. As the college becomes familiar with the potential of the computer system, more and more uses are found for it and it services more and more activities of the college. That will happen on both the academic and the administrative sides of the system. When a dual-function computer system fills up, the universal loser is the academic activities. Registration, testing, reporting, and other administrative activities will always be given the priority. Therefore, it is best to keep the functions and the systems clearly separated and distinct from one another. In the planning phase, it should be made clear that this particular computer system is dedicated to computer-based instruction and can serve no other role on campus.

CBI in Community Colleges

The environmental change that is most often anticipated by groups considering a CBI implementation is a change to the physical environment. Interestingly, the requirement to change the physical environment to accommodate computer equipment has almost disappeared in recent years. Personal computers and local area network equipment generally need only the usual environment found in any office and most college classrooms. The temperature and the humidity of the room should be what is suitable for comfortable human habitation. Electrical requirements are simply standard outlets. In areas that have frequent power failures, power surges, brownouts, or blackouts, it may be necessary to have surge protectors installed. Their costs are nominal. Only when a large mainframe computer is going to be installed is it necessary to plan for special accommodations such as raised floors, controlled air conditioning, and dehumidifiers.

Courseware Design and Control

Two other items must be considered in the initial CBI planning stages. They are the design and, thus, the intended purpose of the courseware and courseware configuration management.

The design and intended purposes of the courseware that is selected or developed are critical to the success of the CBI implementation. One decision that must be made is whether the implementation will be mainline instruction or supplemental instruction. That decision can greatly affect the attitudes of the instructors, especially if they view mainline instruction as a replacement for instructors. If the college is short of faculty and growing or has courses that none of the faculty wants to teach, mainline instruction that changes the instructor's role may be acceptable. When enrollment is declining or when the courseware replaces conventional courses that instructors like to teach, the CBI implementation will be viewed with alarm. When instructors are opposed to the implementation, it will fail. Instructors will suddenly discover that good courseware is flawed or the system is too hard for students to use or the approach to their subject is too simplistic. Instructors must take part in the courseware decisions and must buy into the CBI implementation for it to succeed.

When courseware is selected that meets the faculty's needs, it must be used as it was designed to be used or it must be revised to meet different needs. A course designed as mainline instruction cannot serve as enrichment or remedial supplemental instruction anymore than a grammar textbook can be used for literature study. Instructors who use mainline instruction as a basis for lectures and keep their students in lockstep, need to be enlightened as to the purpose of the instruction.

Earlier in this chapter, the statement was made that courseware should be previewed before it is selected. It is worth repeating that the instructors must preview the courseware early in the planning stages and agree that it meets their needs before selection of a particular program is made.

Once courseware is selected, there must be management of that courseware. During the planning stages, someone must be identified as the person in charge of courseware configuration management. Otherwise, instructors, proctors, student assistants, or anyone with access to the system will quickly learn how to change the courseware and they will use spare time to do just that. Two things can happen to unmanaged courseware that can destroy the implementation. One is that many versions of the courseware can spring up so that there is no longer a single approved course that serves the campus. The other is that the course may stay as a single version, but one that is entirely different from what the faculty agreed to purchase.

Those dangers can be avoided by having the configuration manager be the only person who is allowed to approve changes to the courseware. That can easily be managed through a controlled security system within the CBI system that allows access to coding only to selected people who have the proper passwords. Most CBI systems provide that security within the system. If the system you select does not, reconsider purchasing it.

CONCLUSIONS

Computer-based instructional implementations in community colleges can be successful, cost effective, and instructionally sound. CBI can provide students with a new way to learn that can sometimes handle their problems more effectively than a conventional classroom. It can relieve instructors of the tedious grading and management chores and deliver classes that no one wants to teach. It can permit flexible scheduling within the community college environment. It can provide courses of instruction that might not otherwise be possible. It can deliver high-quality instruction with absolute consistency. It can do all of these things if the implementation is planned fully and carefully. Here is a checklist to use for a CBI implementation. If the community college adds to it those items that are unique to its environment, the college is ready to begin planning the CBI implementation.

- Develop the complete budget for the life of the system at the start, including equipment, maintenance, staffing, software and courseware, and facilities.
- Select field-proven, faculty reviewed, off-the-shelf courseware whenever possible.
- If courseware is to be developed locally, plan the release time for the staff members on the team and a sufficient budget to fund the development.
- Involve the instructors from the beginning of the planning phase.
- Train the staff who will operate and maintain the system.
- Redefine staff roles and full-time equivalencies, as necessary.
- Train the classroom instructors to use the system, to use the courseware, and to operate a self-paced, individualized classroom.
- Develop instruction to teach students to use and care for the system.
- Provide an open facility with a flexible schedule for the system.
- Keep academic and administrative computer applications separate and distinct from one another.
- Use the courseware as it was designed to be used.
- Control the courseware configuration, and maintain the courseware.
- Begin planning the total CBI implementation program well ahead of the date for the installation of the system.

REFERENCES

Alderman, D.L. (1978). *Evaluation of the TICCIT computer-assisted instructional system in the community college: Final report.* Princeton, NJ: Educational Testing Service.

Atkins, J.A., & Lockhart, L. (1976). Instructor-paced college quizzing: A behavioral analysis of preference and performance. In L.E. Fraley & E.Z. Vargas (Eds.), *Behavior research and technology in higher education.* Gainesville, FL: Society for Behavioral Technology and Engineering, University of Florida.

Bunderson, C.V. (1977). *A rejoinder to the ETS evaluation of TICCIT* (CTRC Tech. Rep. No. 22). Provo, UT: Brigham Young University.

Lloyd, K.E., McMullin, W.E., & Fox, R. (1974, October). *Rate of completing unit tests as a function of student-pacing and instruction-pacing.* Paper presented at the Fifth Annual Conference on Behavior Analysis in Education, Kansas City, MO.

Sasscer, M.F. (1977). *TICCIT project 1976–1977: Final report.* Alexandria, VA: Northern Virginia Community College.

14
Design, Development, and Technology Transfer Issues in the Job Skills Education Program*

Robert K. Branson
Center for Educational Technology
Florida State University

INTRODUCTION

This chapter has four purposes:

- To offer general propositions about CBI.
- To describe the Army's Job Skills Education Program (JSEP) ("jay-sepp") CBI basic skills curriculum.
- To describe the transfer of JSEP to civilian education and vocational training settings.
- To describe the lessons learned from JSEP to guide future development and technology transfer efforts.

Attributes of CBI

The discussions in this chapter center on CBI systems that:

- are systematically designed to meet specific organizational needs.
- are controlled by an internal management system.

---

* The views in this chapter are solely those of the author and do not represent the official views of the U.S. Army Research Institute or the U.S. Department of Education.

- assign online and offline lessons based on the progress and achievements of individual students.
- are designed to be dedicated systems.

Why Use CBI?

For CBI to be a system of choice, it should provide some of these advantages when compared to alternatives. CBI should:

- be less costly.
- be more effective.
- take less time to reach criterion.
- provide higher quality instruction.
- be more versatile.
- be preferred by users.

Improvability. In addition, I suggest that CBI has the advantage of greater "improvability"—the capability of adding and retaining improvements through time.

It is my view that teacher-delivered, lockstep instruction is as good now as it will ever be, and probably approached that limit with the introduction of overhead projector, slide projector, and dustless blackboard. Conversely, CBI systems have just begun to realize their full potential.

CBI systems developers provide for subject matter reviews, editorial reviews, and collect user performance data and comments for revisions. Through time, errors and glitches are removed. As the system is revised, lessons work better, and negative user comments decline. The system retains all improvements made; further improvements can be added. Improvement increments are relatively large since few CBI systems have matured. While each improvement adds costs, the system retains the total value. It is this additivity property that defines improvability and separates CBI from teacher-delivered instruction, where there are few provisions for making improvements, and any made remain with the *instructor* not with the *system*. When instructors regularly depart, the investment in them is lost and their replacements must learn the same skills.

Based on normal curve statistics, where half the instructors are above and half are below median performance, the chances of a replacement instructor being better than the previous one is equal to the probability that the replacement will be worse. While some may argue that "good" teachers continue to improve, documentation of these cumulative improvements is unpromising. Even if this argument were valid statistically, only half of the teachers are above average; half the students would still receive below-average instruction. Only small improvements are made through experience because teacher-delivered instruction, a mature practice, it is performing as well as it ever will (Branson, 1987).

Challenging the Propositions

Since CBI research and development is done almost exclusively by advocates with vested interests, we should challenge the seven basic propositions in light of charges made by critics (e.g., Levin & Meister, 1985). Does CBI really offer the benefits claimed? To answer that question fairly, we must conduct a fair, *independent* analysis of instructional requirements. If CBI cannot be reasonably selected using a research-based media selection model, then it should not be chosen (Reiser & Gagne, 1983). Bad CBI selection is management failure, not CBI failure.

Less costly. To compare costs fairly between two forms of instruction requires agreement on the results of interest. I believe that the *unit cost per graduate*, calculated by using a life-cycle (e.g., eight years) system acquisition and management model, is the best way to compare costs. Moreover, the *cost per hour of instruction* is misleading and should never be used; technologies are driven by output, not process.

CBI systems have much higher front-end costs. Whether a CBI system realizes its design potential to be less costly depends largely on how is it managed in day-to-day operations. CBI sytems do not achieve cost and output goals, *managers do.*

Two approaches can be fairly compared only when both are designed to achieve the same objectives. It is rarely possible to find that equality. For example, even when traditional instruction has been systematically designed to meet a specific need, instructors often modify the objectives, thereby reducing the quality and changing the coverage (Baker & Huff, 1981). Traditional instruction is rarely implemented consistently. CBI courses give all students instruction on the same objectives at the same level of quality.

Table 14.1 presents a cost comparison between a CBI system and traditional instruction using three possible student-to-teacher ratios. Notice that for a 15:1 student-to-teacher ratio, the savings per student (graduate) amount to $205, or a total of $830,000 over the 8-year life-cycle. The column headed "Payback period," refers to the length of time required to recover the initial cash investment in the CBI system. The model used permits the user to modify the assumptions and recalculate the results.

Table 14.1 results are based on these assumptions:

- Students paid $3.35 per hour; teachers $12.50 per hour.
- Traditional instruction requires 150 hours. CBI requires 100 hours to achieve equal results.

Table 14.1. Cost Comparison Between Traditional Instruction and CBI* for Three Student-to-Teacher Ratios

Student/Teacher Ratio	Payback Period	Savings per Student (after payback)	Total Savings (over 8-year life cycle)
10:1	15 months	$265	$1,130,000
15:1	21 months	$205	830,000
20:1	26 months	$170	680,000

*MicroTICCIT CBI system

- CBI classrooms have 20 students and one instructor; traditional classrooms have ratios of 10:1, 15:1, or 20:1.
- The CBI system costs $150,000 to purchase and $15,000 per year to maintain for a hardware life span of 8 years.
- Instruction will be offered 12 hours per day, 5 days per week, and 50 weeks per year.
- The traditional classroom materials costs, including books, were assumed to be zero.
- There will be 600 students per year.
- Facility costs were assumed to be equal.

Many other assumptions, implicit and explicit, are made to get enough data to make comparisons. Assumptions and lack of data are two reasons that valid comparisons are rare.

Caution. When the stated assumptions are met, and for practical reasons they rarely are, the results change. For example, we used an annual 600-person throughput in the cost model. If the regular classes are full and if the CBI throughput drops by 10 percent, the potential savings disappear. Of course, when there are empty seats in regular classrooms and the CBI system is full, the savings are more dramatic. That is why it is wise to use best-case–worst-case scenarios in developing CBI life-cycle cost estimates.

CBI systems are virtually always developed on a mastery learning rather than a time-based model. If they are compared to alternative forms of instruction, they must be compared on the basis of costs required to achieve the same results. If students are paid, are required to reach mastery, and there are enough of them, then it is almost always true that the unit cost per graduate for CBI will be less.

When trainees are not paid, and criterion performance is not required of all graduates, then almost any method will do. That is, if students are only required to attend class and the organization tolerates a wide range of scores on final tests, CBI will add to costs, but not to required results since no final results are specified. If true required outcomes are introduced, then CBI will likely be the system of choice.

More effective. To be more effective, CBI systems must provide instruction better in some way than the alternative. I believe that CBI can be more effective under numerous conditions, including: small scale applications using commercial off-the-shelf courseware; training embedded in operations programs; remote delivery programs where trainers are unavailable; and, large-scale dedicated programs (see Roblyer, Castine, & King, 1988).

Less time. Less time can refer to the average amount of time for each student to achieve criterion, or to the total number of instructional hours for all students to reach criterion. Time is another management-sensitive issue. If CBI were on a self-paced basis and if some students could finish the instruction much earlier than others, management must effectively use the time saved or the exercise is trivial. Scheduling students in and out of the CBI system to gain maximum time advantage requires direct management action. CBI provides an excellent means to save time, but it must be managed to that end.

Higher quality instruction. Quality refers to two distinct features of instruction:

1. The instruction matches the objectives specified. It conforms to specifications.
2. The graduates are well prepared for their jobs. The instruction is fit for its intended use.

The principal advantage that CBI brings to item 1, is that the instruction matches the objectives; once the instruction has been approved and judged to meet specifications, it remains constant for all students. For example, in the Navy's Job-Oriented Basic Skills (JOBS) program, where all sailors needed the prescribed curriculum, individual instructors made major changes in the course content—and all instructors did not make the same changes. Thus, some sailors were denied instruction they needed (Baker & Huff, 1981). CBI will always be of higher quality than traditional instruction on this measure.

The second measure of quality is how well the instruction prepares students for their intended futures. I am not aware of any particular advantages that CBI systems have over conventional mastery instruction on this criterion (see Baker & Hamovich, 1983; Baker & Huff, 1981).

More versatility. Instruction is more versatile if it continuously provides more options to individual students than the alternative. In teacher-delivered instruction all students must stay on the same lesson. CBI can provide any lesson to any student at any time—a valuable feature when students are absent or do not learn at the same pace as the average of the class.

Versatility also means instruction such as simulations and "what if" exercises that cannot be readily provided in conventional classrooms. Substitute or untrained teachers can use the CBI system to provide prescribed instruction when regular instructors are absent or unavailable. One example of a CBI system that will be judged on these criteria is presented next.

THE ARMY'S JOB SKILLS EDUCATION PROGRAM (JSEP)

To teach entering soldiers the basic academic skills they need to learn complex jobs, the Army developed JSEP, a computer-based, functional basic skills curriculum. JSEP was based on the results of a job analysis of the 94 Army jobs held by 85 percent of entering soldiers.

In addition to a flexible Soldier Management System (SMS) that routes students, collects data, and generates reports, JSEP has some 300 lessons online, 30 paper-based lessons managed by the SMS, and tests. Examples of topics covered in JSEP lessons include: numbering and counting, degree measures, trigonometry, vocabulary, reference skills, report writing, and graphing in the coordinate plane. JSEP also has numerous lessons that teach learner strategies (Derry, Jacobs, & Murphy, 1986–87).

We tried to design into JSEP all of the available, important, and desirable features of CBI systems to the fullest possible advantage (Branson & Farr, 1984; Dick, 1985). Four years of field testing have yielded important data used to revise the system.

Historical Background

How do large CBI projects like JSEP get started? In the late 1970s, Army field commanders reported that a substantial number of soldiers graduating from training courses were unable to perform jobs satisfactorily and had limited abilities to use maintenance manuals, perform calculations, and do routine paperwork.

These same problems have been reported in the public schools as well (Shanker, 1988). For example, in the late 1980s, only about 4.7% of graduates could read a railroad or airline time table; only 28% could write an acceptable letter to a prospective employer; only 27% could do a simple two-step math problem. Each of these basis academic skills is prerequisite to learning some Army jobs.

Remedial education. When new soldiers lacking basic skills are sent to technical training courses, their instructors must include remedial education in addition to technical training. Thus, in each technical course some time is devoted to remedial education. When soldiers are unable to keep up with their peers, they are given after-hours extra instruction, or are held back to repeat a block of instruction. Both remedial instruction and recycling, while necessary and humane for individual soldiers, are costly expenses for the Army; not all soldiers need it.

The Basic Skills Education Program (BSEP). The Army provides regular classroom-type education in the Basic Skills Education Program (BSEP), with teaching similar to that soldiers received prior to enlistment (Anderson, 1986). Consequently, the Army faces a dilemma. Either provide extra programs like BSEP for those who need it, or use technical training time to teach these skills to all soldiers, most of whom do not need it (see Sticht, 1975; Philippi, 1988; Duffy, 1985).

The Job and Task Analysis

The Army decided that it would be far better to develop a basic skills curriculum that could be implemented on an Army-wide basis, and that related each basic skill to a soldier's job, rather than to include this instruction in all technical training courses (Lieutenant Colonel R. R. Begland, personal communication, 1988; Major Ron Tarr, personal communication, 1988). To proceed, the Army contracted with a team led by RCA Educational Services to conduct the job and task analysis.

That analysis yielded job-specific basic skills prerequisites (Edward Shepherd, personal communication, 1988). Examples of these basic skills uses were called "Indicator Statements;" a description of a basic skill use on the job. RCA then organized these indicator statements into areas of similarity called "Prerequisite Competencies;" for example, "Identify technical words associated with geometric figures," for which an indicator statement would be, "Measure radius using tape measure."

JSEP Development

When the job analysis was complete, the Army Research Institute (ARI) contracted with the team of Florida State University and Ford Aerospace Corporation (FSU-Ford) to design, develop, and implement a CBI curriculum based on the job analysis.

ARI's decision to require CBI was based, in part, on these considerations:

- A computer-based curriculum provides standard, consistent, and high-quality instruction throughout the Army. Previous attempts to provide consistency have met with little success (Pearson, Foertsch, & Moes, 1985).
- Computer-based instruction offered the opportunity to make the system less costly than regular BSEP.

ARI specified that JSEP be implemented on PLATO and one other computer system. PLATO operates on a large mainframe computer with terminals connected via modems and dedicated data lines. The FSU-Ford team proposed MicroTICCIT as the second system. MicroTICCIT is hosted on a midsize personal computer with more than 200 megabyte storage and is accessed by workstations through a local area network. Each has a comprehensive student management system to handle the details of scheduling students, keeping records, and producing records.

Large and Small CBI Projects

Because of the projected size of the curriculum (400 hours of instruction) and the number of soldiers required to use it, large dedicated CBI systems were proposed. When the project was designed, in 1982, it was not feasible to operate a learning center with multiple copies of more than 300 lessons on removable discs: It is still not. It was far better to store lessons internally and provide an internal management and reporting system for each. The management, control, and reporting problems would have been insurmountable if removable discs had been used. This same management problem will be faced by schools, universities, and industries as well.

Qualitative differences. Whether one works with the Army or a school district, we have come to believe that there are qualitative difference between large and small CBI projects. These differences are found in three areas: formative evaluation, quality control, and configuration management (Branson, 1989). While there is considerable overlap among formative evaluation, quality control, and configuration management, their purposes are different. These processes will be discussed separately.

Formative evaluation. It is critical to establish clear revision priorities in advance because it is not economically feasible to make all the revisions that any reviewer or evaluator might suggest. For large projects like JSEP, it is absolutely essential that rules be established that specify which kinds of revisions must be done first, which kinds should be done second, and which kinds would be done if there were enough time. All "must" revisions are done in all lessons first, then the second priority is addressed, and finally, those third priority changes that can be made are made.

If firm interlesson priority categories are not established, the resources dedicated to revision will be applied on a first-come–first-served basis, rather than on a systematic, programwide, priority basis. Some problems and errors are much more important than others. For example, a consequential error in content would receive first priority; a badly performing test would be second priority; making the ethnic mix in graphics more equitable would be third priority.

Configuration management. The configuration management issue centers around making sure that reviewers, designers, programmers, artists, and the quailty control staff are working from the current and approved version of the design document. When artists, designers, and programmers are working from different versions, the revision process is endless and emotional outbreaks among staff members occur often. For example, if one subject matter expert (SME) says that there is a content error in a lesson, that claim must be validated with another SME before changes are made. Some assigned SMEs are not. The SME problem does not occur when there is only one course or lesson, one reviewer, and one SME. JSEP configuration management took considerably more time and effort than we anticipated.

Each computer system has its own peculiarities and attributes. It is essential that designers be aware of these features and limitations.

Quality control. The quality control (QC) issue is centered around inspection standards that require comparing the lessons with the design documents. Changes in lessons that are made during the final QC check are the most expensive ones. Unlike printed text, in which each page can be seen sequentially, CBI lessons branch to different "pages" as a result of student responses. Thus, QC inspectors must go through the lessons repeatedly, checking all right and wrong choices. Further, even the simplest appearing changes can cause numerous other unintended changes to occur.

JSEP quality control took considerably more time and effort than we anticipated.

Army review. Regardless of the context, Army or civilian, lesson review is a big issue. Although the ARI had built in to the project a review of all lessons, the amount of work involved in reviewing that many lessons, in that much detail, was well beyond their expectations. However, the requirement does exist that someone must speak finally for the Army to approve and release the lesson.

Partially because Army SMEs were not available, the ARI review of JSEP took considerably more time than they had anticipated.

Evaluation Issues

We collaborated with ARI to design the JSEP system and to identify the major dependent variables to be used to judge program success. Two major questions of interest are: Did JSEP meet its design specifications; that is, did the soldiers learn what they were supposed to learn; and, in producing those results, did it do so in a more efficient or less costly manner? The questions are simple enough—the difficulty lies in obtaining good answers.

The dependent variables that could be used to measure JSEP effectiveness include:

- Job performance, including how well a soldier continues to learn a new job requirement
- Whether the soldier is able to pass the promotion test
- Whether the soldier is eligible to reenlist in the Army, based on educational achievements
- How long the soldier stays in the Army (see Baker & Hamovitch, 1983).

To answer questions like these requires longitudinal studies well beyond the scope of the project, however, the Baker and Hamovitch (1983) study does address these questions for the Navy's JOBS program. Similar questions are of critical interest to sponsors of civilian CBI sponsors as well.

Next, JSEP will be judged on the seven CBI advantages from the first part of this chapter, using data from the tryouts. Remember that there are large differences among experiments, tryouts, and full implementation. The results reported here are from a tryout and would neither meet the rigorous control requirements of experiments nor the broad cost criteria of full implementation. Much of the data reported are from a third party evaluation conducted by the American Institutes for Research (AIR) (Hoffman, Hahn, Hoffman, & Dean, 1988), and were collected on lessons that had not been through the final revision process.

JSEP is less costly. The tryout sites had hardware systems sized according to development contract budgets, not according to estimated operational efficiency. Consequently, it is not realistic to use cost data from tryout sites as bases for projecting Army-side results (Branson, Allen, & Hayes, 1985). With properly sized installations, both the PLATO and MicroTICCIT systems appear cost less than regular classes.

JSEP is more effective. According to the AIR evaluation, "Almost four-fifths of the online computer lessons were passed by 75% or more of the soldiers who failed the pretest and then took the instruction" (Hoffman, Hahn, Hoffman, & Dean, 1988, p. viii). Based on documented content validity, established by the job analysis data, we concluded that JSEP is more effective in providing consistent instruction relevant to job requirements.

JSEP takes less time. The evaluators presented data from which we can infer time efficiency. "Many soldiers were already competent in the skills of the JSEP lessons prescribed for their job. About three-fifths of the lessons were passed on the pretest (that is, without any instruction) by half or more of the soldiers attempting them" (Hoffman, Hahn, Hoffman, & Dean, 1988, p. viii).

In JSEP, soldiers take only those lessons required by their jobs and they took lessons only if they failed the pretest; they do not take a block scheduled curriculum. Based on these results, we concluded that JSEP was more efficient than traditional classes.

JSEP is of higher quality. The two standard questions used to define quality were applied to JSEP. The evidence suggests that the program met the design specifications; the system works well in the environment, and the users learned what they were supposed to learn. The Soldier Management System routed the soldiers to the correct lessons and kept track of their progress. The content validity of the lessons is much higher than for BSEP programs (see Pearson, Foertsch, & Moes, 1985; United States General Accounting Office, 1983).

Was it fit for intended use? The program can present the identical curriculum to soldiers at any Army installation in the world. Modifications and improvements can be implemented immediately with virtually no staff training.

Follow-up studies had not been conducted at the time of this writing either for BSEP or JSEP. Consequently, it is not now possible to say whether the Army received the planned benefits, that is whether either program improves job performance, promotion rates, retention rates, or other desired outcomes. Even lacking followup data, we concluded that JSEP was a higher quality program than those it was intended to replace.

JSEP is more versatile. Two measures of versatility can be found in the data: adapting the lesson prescriptions to the needs of individual soldiers as described earlier; and, any soldier can take any assigned lesson on any day. When soldiers are absent for an hour or a week, they begin where they last stopped.

The AIR evaluation provides evidence that JSEP accomplished desirable unstated purposes: "Among these [unstated purposes], reading improved by about 0.6 grade levels and mathematics improved about 1.6 grade levels on the average [on the Test of Adult Basic Education]" (Hoffman, Hahn, Hoffman, & Dean, 1988, p. viii). These appear to be good gains from only 80 hours of instruction; we conclude that JSEP is more versatile than alternative programs.

JSEP is the choice of users. The AIR summary: "Soldiers almost invariably liked JSEP. They stated that the computer-based instruction was enjoyable, held their attention, allowed them to progress at their own pace, forced them to persevere in a task until they had mastered it, and allowed them to make mistakes in private" (Hoffman, Hahn, Hoffman, & Dean, 1988, p. vii).

When asked whether the lessons should be taught by a teacher in the education center, percentages of "No" responses ranged from 64% to 85% depending on where soldiers were stationed. We concluded that JSEP was the majority of soldiers' clear preference over traditional treacher-led classroom instruction.

JSEP has greater improvability. The Army's BSEP curriculum is a good traditional program that has been in place for many years, but a recent evaluation reported that it was not getting better (Pearson, Foertsch, & Moes, 1985).

During a 1988 conference of JSEP site directors and ARI reviewers, I asked if JSEP was better than it was in 1987. The consensus was a clear "Yes." There has been one revision since that meeting. Further, the improvements have added value to the system that will remain, even when the current JSEP instructors leave; JSEP has the critical characteristic of additivity.

Even with soldier acceptance and a good curriculum, the program must be implemented. Important implementation issues will be discussed next.

IMPLEMENTATION ISSUES

Top-down vs. Bottom-up-Issues

Since Ned Ludd (his followers were "Luddites"), an early nineteenth century Leicestershire workman, destroyed labor-saving machinery to protest against technology, managers have been concerned about the problem of organizational change. A basic conflict exists between executives, who must achieve results in a competitive environment, and staff members who generally prefer any changes to be oriented toward making the status quo more attractive (e.g., shorter hours or increased pay).

As the information society became more a reality, the knowledge base for organizational survival moved from the accumulated knowledge of craftsmen to the scientific and technical literature. Managers, who know about new processes to improve the efficiency of their organizations, must make these changes while maintaining a cooperative workforce. Staff members see no benefits to themselves if they are replaced or reduced in status by technology and tend to resist or sabotage new approaches.

Top-down issues. Often, the conflict centers around these issues for managers:

- They must move the organization into the future and insure its survival.
- They must address problems from an overall perspective, not from a local view.
- They are responsible for implementing legislative and policy mandates, even though these may not have popular support.
- While they are responsible for all of these issues, they are usually not closely in touch with local issues and problems.

Bottom-up issues. The operations staff members have different views:

- They do not want advances to be made at their expense.
- They prefer predictability, relative constancy, and maximum autonomy.
- They generally dislike measures of performance and productivity.
- They have a problem orientation centered on easing and preserving the present.
- While they seek control over organizational methodologies, they are not usually trained in solving organization-wide problems.

The dilemma. While local projects are more acceptable to staff, they rarely address system-wide problems. Conversely, system-wide approaches, implemented with a top-down orientation, are far more likely to address system-wide issues, but are less acceptable to staff.

Thus, the dilemma: Try to implement field-initiated suboptimal approaches that have limited impact; or design and implement a technologically sound, system-wide, optimal solution and face considerable local resistance, if not direct sabotage (see Seidel & Baker, 1985; Burkman, 1987; Back & McCombs, 1984).

Consultation and collaboration. To be effective, changes must be embraced by staff members. Consequently, change agents have moved toward more consultative and collaborative approaches to technology implementation. Consulting with staff members who must use any new technology, and seeking their help in designing and implementing it, is replacing the rigid top-down power model. If major issues can be cast in the context of how to make them work, rather than whether they should be done at all, a significant step has been taken.

If one casts the question as, "How can teachers use computers in their classrooms?" the answer is likely to generate suboptimal solutions. If, on the other hand, the question is, "How can CBI improve the quality of education?", the range of answers will more likely lead to an effective outcome. It is essential to define problems in terms of outcomes rather than staff processes. We have found no evidence that the nature of these design, development, and implementation problems is different in the Army, the public schools, or industry.

JSEP implementation issues. At issue in the design of Army basic education programs is whether these should be top-down or bottom-up. In the top-down model, when military leadership is changed through rotation, priorities change, resources are reallocated, and planned program development rests with the interest of lower echelons of management who must seek resources and continue development as best they can (Anderson, 1986).

Even if large programs are successfully completed, they may not be fully implemented successfully. Management, instructor, and learner factors largely determine the operational success or failure of various methods of instruction regardless of top-down demands (Anderson, 1986; see also Baker & Hamovitch, 1983).

As a practical matter, if new programs cannot be institutionalized during the tenure of the originating manager, they are often destined to end on the back burner. The nature of performance appraisal systems virtually guarantees that replacement managers will change priorities; often to give the impression that they are making important things happen (Branson, 1979).

Local authority. In JSEP implementation, FSU-Ford rediscovered, again, that each major Army installation is headed by a commander whose authority is analogous to that of a local school board or superintendent. Local officials must be constantly sold and their post-decision anxieties addressed. It is a continuing process that is highly dependent on the personal relationship between the developers and users. No matter how often local officials change, the new officials must be given the same treatment until they are comfortable.

Tryout issues. In an earlier section on formative evaluation, I urged that strict revision priorities be specified before revising. These priorities are established by analyzing the data from tryouts and classifying them according to their importance. Tryouts must reveal all significant problems and errors to permit complete system debugging. To the JSEP developers, a tryout site meant a place to use draft materials with soldiers as a means of gathering data for revisions. JSEP draft materials contained numerous typographical errors, system errors (such as failing to accept the correct answer for an item), and content errors.

While developers view tryouts of draft materials as a necessary step to making the program work well, local users expect to see a finished product. Developers want to make corrections after soldiers have used all lessons; local users want all errors corrected before the materials are tried out. Writing "draft" on lessons does not change expectations. I am not at all confident that this inherent conflict is generally resolvable; we certainly made an abundance of errors and gained no insights into how to field test the unfinished JSEP without protests from users.

We did learn that when we made revisions on a first-come–first-served basis, more revisions were made to lessons tried out first than to later ones, though all lessons were equally important.

TECHNOLOGY TRANSFER

Some technologies, such as chemical processes, alloys, and computer software, can be directly converted to new uses, but those for education and training present difficult technical issues.

While these technical issues are formidable they are not insurmountable. One principal difficulty lies in finding materials that offer reasonable opportunities for commercial success. The military services have developed numerous well designed, technology-based, education and training programs that are suited for the civilian education and training world. However, the existence of high technology products does not mean that they can be exploited commercially.

Public domain. One reason that commercial exploitation has been difficult is that materials developed for the government are often in the public domain. It is intuitively appealing for government-sponsored, innovative curriculum materials to be placed in the public domain. Technically, these materials are "free" to users. Public domain materials *can be* copied and distributed by anyone, but they rarely are. For example, many products developed by the National Science Foundation and the U.S. Office of Education were put in the public domain to promote free access.

Both organizations soon discovered that something belonging to everyone literally belongs to no one. Once the first hundred copies were distributed, the materials vanished. The sponsors did not provide for promotion, reproduction, warehousing, distribution, maintenance, revision, and servicing; functions considered essential by customers. When no one is in charge of marketing them, the materials, no matter how effective and well conceived, remain on the shelf unused. Technology has not been transferred. Licensing and protection of copyrights and trademarks are essential features of transferring technology from Federal to private use.

The Haigler Initiative

If vocational and adult educators are interested in military materials, if the Congress wishes to see these materials successfully used by civilians, and if there are creative and persistent Federal executives dedicated to making such programs work, then it should be possible to transfer this technology successfully.

The necessary conditions for successful transfer include:

- the availability of materials that have civilian educational value
- the legislative authority and bureaucratic engineering necessary for civilian adaptation of the materials
- a promoter who provides for a civilian demonstration.

In 1986, Karl Haigler, a senior executive in the U.S. Department of Education, brought together representatives of the Departments of the Army, Education, and Labor, to initiate a plan to transfer JSEP to the civilian education community. The first consideration was to find civilian needs that JSEP could fill (K. M. Haigler, personal communication, November, 1988).

The Army was key since it owned the JSEP program. Labor had an interest because of its training commitments under the Job Training Partnership Act. Education wanted to promote both vocational education and adult basic education. This federal interagency group collaborated to obtain the funds that would provide for civilian adaptation and demonstration of JSEP.

After making the arrangements to have JSEP revised for the civilian community, Haigler left the Department of Education and undertook a project with the state of Mississippi to use JSEP. The civilian transfer of JSEP was brought about by unlikely circumstances. Haigler had previously served in the Army as a basic training company commander, an experience that provided him with firsthand knowledge of the problem of functional literacy in the Army. As a federal official, he was aware of many of the same problems in the civilian community and was particularly concerned with finding ways to improve productivity and the quality of life through vocational training. Finally, he was dedicated to providing JSEP to the civilian community.

The Civilian Demonstration

In 1988, the Department of Education awarded a contract to the FSU-Ford team, working with the New York Department of Education and the Rochambeau Adult Education Center in White Plains, New York, to provide the civilian demonstration of JSEP. A description of the complexities of curriculum design and technology transfer in that environment will be presented next.

Selecting occupations. Jobs in the Army are not the same as those in the civilian world. For example, there are no civilian equivalents of combat infantry and field artillery jobs. Emerging civilian jobs are highly service oriented. Since the JSEP curriculum was fixed and no new lessons were planned, the problem became one of finding civilian jobs that the JSEP curriculum could support. While the RCA analysis provided fine-grained detail of Army jobs, we could find no equivalent documents for civilian jobs.

Our approach to matching occupations was to compare Army jobs to civilian jobs in enough detail to identify common basic skills. When there were good matches, such as in military police, correctional specialist, and machinist, it was a simple process of substituting civilian job titles for Army job titles in JSEP's Soldier Management System.

The NOICC Crosswalk. Next, we analyzed civilian prerequisites to see if they were the same as Army ones. To do that, we compared civilian job titles from the *Dictionary of Occupational Titles* (DOT) with Army job titles. The National Occupational Information Coordination Committee Crosswalk (NOICC) database was consulted to identify matching DOT and Army titles. We found many multiple matches yielding more than 180 DOT titles corresponding to the 94 Army job titles.

To assess the degree of match and to identify possible overlap among the 180 DOT titles, a more extensive description of the occupations was needed than the NOICC database provided. By consulting other sources, we brought the matches down to 125 truly civilian occupations. From those 125, we selected 20, including: accounting clerk, cosmetologist, computer operator, electrician, corrections officer, and 15 others.

Nonequivalent occupations. There are some civilian growth occupations for which there are no military equivalents (e.g., floral designer and cosmetologist), but for which we believed JSEP had valid lessons. The degree to which lesson content matches the prerequisites for the subsequent training program can be answered reasonably well by the consensus of experts. For nonequivalent occupations, this match was accomplished by having vocational instructors rate each JSEP lesson objective on the Training Emphasis Scale (Ruck, Thompson, & Thomson, 1978) for each occupation.

These instructors were asked to indicate the degree to which each JSEP lesson should be emphasized in the pretraining curriculum for their occupation. The use of this scale represents a second instance of military-to-civilian technology transfer since the scale and its analysis procedures, called the Comprehensive Occupational Data Analysis Programs (CODAP), were developed by the U.S. Air Force Human Resources Laboratory (Christal, 1974).

We believe that the CODAP rating procedure provides an effective approach to assess the match of each JSEP lesson to civilian occupations. Further, we believe that this procedure could be used as an efficient means for reviewing all potentially valuable training materials. However, even with the content match, the functional context may vary from Army to civilian jobs. Here, functional context refers to the location and examples used to elaborate principles and concepts.

Next, I will describe how we modified the lessons to make them more relevant to civilians. There are far more contextual cues in the military than in the civilian community because all soldiers have the vivid and recent common experience of Army Basic Training.

Degreening. To remove the Army context, we developed guidelines for instructional designers to follow. One constraint was to change the lessons as little as possible. This process is referred to as "degreening" (Army uniforms are green). Examples of guidelines are:

- Remove or adapt military context references when they have no civilian equivalents. Assembling a Light Anti-tank Weapon would be changed to a generic civilian procedure. A military policemen giving a ticket would not be changed.
- Convert all military spellings to civilian. For example, aline = align, gage = gauge.
- Convert military ranks and titles to generic, civilian terms by substituting supervisor for sergeant, manager for captain, and president for general.
- Change graphics and illustrations only when they might confuse civilian students, or when changes in text require corresponding changes in graphics.
- Lower the text readability level with shorter sentences, familiar vocabulary, and by changing multisyllable words to simpler forms, for example, change howitzer to gun.

Does JSEP Help Civilians?

Both the civilian and Army versions of JSEP are designed to *prepare* the students for job training, not to provide it. To judge whether this design requirement has been met requires adequate data collection. Two approaches are normally followed: consensus judgements and follow-up studies. Content validity can be verified by measuring consensus with the Training Emphasis Scale.

Conducting follow-up studies is more difficult. First, large numbers of graduates are needed for each of the occupations. Second, graduates must then go to the training programs for which they were prepared, a condition that requires either subsequent occupational training courses, or jobs to be available in the economy within a short period of time after graduation. Finally, acceptable criterion measures of success must be used—something other than supervisors ratings—and these are rarely available.

At the time of this writing, the civilian demonstration was going on in White Plains and in Mississippi. Since the degreening process was done only on the MicroTICCIT version of JSEP, both sites use that hardware configuration. In White Plains, two 18-terminal systems were installed; in Mississippi, one 8-terminal system was used. Follow-up studies are planned in both locations.

When is technology transfer complete? Is it complete the first day students use the system? Does the process require the system to achieve the planned results in the new location? For our purpose here, I believe that the technology transfer process is complete when the system is working as planned with students; everything after that depends on effective management. According to that criterion, JSEP transfer was completed in early summer of 1989, about one year after the contract was awarded.

FINAL OBSERVATIONS

In this chapter, I have described a CBI program from its inception in the Army to its implementation in the civilian education community. One purpose of this description was to show the magnitude of the time and effort required, and some of the potential pitfalls. If our experience can be generalized to make other transfer programs easier, and we believe that it can, the purpose of this chapter will have been well served.

What are the key factors that have been learned from this process? I believe these major issues are critical.

1. Make certain, through careful analysis and planning, that there is a valid requirement CBI can satisfy.
2. Assess the degree to which the user can operate and maintain the system once it is in place. Design accordingly.
3. Make implementation plans based on the characteristics of typical users, not on the enthusiastic response of early adopters.
4. Maintain regular, personal contact between the development staff and the intended users. Try to address their concerns specifically and deliberately.
5. Be particularly sure to initiate contact with any new leaders or managers to get their support.
6. Be sure that all departments and stakeholders are consulted and have opportunities to make input to the design, development, and implementation process.
7. Address the concerns of users, but try to keep project priorities on schedule. Avoid reacting to every negative comment and complaint that would change schedules or priorities.
8. Early adopters will begin to question their decision to participate when the first small, but predictable, problems arise. Stay in touch with them to reassure them and address their concerns.
9. Problems inherent in working with any large bureaucracy are about the same, regardless of whether one is working with the Army, the public schools, or industry. Be prepared for delays, priority changes, and confusion.

10. Remember that the local managers have different needs than the senior management group sponsoring the project. Be prepared to negotiate with each, to provide full airing of issues, and accommodate both interests as best you can. Do not be surprised if you find yourself in the center of organizational conflict.
11. Quality control and configuration management are difficult issues on large projects. Plan carefully to commit sufficient resources to each. Both of these functions must adopt and follow clear priorities on schedules and revisions.

REFERENCES

Anderson, C.L. (1986). *Historical profile of adult basic education programs in the U.S. Army.* Unpublished doctoral dissertaiton. Teachers College, Columbia University, New York, NY.

Back, S.F., & McCombs, B.L. (1984). *Factors critical to the implementation of self-paced instruction: A background review* (Tech. Rep. TP 84-24). Lowry Air Force Base, CO: Air Force Human Resources Laboratory. (AD A145 143).

Baker, M., & Hamovitch, M. (1983, January). *Job-oriented basic skills (JOBS) training program: An evaluation* (NPRDC Tech. Rep. 83-5). San Diego: Navy Personnel Research and Development Center. (AD A124 150).

Baker, M., & Huff, K. (1981, November). *The evaluation of a job-oriented basic skills training program-Interim report #1* (NPRDC Tech. Rep. 82-14). San Diego: Navy Personnel Research and Development Center. (AD A124 150).

Branson, R.K. (1979). Implementation issues in instructional systems development: Three case studies. In H.F. O'Neil, Jr. (Ed.), *Issues in instructional systems development* (pp. 181-203). New York: Academic Press.

Branson, R.K. (1987). Why the schools can't improve: The upper limit hypothesis. *Journal of Instructional Development, 10*(4), 15-26.

Branson, R.K. (1989). Large scale ISD programs. Two case studies in the military services. In W.H. Hannum & C. Hansen (Eds.), *Instructional systems development in large organizations* (pp. 225-254). Englewood Cliffs, NJ: Educational Technology Publications.

Branson, R.K., & Farr, B.J. (1984). The job skills education program: Issues in design and development. *Proceedings 26th Annual Conference of the Military Testing Association* (pp. 791-796). Munich. (AD B096 442).

Branson, R.K., Allen, P.J., & Hayes, M. (1985). *U.S. Army Job Skills Education Program: Implementation and management plan.* Alexandria, VA: U.S. Army Research Institute.

Burkman, E. (1987). Factors affecting utilization. In R.M. Gagne (Ed.), *Instructional technology: Foundations* (pp. 429-455). Hillsdale, NJ: Lawrence Erlbaum.

Christal, R.E. (1974). *The United States Air Force Occupational Research Project* (AFHRL TR-73-75, AD-774-574). Lackland AFB, TX: Air Force Human Resources Laboratory.

Derry, S.J., Jacobs, J., & Murphy, D.A. (1987-87). The JSEP Learning Skills Training System. *Journal of Educational Technology Systems, 15*(4), 273–284.

Dick, W. (1985). *The design and development of the U.S. Army computer-based Job Skills Education Program.* Paper presented at a seminar on Multi-Media Authoring Systems. London, England.

Duffy, T.M. (1985, Spring). Literacy instruction in the military. *Armed Forces & Society, 11*(3), 437–467.

Hoffman, L.M., Hahn, C.P., Hoffman, D.M., & Dean, R.A. (1988). *Evaluation of the job skills education program: Part I, learning outcomes.* Washington, DC: American Institutes for Research.

Levin, H.M., & Meister, G.R. (1985, November). *Educational technology and computers: Promises, promises, always promises* (Project Rep. No. 85-A13). Stanford, CA: Stanford Education Policy Institute.

Pearson, P.D., Foertsch, D.J., & Moes, M. (1985). *An evaluation of the BSEP II remedial curriculum.* Champaign, IL: Center for the Study of Reading, University of Illinois-Urbana-Champaign.

Philippi, J.W. (1988, April). Matching literacy to job training: Some applications from military programs. *Journal of Reading, 31*(7), 658–666.

Reiser, R.A., & Gagne, R.M. (1983). *Selecting media for instruction.* Englewood Cliffs, NJ: Educational Technology Publications.

Roblyer, M.D., Castine, W.H., & King, F.J. (1988). Assessing the impact of computer-based instruction. *Computers in the schools, 5*(3/4).

Ruck, H.W., Thompson, N.A., & Thomson, D.C. (1978). The collection and prediction of training emphasis ratings for curriculum development. *Proceedings of the 20th annual conference of the Military Testing Association.* Oklahoma City, OK: U.S. Coast Guard.

Seidel, R., & Baker, J. (1985, May). Technology transfer project. *Proceedings of Technology Transfer Workshop* (pp. 7–14). Washington, DC: United States Office of Personnel Management.

Shanker, A. (1988, November). *Proceedings of the School Year 2000: An International Seminar on Creating Effective Schools of the Future.* Snowmass, CO.

Sticht, T.G. (1975). *A program of Army functional job reading training: Development, implementation, and delivery system.* Alexandria, VA: Human Resources Research Organization. (AD A012 272).

United States General Accounting Office. (1983). *Report to the secretary of the Army: Poor design and management hamper Army's basic skills education program* (GAO/FPCD-83-19). Washington, DC: Author.

15
Implementing Computer-Based Instruction for Severely Disabled Students

Fred Romney
Jefferson County Public Schools
Louisville, KY

As discussed throughout this volume, CBI holds great promise as an instructional medium. However, unless computer systems are augmented with appropriate control mechanisms and software, CBI is only a remote possibility for students with severe physical or mental handicaps. Computer systems modified for the severely handicapped are termed, "augmentative or alternative access systems."

The best way to learn about the promises and problems of using computer systems to help severely disabled children is to work with these children. The next best way is to read or hear about case studies that describe the troubles and triumphs associated with using such systems. This chapter then presents several vignettes of using augmentative computers to teach and help children with one or more of the following problems: blindness, deafness, inability to control muscular movements, the inability to talk, severe emotional problems, and severe mental retardation. The names of the children involved in these vignettes have been changed in an effort to protect their privacy; however, the descriptions of their experiences and etiologies are authentic.

Before presenting these cases, I briefly discuss my history with using different types of technology in the Jefferson County Public School District in Louisville, Kentucky to help and to teach the severely disabled. Like most teachers, I have been student-oriented, not machine-oriented. Years ago, I decided to major in speech pathology rather than audiology because my perception was that the latter career would have mainly consisted of using audiometers, dials, and knobs. No machines for me! Indeed, years later, it took considerable goading before I could even write a grant for a computer. Many teachers, especially those in special education, have a similar "avoidance mindset" toward technology. However, a positive mindset by the teacher(s) is needed for computer-based technology to work with the severely disabled. A teacher's feelings about using computer-based technology may be transmitted to students which in turn affects the students' motivation to use the computer system. My experience evolving from a mindset of total avoidance to one of using computer-based technology to teach severely disabled students could thus help others to develop a more positive attitude toward using this technology to help these students.

MY HISTORY WITH USING TECHNOLOGY TO HELP THE SEVERELY HANDICAPPED

Teletypewriters (TTYs)

In 1972, I was teaching a class of students with severe-to-profound hearing impairment. I noted that these students said practically nothing during their five-minute breaks between classes. During such breaks, the hearing students from other classes were always chattering about phone conversations and other experiences from the previous evening. If only my students could use the telephone, their communication and social skills would improve markedly. Researching this possibility, I read that TTYs could be converted to relay telephone conversations for the hearing-impaired.

I then embarked on a project to prepare TTYs and telephone modems for my students. They would then be able to converse over distance with friends and report emergency situations. With some hard work and assistance from various sources, this project came together. Western Union donated all the obsolete TTYs from Churchill Downs. The Jefferson County Board of Education provided a truck to haul the units to my classroom. With the volunteer assistance of an electrician and his son, it took three months to rebuild several of these machines for future telephone communications.

Money was needed to buy modems which would link the TTYs to the students' home phones. At that time, these modems cost $130 per phone. The students sold everything from jar openers to hair brushes in order to raise this money. TTYs with modems were then placed in each of their homes. TTYs were also placed in their (hearing) friends' homes, the school office, and my home. The students were to call me to report any "emergencies." They had many extremely minor emergencies which tended to occur at dinnertime! A short time later, the police department provided

TTY service for the deaf. As far as I could determine, we were the first class of hearing-impaired students with TTYs in each home.

Students were quickly able to engage in extremely lengthy "conversations." I received printed transcripts which must have taken hours to produce—single-spaced $8\frac{1}{2}'' \times 36''$ typed transcripts. It was apparent that their ability to communicate was constrained by their limited typing skills. More efficient typing would lead to more and more efficient communication with others. Every student was then enrolled in a beginning typing course. By the end of this course, the students were able to engage in longer, more varied, and more interesting conversations without taking so much telephone time. As one parent stated:

> You got these teenagers their TTYs and now we can't get our son off the phone...Now he is a normal teenager! Isn't it wonderful!

All of the students benefitted from using the TTYs. They developed lasting skills in typing, writing, and interacting with other peple. In fact, one student worked for several years as a computer input specialist for the local newspaper.

Computer-Based Training

Initial experience. In 1975, the Jefferson County Public School System advertised several new positions which were designed to provide new and innovative services to children within the school district. One position was, "Program Development Specialist for Physical and Communication Disorders." It was a 12-month job with a great title and benefits. I could not pass it up, and much to my surprise and delight, I got the position.

During my first year in this job, a teenage boy was brought to my attention by his principal. This student expressed a desire to commit suicide, but he did not have the muscle strength nor the dexterity to use a razor. His depression was due to a complete physical dependence on others. Since his neck was broken in a childhood fall, he had extremely limited arm and leg movements. He had, however, enough mobility in the right hand to operate a miniature calculator.

I thus submitted a grant to the Kentucky State Department of Health in an effort to get him some tools which would allow him to be more independent. For that year only, this state agency was offering grants to assist handicapped people who desired to be physically independent. I asked for the following items: (a) a page turner @ \$450, (b) a computer @ \$4000, (c) a special miniature keyboard @ \$1000, and (d) an automatic telephone dialing and answering device @ \$600. Unfortunately, my grant was rejected because I had requested too much money. I resubmitted the request, without the computer, but with a Sharp Memowriter instead. The grant was then approved.

Since the time of the grant, he has been able to operate computers, read books, make and answer phone calls, graduate from high school, and become a positive and productive member of society. His story served as an example to me that severely handicapped people can have a productive life with the appropriate technological assistance.

Morse Code and the severely handicapped. As discussed, the Jefferson County Public School System has attempted to provide alternative access to computers for its severely handicapped children. We have found that using Morse Code has helped make computers more accessible to dozens of severely handicapped children. Illustrations of severely disabled children using Morse Code and other input systems are presented in the case study section.

Using Morse Code to input information into the computer is often much easier for these children, provides faster access to the computer, and is less expensive to the school system than many scanning input systems. However, teaching Morse Code to severely disabled children by traditional methods is very time consuming. In order to develop a faster system, Dixon Romney was commissioned to produce graphics which would assist in teaching the code. With a picture system, it became possible to teach the Morse Code alphabet within 15 minutes. A sample of these graphics is presented in Appendix B.

Funding issues. Funding constraints present a serious obstacle to any attempt to use computer-based technology. The Jefferson County School District has thus provided an atmosphere which encourages and enables its employees to write grants. And grants have been the primary source of funds for obtaining the computer-based tools needed to help severely handicapped students.

Our grants have been of various amounts from diverse sources. A modem for hearing-impaired students was the result of a grant from the women's auxiliary of a local volunteer fire station. A local machinery company provided funds for several TTYs. We received a package grant of hardware and software equipment valued at $80,000 from the Kentucky State Department of Education. The State Department of Education with federally provided funds was able to create hardware and software packages for students with the following types of low-incidence handicaps: (a) blind and visually impaired (VI); (b) deaf and hearing impaired (HI); (c) physically handicapped and other health impairments (PHOHI); (d) severely and profoundly mentally handicapped (SPH); and (e) severely language and speech handicapped students.

Package grants can be problematic, as the "packages" are not always complete. Our package from the State Department of Education included several IBM computers without any Disk Operating System (DOS) disks;

printers came without the needed electrical cords. Evidently, the ordering by the State Department of Education was accomplished in such a hurry that some pieces were not requested. We acquired, locally, many of the missing elements, and eventually the State Department of Education supplied the rest. A smaller school system, without many local resources, might have been caught with a completely unusable $4000 computer system because of the lack of a $400 interface or a $30 electrical cord. Local communities must then explore ways of developing resources to meet their special needs, even when the majority of supplies are provided by the granting agency.

The Louisville metropolitan area has a most exciting program for raising money for needy children. A local radio and TV station (WHAS Radio and TV) conducts a yearly, "WHAS Crusade for Children." This Crusade is a most thrilling local phenomenon as the entire region for one late spring weekend becomes embroiled in this fund-raising tradition. During this entire special weekend, volunteer fire personnel can be found on their local street corners with hats inverted and boots in the air collecting coins and dollar bills from passing motorists. On Sunday, the fire personnel empty their boots and hats into a large container at the WHAS-TV studios. Sirens, bells, clapping, and shouting accompany the words of thanks from the Crusade personnel as each fire department pours in its collections. Money is also raised for this Crusade by churches and other organizations through such activities as softball games and cookouts. In recent years, this Crusade has raised over $2,000,000 annually to help the children.

We have been very fortunate to receive several hundred thousand dollars over the past several years from this Crusade. These grants have been used to establish the WHAS Crusade Technology Center, which is the source of computer equipment for the Jefferson County Public Schools. From this center, teachers check out various special keyboards, interface cards, and augmentative devices that allow their students to access computers and other devices.

Because of the grants cited in this section, severely handicapped students have been better able to cope in school and in their daily lives. For example, they can actively turn on a radio or TV by hitting a switch in close proximity to movable parts of their bodies. Other examples are discussed in the next section.

CASE STUDIES THROUGH THE 1988–89 SCHOOL YEAR

Mark (age 8). At first glance, Mark appears to be the prototypic golden boy with pure blonde hair and a fair complexion. However, he has cerebral palsy which makes it difficult for him to talk clearly and to control his limbs. During his preschool years, Mark tried to use a computer-based communication system, but his fingers just would not cooperate. Nevertheless, it was evident that he had a strong desire to make the unit speak and print.

The Occupational Therapist (OT) said, "Oh, if only there were the possibility of his using the device." The Physical Therapist (PT) said, "Wouldn't it be nice if only. . ." His mother said, "It is obvious that he wants to operate this unit so much that we are getting one for him. He will learn to use it!" Mark, through much practice, developed the ability to use the system by typing the desired letter with the little finger of his left hand.

Using one finger, however, was not the most efficient way to use a computer. Mark then started to learn Morse Code in an effort to increase response speed through the use of one or two movements rather than the multiple movements required to use the whole keyboard. Unfortunately, he did not have sufficient muscular control to use a single- or dual-switch Morse system.

Fortunately, laptop MS-DOS units came to be available with software that permitted use by any external movement possible. We purchased such a device for Mark and discovered an input system which would allow him to use it. This input system involves using an on-screen keyboard and a cursor that highlights the keyboard items. Mark's typing speed dramatically increased with this input system. He was quickly able to use the same software program used by Professor Stephen Hawkings of Cambridge University, who has Amyotropic Lateral Sclerosis-Lou Gehrig's disease.

Mark is currently using a Toshiba T1200 computer with a single-switch scanning keyboard emulator. He types information into this computer by using his elbow to hit the switch. His work has continually improved to the point that Mark is expected to develop the writing skills necessary for college.

Two important lessons were learned from the experience with Mark. First, early intervention was important. Without such early intervention, Mark might not have begun the development of writing skills necessary for more advanced classes. People with severe speaking problems usually have jumbled syntax, as their words and thoughts come out in a curious order. Teaching proper syntax to people with severe speaking problems is a most tedious and time-consuming process. Second, much work is needed after the system is implemented to derive the greatest possible advantage of the equipment. Mark continues to need much assistance from language development specialists, speech therapists, teachers, and the technology consultant in order to successfully gain the greatest advantage of the augmentative tools.

Sheri. Sheri is a sweetheart, who unfortunately has a debilitating disease that causes her to go downhill from day to day. Her voice seems to be the only thing that has remained constant. A voice input module was thus ordered for her.

After the voice system was installed, we proceeded to train the computer to recognize Sherri's voice. All went well the first afternoon with using the system. Using the voice input module in combination with the basic math program allowed her to do the homework assignment in mathematics. She would simply speak the number and it would be printed on the screen. We had seemingly found the technological solution to Sherri's problem. We soon discovered, however, that the voice system had to be continually "re-trained" to recognize Sherri's voice. Eventually, Sherri was trained to use another system which is activated by muscular movements.

We have learned through this experience that inexpensive voice systems (under $1000) are not much use to severely disabled students. The voice systems needed for such students cost up to $24,000 and are still in the developmental stage. As in the case of Sherri, a system which is tied to perceptible muscular movements is preferable to an expensive voice operated system. The former type of system can be operated by either a switch or a sensor placed over a muscle. Muscular movements then serve to command the technology. And the technology then becomes the servant of the child.

Samantha (12). Samantha has the worst case of infantile arthritis that I have ever seen. Her little hands have gradually become deformed until they resemble balls of jelly. For many years, she was able to keep up with the "normal students" in a mainstream classroom by writing with a pencil strapped in her hand. As Samantha's condition deteriorated, it was evident that technological assistance was needed for her to keep up with the other students. A single switch laptop computer seemed to be best for Samantha. Being a very bright child, she quickly learned to use this system and was able to type her first homework assignment on the first day of use. This technology has allowed Samantha to continue being the academic equal of the "normal" students in her class.

Kent (16). Kent was born with a form of cerebral palsy which causes very sharp uncontrolled movements. In an effort to assist him with written tasks, several interventions were attempted. He initially used a portable laptop unit (SpeechPac/Epson). He could have theoretically used this system to do all class assignments; however, he continually crashed this system.

He crashed every computer in our center—even an "uncrashable" Apple 11e computer. We had never encountered such a child. Kent's propensity for zapping computers would have been an item of fascination if it had not been so troublesome. When we determined that Kent's body was generating enough static electricity to crash the different systems, we procured an external keyboard which only requires the use of a wooden dowel to move the cursor. Physical contact with this keyboard was not needed. Using this keyboard enabled Kent to do his work without crashing the program. Later we discovered that Kent was able to use regular keyboards to play games on the computer. He must have discovered a way to inhibit his production of static electricity for these computers, or perhaps he found ways to crash the programs which were associated with school work.

At this point we thought that Kent was able to use a computer for school work. He was then presented with a laptop Datavue Spark computer which has a joystick similar to the one used in the lab, and Kent was ready for action. By the way, he was instructed to touch only the plastic joystick.

Solving one problem sometimes leads to the discovery of other problems. After a few weeks of use, Kent's computer was continually shutting down because the battery was not taking a charge, a problem we should have expected. The temporary solution was to operate the laptop as a standard plug-in unit. A lack of staff time has precluded the possibility of discharging and charging the battery periodically, which is the ideal solution to this problem.

Betty (12). Betty is about 12 years of age and has multiple handicaps. She cannot speak nor has she much control over her limbs. As an infant, Betty was diagnosed as being severely mentally handicapped.

Betty was initially placed in a class for severely and profoundly mentally handicapped children, but was soon moved to a class for children with multiple handicaps. There were several reasons for this move. First, her performance on intelligence tests indicated that she was not so mentally handicapped. Second, her visual responses to the environment revealed that she was thinking and reasoning near her appropriate developmental level. Third, bathroom services were also available in the multiple handicapped classroom. Fourth, her parents and the staff agreed that this move was the right thing to do.

To function as a member of this class, Betty needed a way to communicate with others. As previously stated, it was not possible for her to speak nor control the movement of her hands. She could, however, move her right arm from the left to the right. The Morse Code response system was then proposed as an avenue to follow. This proposal was met with stares of disbelief as it is very hard to teach Morse code to a child with an SPH background, especially one who does not know the alphabet. Over a period of time, Betty was able to learn Morse Code well enough to type some basic phrases into the computer. She can now communicate with others!

By learning Morse Code, Betty has developed some reading skills. We may now investigate the possibility of having her use an MS-DOS unit, which has many advantages. One, this system has a greater memory capacity than the RealVoice/Epson system. Betty would then be able to store stories and assignments for later use. Two, word prediction can be incorporated into the MS-DOS system. That is, the words that Betty would most likely want to use would be available on the screen. A third advantage is that a full-size screen would provide more feedback. Disadvantages of the MS-DOS system as compared to the Real Voice/Epson system are its greater complexity, lack of a built-in printer, greater expense, and shorter battery time (2–6 hours vs. 10–20 hours) for the MS-DOS system.

Cathy (15). Cathy is a beautiful but legally blind teenager. She is lucky in that her teacher understood the importance of using computers to help visually impaired students. This teacher had obtained a grant which provided a voice module for Cathy's home computer. Unfortunately, the voice synthesizer was relatively worthless because it would not "read" text from the screen nor from a disk. Contacts with the supplier of the voice module did not result in a trade for a more appropriate system.

Cathy thus came to school to do her work with a special IBM computer equipped with a "Speaqualizer." The Speaqualizer includes a separate keyboard with keys to control a second cursor, which indicates the start of the spoken text. Through the use of this keyboard, Cathy can also determine whether each key will speak its name and whether each word will be spoken. This keyboard also controls: (a) the type of speech, (b) the speed of speech, (c) the speech mode, (d) the pitch, and (e) the amount of punctuation which will be spoken. The Speaqualizer is a very versatile and useful system to the visually impaired individuals who use MS-DOS units. The Printing House for the Blind manufactures and sells the Speaqualizer system for under $1000. We wish that Cathy could have one at home. Unfortunately, we have not yet been able to fulfill this dream as there are a limited number of these systems.

Sally (7). Sally Jones is a precious child. When Sally first used electronic technology, she could not apply enough pressure to depress standard keys and switches. Hence, keys and switches with very weak springs had to be used.

She eventually developed the ability to move ever-so-slowly from one key to the next. However, it was still a most laborious process for her to use a standard keyboard. Since she could spell and understand the concept of directionality, Sally was expected to be able to grasp the idea of using an on-screen matrix with a directional "joystick" or trackball. It was hoped that Sally could develop the ability to type the letters into the computer by turning the joystick in the direction that the cursor should go. A keyboard superimposed upon the screen would provide the targets for the cursor movements. The production of a prototype system for Sally began.

A trackball and joystick emulation program was soon discovered. The trackball would provide the rotating sphere for Sally's fingers to turn. Also, this trackball would easily fit on the top of the lap tray of her wheelchair. A MacIntosh computer was provided by the WHAS Crusade for Children. We then started to train Sally to operate this system. However, Sally was unable to see the standard size print of the MacIntosh's screen keyboard. The computer supplier was then able to provide a copy of a program called "Fat Bits" which provided a larger-then-normal screen keyboard. Now, at last, our work with Sally on the computer system could begin in earnest.

As the MacIntosh Computer, peripheral devices, the different programs, and electrical cords were brought into Sally's classroom, the teacher and teacher assistant showed their hesitancy to have this computer unit in the classroom. They were not adequately trained to change the classroom routine and environment to accommodate the computer technology. More importantly, they were not emotionally prepared for the "intrusion." The predictable result was that the unit was not used within the classroom. The computer was then moved to the computer lab where Sally used it only once or twice a week. This amount of use was not sufficient for Sally to develop the desired "typing" proficiency for using the MacIntosh computer system.

Luckily, Sally is now enrolled in a different classroom . She now uses a single-switch selection mechanism to access an Apple IIe computer through an Adaptive Firmware card as well as a RealVoice/Epson system. Sally is also learning to use a Toshiba (MS-DOS) computer with a single light pressure switch. Unfortunately, her entry rate for the Epson system, for example, is only about one word per minute. Hopefully, if the proper muscular movements can be defined or developed, Sally can eventually learn Morse Code to increase her speed in using computer technology.

Sally's story could not be completed without talking about her mother: This women seems to be the "ideal mother" for a handicapped child. She is supportive to the extent of building slant boards for Sally's wheelchair, covering them with Dycem, and modifying them to meet Sally's changing needs. The school system may not yet have a rehabilitation engineer, but Sally has one in her mother. Mrs. Jones also arranges to meet with anybody who can help Sally—therapists, teachers, or consultants. In fact, the staff often learns as much from Mrs. Jones as she from them. For example, Mrs. Jones suggested the use of disposable ice-maker plastic tubes as an inexpensive but safe straw for the handicapped children to use. Regular straws are too sharp and stiff for these children to use. Thank heaven for such mothers!

Karri. Karri is one of my favorite students. Her coal-black almost horizontal pigtails accenturate a broad hopeful smile. Unfortunately, Karri seemingly did not have enough control over her muscular movements to operate any computer-based technology. Her arms were always, involuntarily held out at a right angle to her sides, and her feet were fastened into foot rests with velcro.

The OT, PT, and technology consultant took almost a year to find a muscular movement which Karri could control well enough to use a comuter system. We discovered that Karri could grasp objects with her fingers. A special grasp-switch was built for Karri which could be activated by very slight bodily pressure. However, Karri was unable to release the switch to take advantage of multiple activations nor could she use computer programs which required several switch closures. It was back to the drawing board with more observations of Karri's muscular capabilities and more trials of various switches.

We finally found that Karri could move her left elbow with enough accuracy and pressure to activate and release a leaf switch. She was immediately connected to a computer so that she could scan through the alphabet and hit a switch when each of the letters of her name was highlighted. Karri now was typring by wiggling her elbow. The excitement was evident in the faces of everyone involved with Karri—therapists, teachers, technology consultant, and Karri.

A number of possibilities became evident with Karri:

1. If Karri could develop greater timing skill in releasing the leaf switch, she might eventually be able to use Morse Code as an entry system.
2. If Karri could develop accurate movements with her other elbow, she could use a two-switch system with the left elbow for dashes and the right for dots.
3. Even if Karri does not develop the capability to use Morse Code, she will still be able to operate Apple computers, IBM compatible computers, and any other computer which allows external switch scanning. She also will be able to operate items (e.g., the telephone, a light, and the television) by using the external switch scanning system to select those items on the computer screen.

Jonathan (15). Jonathan was born deaf 15 years ago. His parents soon realized that Jonathan was deaf when he did not react to any loud noises, for example, ringing of the telephone or the barking of the dog. Jonathan was enrolled in the Louisville Deaf-Oral Preschool where he gained skills in speech reading and auditory training. Later, he attended regular classes with tutorial help after school.

Around Jonathan's thirteenth year, I suggested to his family that a home computer would allow Jonathan to more easily write and rewrite papers. Additionally, the computer with a telephone modem hookup would allow Jonathan to participate in telecommunication activities with correspondents throughout the United States. The Christmas season brought the desired computer. During the next few months, Jonathan was on the phone so much that his teenage brother and sister had difficulty conducting their normal social lives.

The local newspaper was then providing a toll-free number to permit computer users to view newspaper articles on their computers. Jonathan was able to get scores of ball games before the newspaper was delivered, which allowed him to tell Dad the scores before anybody else. His parents were astonished by the amount of reading that Jonathan was now doing. With the termination of the newspaper service, Jonathan discovered other local bulletin boards. He began to trade jokes and messages through these services with other computer devotees. The school system was soon able to obtain a membership for Jonathan in "Kendallnet"—a telecommunication network for the deaf and people associated with the deaf. Jonathan could now correspond with deaf students throughout the United States.

Jonathan presently uses the computer to do school papers, correspond with others, and play games. He also uses a TTY to convey messages to friends who do not have a computer modem system. Finally, Jonathan is an honor roll student in a private school which his brother and sister had also attended.

Jerry (16). Jerry was born with cerebral palsy which left him unable to speak, walk, or control his movements. Jerry's case of cerebral palsy is so bad that he cannot hold a crayon or even have it mounted in his hands. In fact, Jerry's arms and hands are often unwieldy "weapons" which unwittingly become entangled with loose wires, materials, or other people's arms. He also has a form of dyslexia which makes it very difficult for him to deal with printed words. His language problems appeared to be insurmountable for many years. With all these problems, Jerry has still been able to attend public schools and he drives an electrical wheelchair with an inverted suction cup in his mouth.

His high school teachers recognized that Jerry would need to use the alphabet in order to produce written work. We thus began to teach him the Morse Code system. The most difficult task is not teaching the code but selecting and mounting the most appropriate and comfortable input switch for the individual to use. Since Jerry's only controlled movements have been with the head and chin, the input switch was placed just under his chin. Jerry was then taught Morse Code so that with one head and chin movement, repeated in various sequences, he could type the 26 letters, 10 digits, and various ASCII codes needed to run a computer.

Soon after learning the code, Jerry expressed a desire for another type of responding mechanism. Perhaps he had seen the new video presentation that Apple Corporation produced to show what handicapped individuals could do when given technological assistance. Or perhaps he had just heard of other switches. Whatever the reason, he wanted to try a "sip-and-puff" switch in which the computer was operated through air movements. We surely did not want to douse his enthusiasm, but he lacked the sufficient lip closure to use that device. After many attempts with the "sip-and-puff" switch, Jerry concluded that there must be a better responding mechanism for him.

He then wanted to try using his hands to enter information into the computer. We would like nothing better than to have students use their hands to operate the computer, but it was evident that Jerry did not have the necessary control over his hands. After all, these hands were "dangerous weapons" as they inadvertently abused all who came close. Nevertheless, we tried to assist him in realizing this dream. The OT and PT were summoned to check the different ways in which Jerry could control his arms or hands in order to run the computer. After trying all the options, Jerry conceded that a chin movement system would be best.

It was not time to make decisions about specific features of the input system. We needed to know if a single switch or a dual switch system would be best. We also needed to know the optimal amount of spring pressure for providing proprioceptive feedback without causing fatigue. We also had to use a mounting system so that the computer switch would not be in the way of the wheelchair controls. After working through numerous options, Jerry is using a Round Pad Switch" which is mounted on an Able-net "Universal Switch Mount." He can use this single-switch system to operate the Words + Software Keyboard Emulator (WSKE), which in turn runs standard commercial software.

CONCLUSIONS

My experience has demonstrated the importance of being creative when using technology to help and teach the severely handicapped. As indicated throughout this chapter, one must find creative technical solutions for each child. For example, the leaf switch was a creative solution to Karri's problem. One also has to develop alternative language and communication methods for these children, for example, Morse Code. Also, in this day of dwindling resources, one has to discover alternative methods of raising money. These fund-raising methods can range from obtaining small grant money from the women's auxiliary of a local volunteer fire station to obtaining large grants from federal and state sources to having a community-wide charity event.

My discussion has also indicated that perseverance and dedication are important attributes for the severely disabled, their parents, and the professionals who are trying to help them. As stated, it took the OT, PT, and technological consultant over a year to finally find a muscular movement that Karri could control well enough to use a computer system. She never quit smiling and trying which gave the staff additional incentive to keep trying to help her.

There are also great rewards inherent in dealing with the severely disabled. Everybody involved with Karri will always remember the elation when a technological solution was found for her. And a great feeling of satisfaction occurs when you have helped children like Mark and Jonathan to reach high levels of academic performance. Even children who are so severely mentally handicapped that we don't know if their process language can benefit from computers, we can present them with talking pictures that change on the monitor as the children move a muscle. The children are thereby given the opportunity to learn concepts of (a) cause and effect, (b) sequencing, (c) matching, and (d) choicemaking—all skills that can be developed without speech.

In closing, computer-based technology may be the best known answer for helping the severely handicapped to live "happy" and "productive" lives. Computer technology has allowed the severely disabled to live less limited lives than ever before. They can now do more of the things that the rest of us take for granted. Finally, the severely disabled are now better able to help us TABs (temporally able-bodied individuals) when we may need their assistance.

APPENDIX A

For more information regarding the equipment and programs discussed in this chapter, the reader is referred to the following sources:

1. Ablenet, 1081 10th Ave. S.E., Minneapolis, MN 55414. Phone: (800) 322-0956 (distributors of switches and mounting devices).
2. Adaptive Communication Systems, 354 Hookstown Grade Road, Clinton, PA 15026. Phone: (412) 264-2288 and (800) 247-3433 (national distributors of RealVOICE Epson and MS-DOS systems).
3. American Printing House for the Blind Inc., 1839 Frankfort Ave., P.O. Box 6085, Louisville, KY 40206. Phone: (502) 895-2495 (distributors of the "Speaqualizers" and other products for the visually impaired).
4. IBM National Support Center for Persons with Disabilities, P.O. Box 2150, Altanta, GA 30055. Phone: 1-800-IBM(426)-2133 (a resource of information for computers and the handicapped).
5. Apple Computer Inc, Inc., Office of Special Education (NSEA), 20525 Mariani Ave., M/S 43-F, Cupertino, CA 95104. Phone: (408) 947-7910.

6.   Hawking, Stephen W. CBE, FRS: Lucacion Professor of Mathematics, Department of Applied Mathematics and Theoretical Physics, Cambridge University, Cambridge, England, CB3 9EW (ALS victim who uses an augmentative system).
7.   Jefferson County Public Schools, 3333 Newburg Road, Louisville, KY 40217. Phone: (502) 473-3011 (school system which the children described attend).
8.   Don Johnston Developmental Equipment Inc., P.O. Box 639, 1000 Rand Rd., Bldg. 115, Wauconda, IL 60084. Phone: (312) 526-2682 and (800) 999-4660 (distributor of the Adaptive Firmware Cards and other adaptive devices).
9.   Dixon B. Romney (son of the author), 221 West Carter Avenue, Clarksville, IN 47130. Phone: (812) 282-3212 (designer of the Morse Code Graphics).
10. WHAS Television and Radio Stations, 520 West Chestnut Street, Louisville, KY 40508. Phone: (502) 582-7840 (organizers of the "WHAS Crusade for Children").
11. Words + Inc., P.O. Box 1229, Lancaster, CA 93534. Phone: (805) 949-8331 and (800) 869-8521 (developers and international distributors of software for IBM and computer systems).

APPENDIX B: WHY MORSE?......AND HOW?

By remembering pictures instead of dots and dashes, children, adults, almost everyone can learn Morse Code in just a few minutes. The computer can then be operated with one or two muscle movements, even the blink of an eye will do!

Advantages of a one-switch (or of a two-switch) system include:

*   The eliminating of hunting for keys, thus reducing typing time in many cases.
*   Because switches can be mounted where movements are most easily made, there is a reduction of posture problems caused by leaning over the keyboard and looking downward.
*   Eye-to-eye contact is easier to maintain because the need to look at the keyboard is eliminated.
*   Notes may be taken easily because there is no need to look down from the blackboard...just keep keying.
*   Morse code is almost universal...it can be used with IBMs (and their clones), Apple computers, Epsons, Toshibas, and so forth.

Letters and their corresponding pictures are below: (Read icons top to bottom or left to right.)

A = Arrow	N = Nose
B = Butterfly	O = OVER the candlestick
C = Grocery CART	P = Packard (2 running boards)
D = Door	Q = Queen's crown
E = Egg	R = Renault (1 running board)
F = Frog with dimple	S = Stop light
G = Girl	T = Table
H = House	U = Umbrella
I = Eyes	V = Beethoven's 5th
J = Jack-in-the-box	W = Wagon
K = Kitten	X = Xylophone
L = Locomotive	Y = YoYo
M = Money	Z = Zipper

 JACK IN
THE BOX

  OVER

 KITTEN

 PACKARD

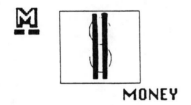 LOCOMOTIVE

 QUEEN

 MONEY

 RENAULT

NOSE

16
CBT:
Its Current and Future State

Barbara L. McCombs
Mid-continent Regional Educational Laboratory
Aurora, CO

We've seen throughout this volume both a diversity and similarity of problems and promises when computer-based technology (CBT) and related instructional technologies are applied in a variety of real-world educational and training settings. Our challenge as educational technologists is to assess the current status of CBT and analyze the implications of this status—complete with its problems and promises—for future research and practice. Particularly important in the context of the current need and motivation for educational reform in America's schools is to point a future direction that can both clarify our role as educational technologists in this reform and maximize technology's potential to contribute to educational improvement for the wide spectrum of learners in our society. My purpose in this chapter is to address this challenge.

I want to begin by briefly summarizing where we are now in light of the problems and promises presented in this volume. The current status of CBT and the design, development, and implementation issues outlined in each chapter are briefly summarized with the goal of highlighting the areas of consensus regarding CBT's problems and promises. I next summarize what we have learned from diverse implementations of CBT and draw out further remaining issues regarding our roles as educational technologists in school redesign and the resulting implications for the role of technology in education and training. Finally, I address what's next in terms of future directions for practice and research. Our time is an exciting one. We have the potential of playing a leadership role in addressing technology's role in the redesign of today's schools.

WHERE ARE WE NOW?

In the Overview section of this volume, Shlechter (Chapter 1) notes that from a historical perspective, CBT in large part emerged as a viable educational and training medium from applications of computers to instruction by the military. These applications were driven by the military's need to provide standardized training to vast numbers of personnel in a cost-efficient manner, beginning during World War II and escalating during the Vietnam War. Societal demands to educate a growing student population and reduce increased costs of schooling during the 1960s further contributed to the development and implementation of CBT in the schools. The early excitement about the potential of CBT, however, has not led to the continued widespread use of computers in either military training or public education. As we learned from Sugrue (Chapter 2), the situation is now changing both in Europe and the United States with recent increased interests in using computers to better prepare students for life in the "information age." The interest in using computers to provide more effective instruction is particularly high among educators of students with special needs, as exemplified by Robinson's (Chapter 3) account of the suitability of CBT for special education students. On the other hand, Reeves (Chapter 4) pointed out that although there is increased research support for computer applications, CBT continues to have limited instructional use in higher education.

In assessing the complex set of issues that surround this state of affairs, we learned from Carrier and Glenn (Chapter 5) that insufficient and inadequate technology training for teachers is a major contributor to limited and/or inappropriate uses of computers in the classroom. This training remains an "add-on" in the majority of preservice teacher preparation programs, is introductory and limited in duration, and is often out of date and missing essential training elements (i.e., instructional design, teacher roles with technology, modeling of appropriate usages, and opportunities for experiential classroom applications). The issue of inadequate teacher training programs is one echoed nearly unanimously by all the contributors to this volume. It is a major problem in the acceptance and utilization of CBT at all levels of schooling (elementary through postsecondary) and for all special applications of CBT (in military training, in special education and gifted programs, in specialized content areas). Carrier and Glenn propose that the need for teacher training in technology takes on even more critical proportions in current school redesign efforts, as teachers are being encouraged to make more decisions about how technology will be used. Changes in both preservice and inservice technology training for teachers is essential, along with long-term commitments from schools of education and school districts to provide this training in a complete and comprehensive manner. Collaborations between educational institutions, businesses, and professional technology groups are recommended as strategies for designing and delivering this training.

Issues of both CBT design and implementation were raised by Hativa (Chapter 6) in discussing the special use of computers in the teaching of arithmetic. On the design side, issues center on the careful matching of CBT capabilities and content learning needs. On the implementation side, issues are focused on providing sufficient resources (having enough computers for all students so that individualized instruction is possible), efficient classroom management (operating an individualized system for the whole class concurrently, with the system managing student learning via a central computer), and teacher roles (facilitating and improving what the teacher already does without introducing major changes, providing reports of individual student and class rank data that can influence teachers to conduct individualized vs. group instruction). It is in this area of teacher roles and how the computer is integrated with teachers' existing subject matter and pedagogical expertise that many critical issues are centered for a number of contributors to this volume.

For example, Semb and his colleagues (Chapter 7) concur with the importance of the teacher and argue that even though the computer can do much, it can't replace the instructor. They also raise the issue of policy changes that are needed if self-pacing (or other forms of individualized instruction) are to be used effectively in traditional education. The focus of these forms of instruction is on the student and is in keeping with the instructional technology movement's attempt to adapt to individual differences. In spite of this student-centered focus, however, Semb et al. point out that these innovations have frequently failed in military and civilian contexts for reasons that include failures to distinguish the method of delivery from content or instructional design issues and failures to provide adequate instructor role training. The issue of teacher training thus pervades a range of educational and training contexts where CBT has been used. Additional issues, however, from Semb et al.'s point of view include the design of quality materials, appropriate matching of content and methods of delivery, advance planning, and the inclusion of student performance monitoring systems in self-paced systems.

The issue of matching technology to the special talents and characteristics of the gifted is emphasized by Pyryt (Chapter 8) as essential if the benefits of CBT are to be achieved. We see in his discussion of gifted students the kind of attention to student needs that has often been missing in those attempts that either fit existing technology to the learner or focus on a technology that is a solution to instructional design goals rather than one that meets the student's learning needs. In Pyryt's discussion of the recommended approach to software design for gifted students, however, the focus is on what is to be taught (content) and matching technology to desired content goals rather than learner and learning goals. Nonetheless, the importance of not only *matching* technology to special student needs but also *designing* technology that fits these unique needs is especially recognized by those who deal with special populations and/or approach technology applications from an individual differences, student-centered perspective.

Coming from just such a perspective, Derry and Hawkes (Chapter 9) suggest that the capabilities of technology can now allow for the advanced design of systems that address the whole person and incorporate more "human" concepts. Intelligent tutoring systems offer the promise of helping students develop specialized capabilities in a way that is compatible with their prior knowledge, motivation history, current goals, and task performance. A system for developing students' strategic problem-solving capabilities that incorporates many teacher functions such as expert guidance, correction, encouragement, and coaching—all in the context of individualized communication during the problem-solving process is described by Derry and Hawkes. Even more sophisticated personalization and individualization strategies are envisioned for intelligent computer systems of the future. Obviously, then, the issue is not *whether* systems can be designed to provide vital human functions and meet broadly based individual needs; in fact, intelligent systems can actually help in the analysis of learner needs. Rather, the issue is *how best* to guide this design process in the larger context of school redesign and what conceptual framework best serves this redesign goal.

Additional issues that were raised in the Overview section of this volume include the following:

- Early promises of CBT did not match up with realities, for example, there is limited evidence (a) for educational or training costs being stabilized or reduced by CBT, (b) for increases in student achievement and motivation, or (c) for the ability of CBT systems to effectively handle individual differences (Shlechter, Chapter 1; Reeves, Chapter 4).
- Inadequate funding, software, planning and preparation (incuding feasibility studies) have further limited the potential of CBT acceptance and effectiveness (Shlechter, Chapter 1; Robinson, Chapter 3; Reeves, Chapter 4).
- CBT has been seen as a panacea and has not been understood as a tool that needs to be carefully integrated with established instructional programs, the needs and conditions of classroom teaching, and the mainstream of classroom activities (Shlechter, Chapter 1; Sugrue, Chapter 2; Robinson, Chapter 3; Reeves, Chapter 4).

With these issues as a backdrop, let's next look at the lessons learned from the perspective of this volume's contributors, at the additional issues that were raised, and at those that remain.

WHAT HAVE WE LEARNED?

In looking across what our contributors have had to say regarding lessons learned, it is particularly impressive to note the breadth of applications in which these lessons took place: CBT in a large school district, in a medium school district, in higher education, in community colleges, in military training, and in education for the severely handicapped. In spite of some differences in the lessons learned, a great deal of agreement also surfaced. Let's look at this agreement from the chapters by Colbert, Schultz, and Higginbotham-Wheat, Deaton, Wilson, Branson, and Romney (Chapters 10–15):

- Large-scale and/or mainline projects require systematic long-term planning.
- Users at all levels (teachers, administrators, etc.) need to be involved in decisions at each stage (design, development, implementation).
- Teachers, in particular, need to be involved in long-range planning about the integration of the computer into the classroom and curriculum as well as in planning their own training programs.
- Uniform standards and quality control procedures need to be developed and adhered to by all participants in large-scale projects.
- Regular evaluations of CBT effectiveness are essential to long-term acceptance and need to be included in early planning, along with a designation of who has responsibility for these evaluations.
- Software needs to be adaptable to teaching and learning requirements, and hardware needs to be easy to maintain and use.

Lessons learned that are more specific to the particular CBT application were also identified. Implementing CBT effectively in a large urban school district is one example. In such an application, Colbert (Chapter 10) discusses the importance of a balance between local control of implementation decisions and central (district level) responsibilities for inservice training and insuring continuity of implementation between elementary and secondary schools in economically and geographically diverse regions that comprise the district. Also critical to the success of this type of application is a phased implementation of CBT in which incremental effects can be documented (e.g., improved student test scores; using technology successfully to teach critical thinking, problem solving, and new concepts). In addition, Colbert stresses the importance of assessing the unique qualities of each school and region for the purpose of concentrating CBT applications in those areas where it can have the greatest impact, thus enhancing user commitment and ownership. Finally, Colbert emphasizes the care that must be taken to produce a policy at the district level that is broad enough to address the diverse needs of schools and regions within the district.

Wilson (Chapter 13), in her discussion of lessons learned in the implementation of CBT in community colleges, raises the additional issue of training students to assume responsibility for managing their own learning rates and for selecting their own instructional methods and strategies. As I have noted in my own work (McCombs, 1985, 1986), preparing students to assume responsibilities for their own learning is critical to the success of self-paced and individualized learning systems. To get the greatest cost-benefit from CBT, Wilson further points out that the system needs to be available for student use many more hours per day than classes are in session. At least in the community college setting, access to the CBT system needs to occur in an open facility with flexible hours.

From the large-scale implementation of CBT in the military, Branson (Chapter 14) adds several other lessons learned that can be applied to a broader range of settings. These include: (a) the ease with which users can operate and maintain the system once it is in place needs to be assessed in advance, and the system needs to be designed accordingly; and (b) implementation plans need to be made based on user characteristics. Branson argues that the issue in planning for CBT implementations is to ask the question: "How can CBT improve the quality of education?" and not "How can teachers use computers in their classrooms?"

Finally, Romney's (Chapter 15) examples of creative approaches to using CBT for the severely handicapped further underscore not only the need to match technologies to the needs of students, but also the need for dedication and perseverance in finding and implementing these matches. This issue is an important one in the broader sense when one considers the multiple needs of not only handicapped learners, but also those of the increasing number of culturally diverse and disadvantaged students in today's classrooms.

In summary, then, it can be said that the current status of CBT is that it continues to be viewed as a viable tool for enhancing student learning and the process of instruction. Many of the promises regarding this technology have been fulfilled, but, drawing upon what has been said by the contributors to this volume, the following can be identified as issues to be resolved:

- How best to provide sufficient and adequate preservice and inservice technology training for teachers.

- How best to match CBT capabilities and content learning needs.
- How best to provide sufficient resources for meeting hardware needs for all students.
- How best to provide adequate software and resources for local software development.
- How best to integrate CBT with teachers' existing subject matter and pedagogical expertise.
- How best to enhance faculty development and use of technology in schools of education.
- How best to use the capabilities of advanced technologies to guide school redesign efforts.
- How best to support the long-term planning required for successful CBT implementation
- How best to involve teachers, and all levels of users, in planning and decision making regarding CBT implementation.
- How best to support systematic and ongoing evaluations of CBT effectiveness.
- How best to support policy changes that can facilitate a balance between local control and centralized support responsibilities.
- How best to prepare both teachers and students for their changing roles in individualized, technology-supported environments.
- How best to provide flexibility and adaptiveness in CBT availability and applications.
- How best to work with users during the planning stage to assess their needs, characteristics, and ongoing support requirements.

WHAT ISSUES REMAIN?

As we focus our attention on our roles as educational technologists in school redesign and the resulting implications for the role of technology in education and training, a number of other issues surface. The first of these issues has to do with the scope and focus of our thinking about the role of technology in education and training, and the need for a conceptual framework that can guide us in our role as educational technologists in approaching this issue. In beginning to examine this issue, I would like to share with you my beliefs about what needs to be done.

Educating the Whole Person

Never in the history of American education has the importance of addressing the needs of the whole person been more apparent. Students in today's schools—from kindergarten through high school—are increasingly the products of dysfunctional families, little parental involvement and emotional support, economic and social impoverishment, and negative ethical and cultural models. With these factors increasing in prevalence, the job of the teacher and the educational system as a whole looms larger and larger.

In support of, but independent from, the preceding negative factors, researchers from a variety of disciplines are converging on an understanding that the optimal conditions for all learning are those that address the needs of the whole individual (cf. McCombs & Marzano, in press). By this it is meant that the experience of schooling must attend to the following dimensions of the individual: self, metacognitive, cognitive, affective, behavioral, and social. For students to be optimally motivated to learn, they must

- see schooling and education as personally relevant to their interests and goals
- believe that they possess the skills and competencies to successfully accomplish these learning goals
- see themselves as responsible agents in the definition and accomplishment of personal goals
- understand the higher-level thinking and self-regulation skills that lead to goal attainment
- call into play processes for effectively and efficiently encoding, processing, and recalling information
- control emotions and moods that can facilitate or interfere with learning and motivation
- produce the performance outcomes that signal successful goal attainment.

To assist students in these need dimensions essential to learning, it is necessary to not only directly address them in the design of learning experiences and instructional materials, but also to provide a context of socioemotional support—a context in which each individual student feels valued and appreciated for his or her unique set of talents or skills. Without attention to the critical dimension of context, students are not freed up to function at higher levels of consciousness that can lead to optimum learning and self-development (cf., Mills, Dunham, & Alpert, 1988; Suarez, Mills, & Stewart, 1987).

In the school environment, the context of socioemotional support students need can best be provided by teachers, with additional support available from peers. For teachers to provide the necessary socioemotional support, the whole person concept applies as well. They, too, need to feel valued and supported in their role; they, too, need attention paid to their own self, metacognitive, cognitive, affective, behavioral, and social needs within their teaching practice.

With the preceding as the starting place for considering both the role of the educational technologist and the role of educational technology in school redesign, our focus broadens and deepens. From this whole person perspective we can begin to more fully identify and understand the needs of learners and teachers. This is the initial issue that should guide our thinking. I would further suggest that two other questions be asked: "What are the desired student outcomes in this redesigned educational or training setting?" and then, "How can CBT help obtain these outcomes?" These questions need to be asked in the context of both the whole person and the supporting systems that lead to desired outcomes (e.g., teachers, curricula, school resources and facilities, community and social resources, etc.). To deal with this level of complexity, we need a framework. A framework that has particular relevance to this problem is discussed next.

A Living Systems Model of Schooling

For the past several years, Dr. C.L. Hutchins, Director of the Mid-continent Regional Educational Laboratory, has been working on what he terms "A Living Systems Model of Schooling" (Hutchins, in preparation). He points out that the concept of "living systems" has been around for some time and is based on systems theory. The seminal work in living systems was done by Miller (1978), but it has never been comprehensively applied to education or schooling. Hutchins argues that this framework is needed because most existing models of education are quite limited and out of date. He further contends that this new model is particularly appropriate to the redesign of schooling because the complexity of the system often blocks our ability to understand and propose constructive redesign strategies. Hutchins also points out that our prior attempts to apply systems theory to education have had only limited success—in large part because they applied principles of physical systems to human or living systems. One can argue, in addition, that earlier work in programmed instruction, instructional design models, and even instructional technology fell victim to this practice. As Hutchins (in preparation) explains,

These applications have failed largely because human systems, as distinct from physical systems, operate volitionally in an open environment. Unexpected interactions can quickly alter an organism or organization's behavior, resulting, for example, in a situation in which single organisms and complex organizations can frequently make choices that result in multiple goals, conflicting goals and sometimes, at least the appearance of no goals at all.

In Hutchin's work, three features of the living systems approach are outlined that I believe have important implications for the role of educational technologists in school redesign:

- Behavior is analyzed from a general systems view, that is, from the perspective of what functions need to be performed by each level of the system, to get beyond current artifacts that limit our thinking about schooling (e.g., classrooms, textbooks, 50-minute periods, grades, etc.).
- Complex systems, such as schooling, have multiple levels: the learning level, the instructional level, the administrative or management level, the institutional or community level, and the external support level.
- Significant improvements in educational practice will not occur until the system is redesigned with the learning level as primary.

Specifically, what these features imply is that our perspective needs to be broadened to a functional general systems perspective, with a focus on the learning level in considering technology's role in school redesign. Our role as educational technologists takes on larger and more meaningful proportions when we consider "disengaging" ourselves from our current conceptions of schooling and technology, and begin to analyze what students need from the learning level. From this perspective, in collaboration with the educational community and others invested in school redesign, we can analyze how technology can best contribute to redesign goals from the learning level up through the instructional level, management level, institutional or community level, and the external support level. A new and exciting vision of schooling and technology's role in this vision can then emerge.

Hutchins (in preparation) further recommends that schooling be responsive to the trends, learning outcomes, and instructional outcomes that are derived from the analysis of the functional needs of the learner in this information age. In his framework, these include:

- *Information accessing,* or student mastery of strategies for accessing and handling diverse types and quantities of information.
- *Understanding,* or student mastery of the diverse ways in which society organizes and creates meaning using the methods and disciplines of science, social science, mathematics, language and literature, the arts and humanities, business and health; at the same time, knowing how to integrate and apply this knowledge to "real world," interdisciplinary situations.
- *Reasoning and problem solving,* or student mastery of reasoning and thinking strategies that enable them to make positive choices and decisions as well as create solutions to problems.

- *Producing*, or student mastery of basic language and mathematical proficiencies and other performance skills that enable them to effectively communicate, compute, create, and produce a variety of intellectual, artistic, practical, and physical outcomes.
- *Using technology*, or student mastery and understanding of a variety of technologies that can assist them in becoming increasingly proficient in necessary skills as well as assist them in developing their unique potentials.
- *Directing self*, or student mastery of strategies for monitoring and regulating their own thinking and learning processes, feelings, and behaviors that will enable them to become socially responsible and capable of setting and making long term commitments to personally satisfying goals.
- *Working with others*, or student mastery of strategies for effectively working with others, including those who are culturally diverse, as well as effectively working with organizations and across institutional boundaries.

Hutchins (in preparation) derives a number of instructional implications from each functional need of the learner that should be considered in school redesign efforts (e.g., increasing the variety and sophistication of information students use, providing opportunities to apply new knowledge to interdisciplinary situations, integrating teaching of thinking and problem solving skills in all disciplines and subjects, providing opportunities for students to create a variety of products related to traditional and nontraditional learning outcomes, providing access to and instruction in the multidisciplinary use of technology, and providing experiences for learning interpersonal and organizational skills that range from working alone to working in groups). What is important from our perspective is that CBT can clearly contribute to these learning and instructional redesign goals. It is clear that technology can support both the process and products of redesign. For example, in support of meeting the needs of individual students, CBT can (a) assist teachers with their functions of student diagnosis, evaluation, prescription, and instructional management; (b) deliver instruction that introduces novelty, challenge, and success experiences that can contribute to students' enhanced curiosity, motivation, and perceptions of competence and worth; and (c) actively engage students in knowledge and skill development while at the same time supporting cooperative learning and social skill development.

Using this framework as a basis for our efforts, let's look at further implications both for our roles as educational technologists in school redesign and for the role of technology in this effort.

The Role of Educational Technologists
and Technology in School Redesign

An active proponent of new roles for educational technologists in school redesign, Kerr (in press) argues that educational technologists need to interact in the daily life of teachers and students in rethinking their role and the role of technology in radical school reform. By working together, he sees four major ways educational technologists can assist with school reform:

1. *Developing models of teaching-with-technology.* Jointly with teachers, we need to develop models of using tools, materials, and processes that recognize the difficulties inherent in everyday classroom work, seek to alleviate their impact, and provide an opportunity for teachers to expand their thinking about what is possible in the classroom.

In this development, Kerr (in press) stresses that teachers' motivations and sources of reward in teaching must be considered in terms of what technology can provide or take away. The constraints under which teachers work need to be accepted while at the same time reducing teachers' burdens, preparing them for their roles as guides and mentors, minimizing additional preparation, and supporting them with appropriate training. Further, a well-articulated view of what is possible needs to be demonstrated to work in a real classroom.

2. *Designing supportive software.* We need to move as far as possible away from the earlier concept of "teacher-proofing" materials. Materials need to be instructive to both teachers and students and be able to support activities teachers see as clearly important.

Kerr (in press) further points out that software needs to allow more direct and regular interactions among students and between teachers and students. Software needs to enhance student motivation, excitement, and interest in learning; it needs to help students acquire a "higher literacy."

3. *Supporting the education and further professional growth of teachers.* Teacher training needs to incorporate more actual experiences with technology, both hardware/software and process.

In this area, Kerr (in press) recommends the modeling of appropriate uses of technology and establishing professional development centers where teachers can acquire education and experience with technology. He also argues that ways need to be provided to help teachers have more routine access to computers. Systems for gathering, collating, analyzing, and disseminating data about student performance need to be part of teachers' environments in order to assist them in making their work more professional.

4. *Improving research on teaching-with-technology.* Field experiments and comparative studies on the application of technology in different contexts are needed.

Kerr (in press) stresses that the research should encourage diversity among schools and foster innovation and improvement. More research is needed on program feasibility, with reasonable estimates of time constraints and difficulties for teachers, students, and administrators with various new systems and approaches. Research also needs to measure more long-term changes in cognitive outcomes and personal well-being.

In support of the need for a different vision of the technologist's and technology's role in school redesign, Kerr (in press) argues that educational technologists have been increasingly distanced from the work of ordinary teachers. This had led to the technologist's vision of precisely engineered materials, controlled experiences, and measured outcomes—all of which are designed to minimize the teacher's contribution. The assumptions made by many educational technologists are contradictory to those of teachers and the reality of their world. These assumptions also contradict the current trends in school redesign toward more building-based management of schools, with teachers (a) playing a more significant role in administration; (b) making more of the professional decisions about curricula, teaching approaches, and research to be carried out; (c) demanding to be more of a guide or coach in the learning process, in order to provide opportunities for students to reflect thoughtfully on what they have learned; and (d) working more closely with colleges in defining teacher preparation courses. Kerr (in press) concludes by saying,

> If radical reform is possible, it requires us to engage in radically new ways of thinking about schooling. It demands that we recognize the importance of schools as social institutions, and of teachers as the agents principally responsible for effecting education. Using technology to define and strengthen teachers' roles, to empower them in their institutional context, to allow them to find and amplify their voice, will lead to a true and more effective linkage of teaching and technology, a linkage that can also contribute to important broader changes now under way in education.

The congruence of this position with my beliefs concerning the application of technology within the context of educating the whole person and within the framework of a living systems model of schooling should be clear.

Further views about the technology's role in school redesign are expressed by Bunderson and Inouye (1987). They argue for total system modification *via* CBT technologies and put CBT at the center of redesign. Their position is that the real deficiencies in the present delivery system cannot be easily changed, that is, limitations that arise out of the very nature of the teacher-textbook delivery system and its inability to solve the problems of work and knowledge. Bunderson and Inouye believe that CBT systems should assist and not supplant educators and teachers. Rather, CBT systems should provide the teacher and student with hardware and software tools to enhance their productivity. They further contend that although CBT systems will require new teacher roles and skills, these can be minimized by fitting the system to existing teaching and learning traditions. For example, group interactive computer-aided educational delivery systems are recommended as approaches that will be more acceptable and effective. From this perspective, the new school environments will need teachers to model and coach as well as schedule and conduct group activities.

Bunderson and Inouye's (1987) position is in keeping with research by Linn and Burbules (1989) which demonstrates that the integration of computer technology and cooperative learning capitalizes on the best of each. In this research, both technologies helped students acquire a more realistic view of science and the scientific enterprise. Linn and Burbules argue that science education should emphasize how we want students to think about science rather than what we want them to know about science. The blending of computer technology and cooperative learning helps students not only move from an emphasis on declarative knowledge to an emphasis on procedural and strategic knowledge, but it also helps them overcome mistaken impressions about how scientific advances happen, for example, by collaborative efforts vs. working alone. In addition, by working in pairs or small cooperative groups, students have an opportunity to emulate the social interactions characteristic of scientists: joint hypothesis formation, generation of alternatives, and negotiation of the tenability of conclusions in a public forum.

These preceding findings thus support the notion that we need to shift our focus on CBT instructional applications from self-contained to those integrated with the wider social, cognitive, and emotional process of learning from the whole person perspective. In addition, this shift in focus can challenge us to explore new and exciting questions we've yet to ask. For example, in my recent conversation on this topic with Howard Sullivan, the editor of the journal, *Educational Technology Research and Development,* he offered a critical question for the future: "What would be the effect of extensive computer usage in the schools on students' desire to read or pursue 'harder' jobs of learning such as research and writing?" (Sullivan, personal communication, September 25, 1989).

With these thoughts in mind, let's now explore our final question.

WHAT'S NEXT?

The exciting promises of CBT's role in school redesign efforts over the next decade lead to some recommendations for future directions in both practice and research. Some of these are drawn from the contributors to this volume and some are drawn from the issues raised in the prior section.

These recommendations build on the notion that the future of CBT is its role in supporting both the process and products of redesign.

Future Directions for Practice

It is encouraging to note that in a recent survey of 1,100 teachers by IBM ("Teachers Say," 1989), teachers report generally positive attitudes toward computers and see the most important promises of CBT in the areas of improving basic skills, reducing dropout and illiteracy rates, and increasing students' problem solving abilities. What they report as problems are lack of funding, lack of materials and space, inadequate training, and inappropriate uses of computers (e.g., for drill rather than to foster thinking). These promises and problems mirror fairly closely those noted by the contributors to this volume. They also help point to fruitful short-term directions for CBT in practice—directions that can capitalize on recent trends for increased teacher decision making regarding curricula and teaching approaches.

First, it is clear that teachers need to be encouraged to take on more of a leadership role in the design and conduct of technology training. Those teachers who have become experts in the use of technology and have integrated computers into their own programs are the leaders and mentors for others. They can become the trainers-of-trainers (as suggested by Colbert in Chapter 10) to help infuse their knowledge and experience in their school buildings, school districts, and regions. Furthermore, those teachers who have either developed creative applications of existing software in particular subject areas (as suggestd by Sugrue in Chapter 2) or have developed their own software can begin to share this expertise by forming networks (electronically facilitated) and working collaboratively with professional organizations, business, and higher education (as suggested by Reeves in Chapter 4 and Carrier and Glenn in Chapter 5).

Second, a related direction is one which challenges us as educational technologists to join forces with teachers, educators, and other leaders in the school reform movement by forming working task groups that can apply the best of what they know—from a living systems, learner-centered framework—to the problem of school redesign and technology's role in that redesign process and resulting product. This further implies that more of us need to get out into the classroom, into the real world of schooling (as Branson implied in Chapter 14), and use our technological expertise to analyze the needs of learners within the context of first, the existing system, and then, in light of a new system that could better fit these needs. We can then be in a position to suggest applications that are capable of moving from those that fit the current operational environment and conditions to those that fit the learner and extend teachers' notions about what is possible.

Additional tasks that we need to take on include assuming more of a leadership role ourselves in educating our peers and others in the educational community about the broader role technology can play in school redesign. This means we continue to write and disseminate our knowledge, and encourage more involvement of publishers, professional groups, and businesses in supporting this effort. It can also mean taking a more active role in securing funding for and setting up demonstration sites (such as those described by Wilson in Chapter 13) where teachers can view changes in their roles, how to integrate computer use into their daily activities, and how computers can make their jobs easier rather than harder (as suggested by Schultz and Higginbotham-Wheat in Chapter 11). As a secondary goal, this effort can help direct attention towards the need for increased funding and better equipment, and at improving software and authoring system quality. Furthermore, to the extent that we can impact thinking in schools of education and higher education, in general, we can begin to make inroads on the problems of limited and out-of-date preservice teacher training programs, and inadequate incentives and support for faculty development and use of CBT (as pointed out by Reeves in Chapter 4 and Deaton in Chapter 12). Finally, this involvement can no doubt assist in guiding policy changes needed to effectively use technology in traditional education (as noted by Semb et al. in Chapter 7).

Future Directions for Research

Research directions that were suggested by contributors to this volume include (a) research that can increase our understanding of the processes of change, integration, and utilization of technology (Robinson, Chapter 3); (b) research on the outcomes of teacher technology training (Carrier and Glenn, Chapter 5); (c) research on special needs of gifted and handicapped learners that technology can help meet (Robinson, Chapter 3; Pyryt, Chapter 8; Romney, Chapter 15); (d) research on advanced technology that can provide enchanced tutoring capabilities (Derry and Hawkes, Chapter 9); (e) research to substantiate the effectiveness of CBT applications (Colbert, Chapter 10, Schultz and Higginbotham-Wheat, Chapter 11; Deaton, Chapter 12); and (f) research on how technology can support grouping and socialization strategies in different content areas (Hativa, Chapter 6).

In addition to these research directions, there is a need for applied research that can intensively study the effects of a holistic application of the living systems framewrok to the identification of technology applications in redesigned schools. This research could address such questions as (a) how does this approach change our conceptions of technology? (b) what are the implications of this approach for identifying new technology designs? (c) what new roles emerge for teachers and students? and (d) what additional system design perspectives are needed? It may be, as Jonassen (1986; Tessmer & Jonassen, 1988) has noted, we need to extend the notion of technology beyond hardware and software, and beyond engineering notions to include "soft technologies" that include the mind and thinking skills. It may also be, as Sullivan (personal communication, September 25, 1989) implied in his earlier question regarding the effects of extensive computer usage, that we will discover a range of unanticipated student learning and development outcomes. This would also be true as we further research advanced technology applications such as simulations and interactive videodisk in teaching complex concepts and interactions among these concepts in multidisciplinary contexts.

Finally, as implied by the research of Linn and Burbules (1989) there is a need to more extensively study the blending of computer technology and cooperative learning approaches in terms of their impact in specific content areas, with students of different ages and social groups, and so on. This research should be of the field experiment and comparative type recommended by Kerr (in press), and should measure long-term changes in both cognitive and personal/social outcomes. By conducting these types of "real-world" studies, we can not only explore the feasibility of various approaches and applications of CBT, but we can also more actively pursue our leadership role as change agents in this era of school redesign.

REFERENCES

Bunderson, C.V., & Inouye, D.K. (1987). The evolution of computer-aided educational delivery systems. In R.M. Gagne (Ed.), *Instructional technology: Foundations*. Hillsdale, NJ: Erlbaum.

Hutchins, C.L. (in preparation). *A living systems model of schooling*. Aurora, CO: Mid-continent Regional Educational Laboratory.

Jonassen, D.H. (1986). Soft technologies: A paradigm shift for educational technology. *Educational Technology, 26*(9), 33–34.

Kerr, S.T. (in press). Teachers, technology, and the search for school reform. *Educational Technology, Research and Development, 37*(4).

Linn, M.C., & Burbules, N.C. (1989, April). *Group problem solving in computer environments: Opportunities and drawbacks*. Paper presented at the annual meeting of the American Educational Research Association, San Francisco, CA.

McCombs, B.L. (1985). Instructor and group process roles in computer-based training. *Educational Communications and Technology Journal, 33*(3), 159–167.

McCombs, B.L. (1986). The Instructional Systems Development (ISD) model: Factors critical to its successful implementation. *Educational Communications and Technology Journal, 34*(2), 67–81.

McCombs, B.L., & Marzano, R.J. (in press). Putting the self in self-regulated learning: The self as agent in integrating will and skill. *Educational Psychologist.*

Miller, J.G. (1978). *Living systems.* New York: McGraw-Hill.

Mills, R.C., Dunham, R.G., & Alpert, G.P. (1988). Working with high-risk youth in prevention and early intervention programs: Toward a comprehensive model. *Adolescence, 23*(91), 643–660.

Suarez, R., Mills, R.C., & Stewart, D. (1987). *Sanity, insanity, and common sense.* New York: Fawcett Columbine.

Sullivan, H. (1989, September). Teachers say lack of money, training dims the promise of computers. *Education Daily, 22*(16), 1–2.

Tessmer, M., & Jonassen, D. (1988). Learning strategies: A new instructional technology. *World Yearbook of Education,* 29–47.

Author Index

Subject Index